W9-AVM-446

NORTH PORT PUBLIC LIBRARY

13800 S. TAMIAMI TRAIL
NORTH PORT, FL 34287

31969023288847

NORTH PORT PUBLIC LIBRARY

13800 S. TAMIAMI TRAIL
NORTH PORT, FL 34287

THE LOVE BUNGLERS

JAIME HERNANDEZ

Editor and Associate Publisher: ERIC REYNOLDS
Original Serial Editor: KIM THOMPSON
Book Design: JACOB COVEY
Production: PAUL BARESH
Publisher: GARY GROTH

Fantagraphics Books, Inc.
Seattle, Washington, USA

The Love Bunglers is copyright © 2014 Jaime Hernandez. This edition is
copyright © 2014 Fantagraphics Books, Inc. Permission to reproduce content
must be obtained from the author or publisher. *The Love Bunglers* was
originally serialized in *Love and Rockets: New Stories* numbers 3 and 4.
Back cover coloring by Eric Reynolds.

ISBN 978-1-60699-729-1
First printing: June, 2014. Printed in Hong Kong.

Fantagraphics Books would like to thank: Jason Aaron Wong, Karen Green, Ted Haycraft,
Secret Headquarters, Eduardo Takeo "Lizarkeo" Igarashi, John DiBello, Andy Koopmans,
Juan Manuel Domínguez, Paul van Dijken, Nick Capetillo, Randall Bethune, Kevin Czapiewski,
Thomas Eykemans, Christian Schremser, Thomas Zimmermann, Kurt Sayenga, Philip Nel,
Anne Lise Rostgaard Schmidt, Coco and Eddie Gorodetsky, Big Planet Comics, Dan Evans III,
Nevdon Jamgochian, Scott Fritsch-Hammes, Black Hook Press, Mungo van Krimpen-Hall,
Vanessa Palacios and Mathieu Doublet.

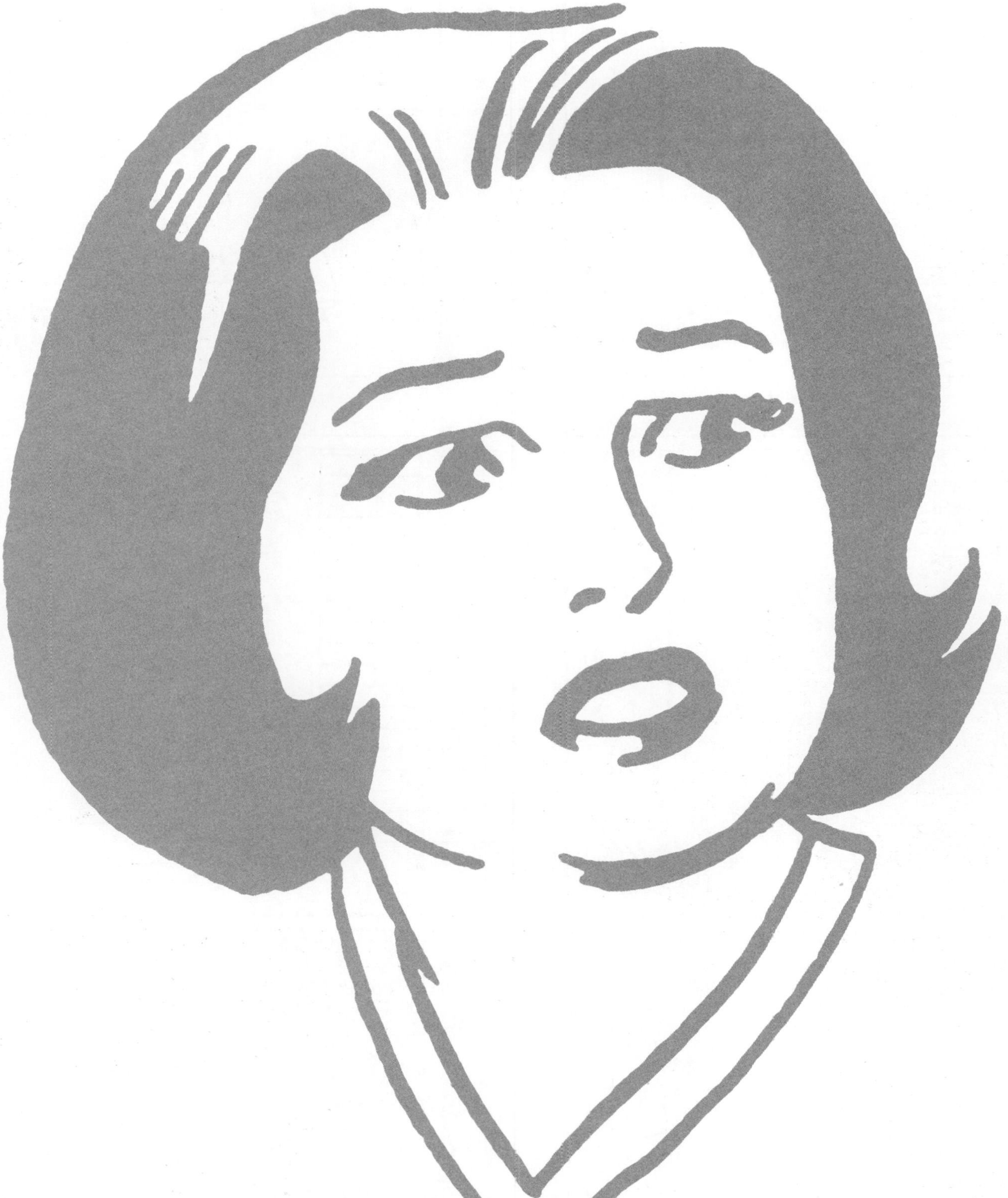

1 THE LOVE BUNGLERS

PART ONE

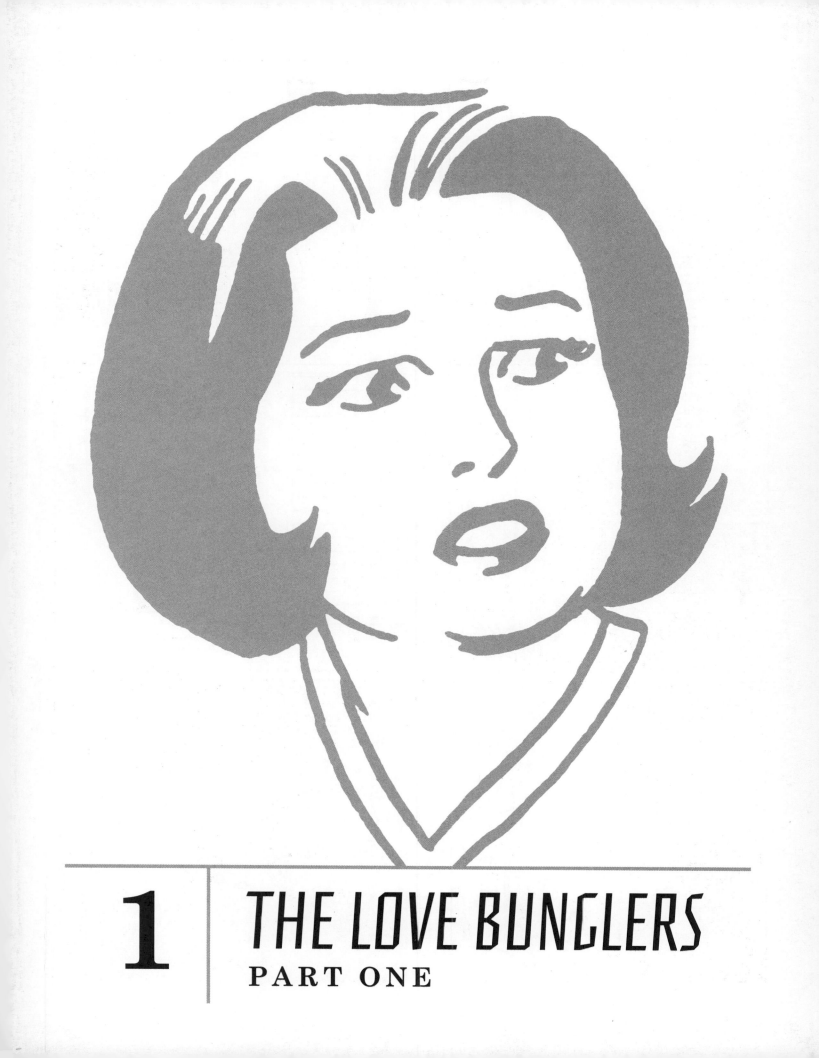

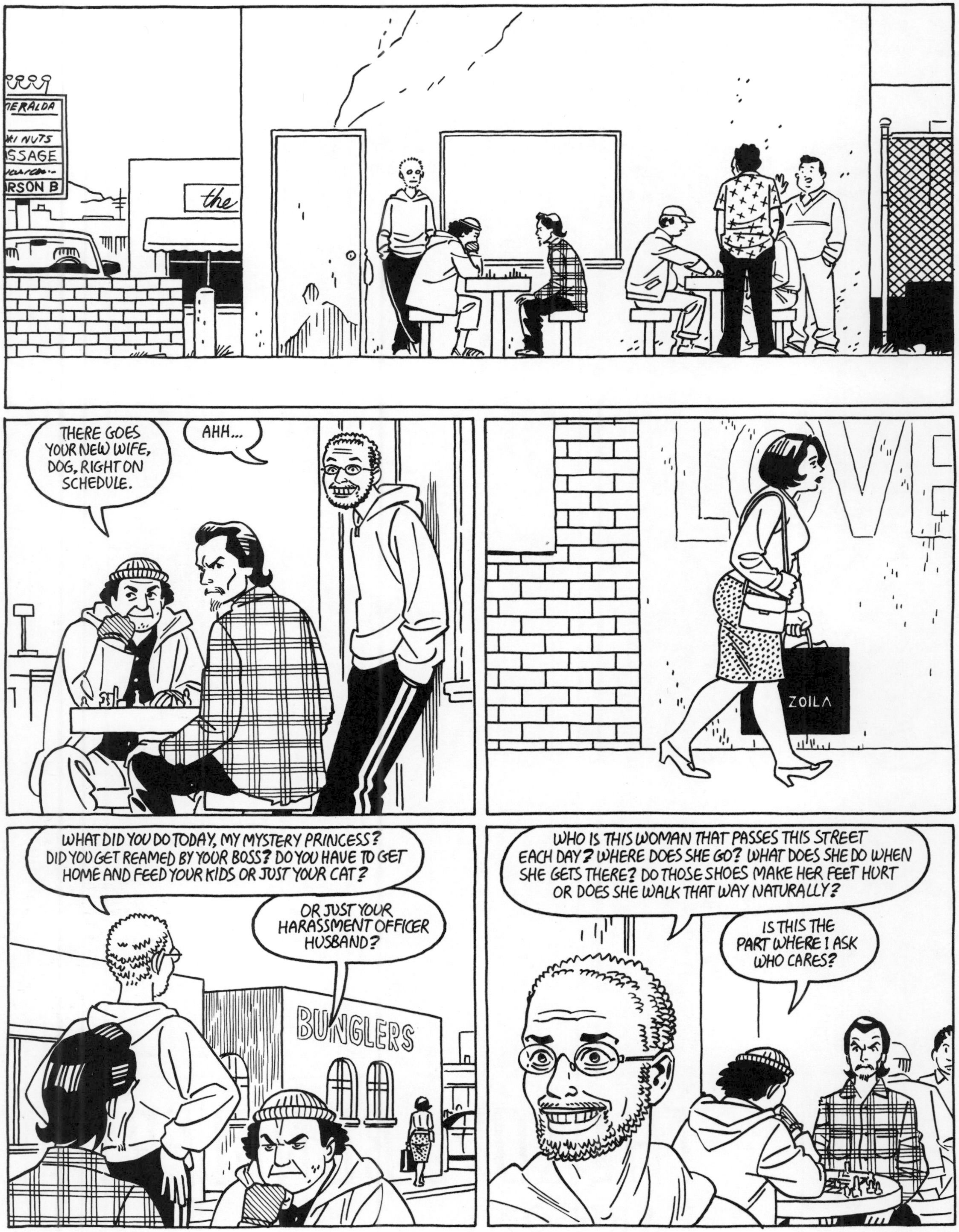
ESMERALDA
NUTS
MASSAGE
ARSON B
the
THERE GOES YOUR NEW WIFE, DOG, RIGHT ON SCHEDULE.
AHH...
ZOILA
WHAT DID YOU DO TODAY, MY MYSTERY PRINCESS? DID YOU GET REAMED BY YOUR BOSS? DO YOU HAVE TO GET HOME AND FEED YOUR KIDS OR JUST YOUR CAT?
OR JUST YOUR HARASSMENT OFFICER HUSBAND?
BUNGLERS
WHO IS THIS WOMAN THAT PASSES THIS STREET EACH DAY? WHERE DOES SHE GO? WHAT DOES SHE DO WHEN SHE GETS THERE? DO THOSE SHOES MAKE HER FEET HURT OR DOES SHE WALK THAT WAY NATURALLY?
IS THIS THE PART WHERE I ASK WHO CARES?

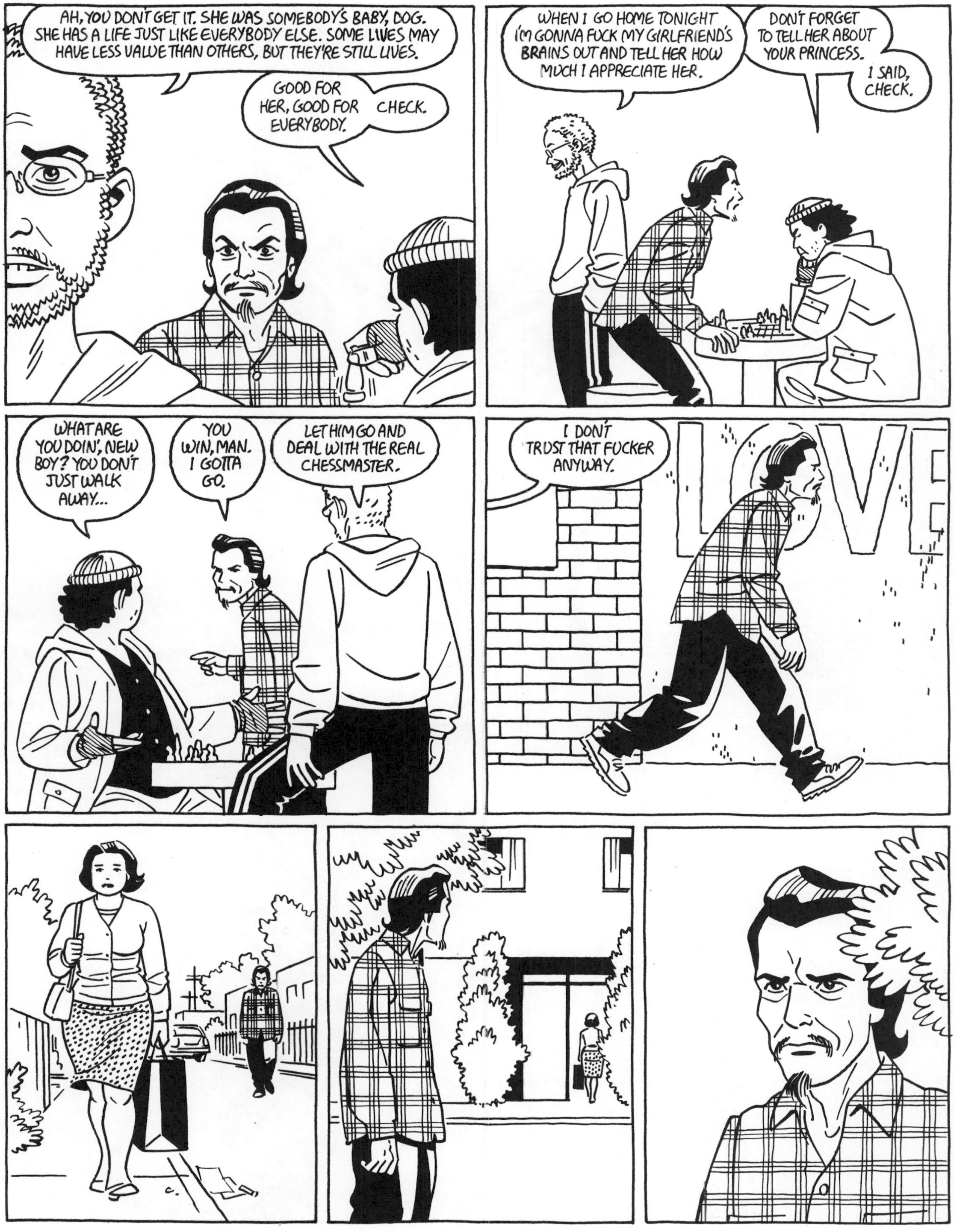
AH, YOU DON'T GET IT. SHE WAS SOMEBODY'S BABY, DOG. SHE HAS A LIFE JUST LIKE EVERYBODY ELSE. SOME LIVES MAY HAVE LESS VALUE THAN OTHERS, BUT THEY'RE STILL LIVES.
GOOD FOR HER, GOOD FOR EVERYBODY.
CHECK.
WHEN I GO HOME TONIGHT I'M GONNA FUCK MY GIRLFRIEND'S BRAINS OUT AND TELL HER HOW MUCH I APPRECIATE HER.
DON'T FORGET TO TELL HER ABOUT YOUR PRINCESS.
I SAID, CHECK.
WHAT ARE YOU DOIN', NEW BOY? YOU DON'T JUST WALK AWAY...
YOU WIN, MAN. I GOTTA GO.
LET HIM GO AND DEAL WITH THE REAL CHESSMASTER.
I DON'T TRUST THAT FUCKER ANYWAY.
LOVE

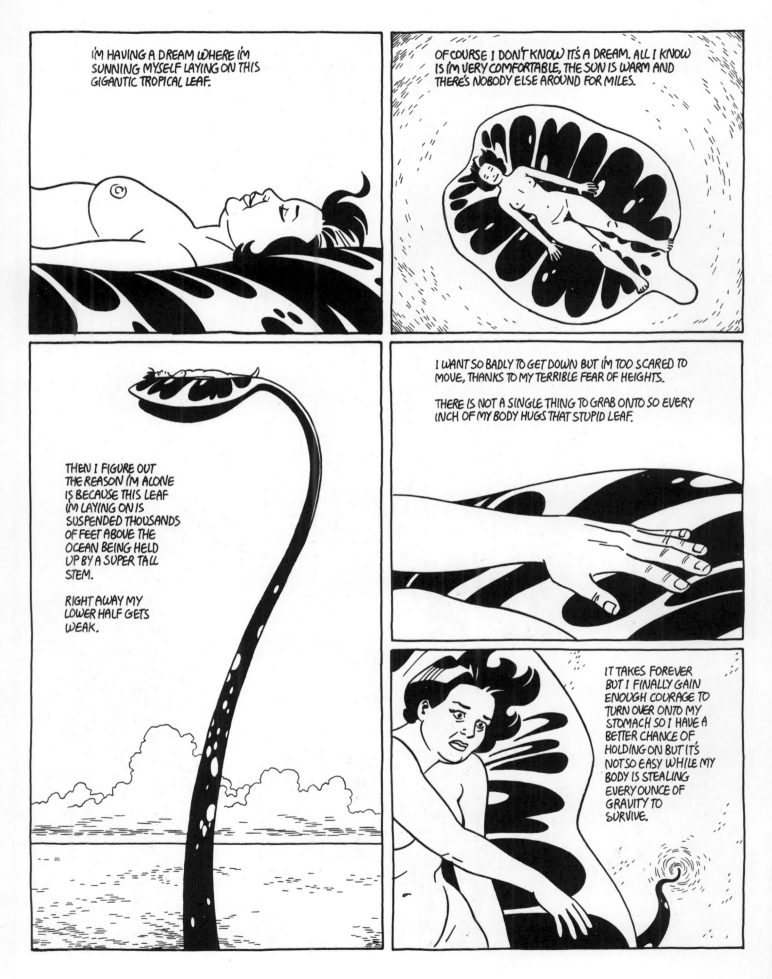

I'M HAVING A DREAM WHERE I'M SUNNING MYSELF LAYING ON THIS GIGANTIC TROPICAL LEAF.

OF COURSE I DON'T KNOW IT'S A DREAM. ALL I KNOW IS I'M VERY COMFORTABLE, THE SUN IS WARM AND THERE'S NOBODY ELSE AROUND FOR MILES.

THEN I FIGURE OUT THE REASON I'M ALONE IS BECAUSE THIS LEAF I'M LAYING ON IS SUSPENDED THOUSANDS OF FEET ABOVE THE OCEAN BEING HELD UP BY A SUPER TALL STEM.

RIGHT AWAY MY LOWER HALF GETS WEAK.

I WANT SO BADLY TO GET DOWN BUT I'M TOO SCARED TO MOVE, THANKS TO MY TERRIBLE FEAR OF HEIGHTS.

THERE IS NOT A SINGLE THING TO GRAB ONTO SO EVERY INCH OF MY BODY HUGS THAT STUPID LEAF.

IT TAKES FOREVER BUT I FINALLY GAIN ENOUGH COURAGE TO TURN OVER ONTO MY STOMACH SO I HAVE A BETTER CHANCE OF HOLDING ON BUT IT'S NOT SO EASY WHILE MY BODY IS STEALING EVERY OUNCE OF GRAVITY TO SURVIVE.

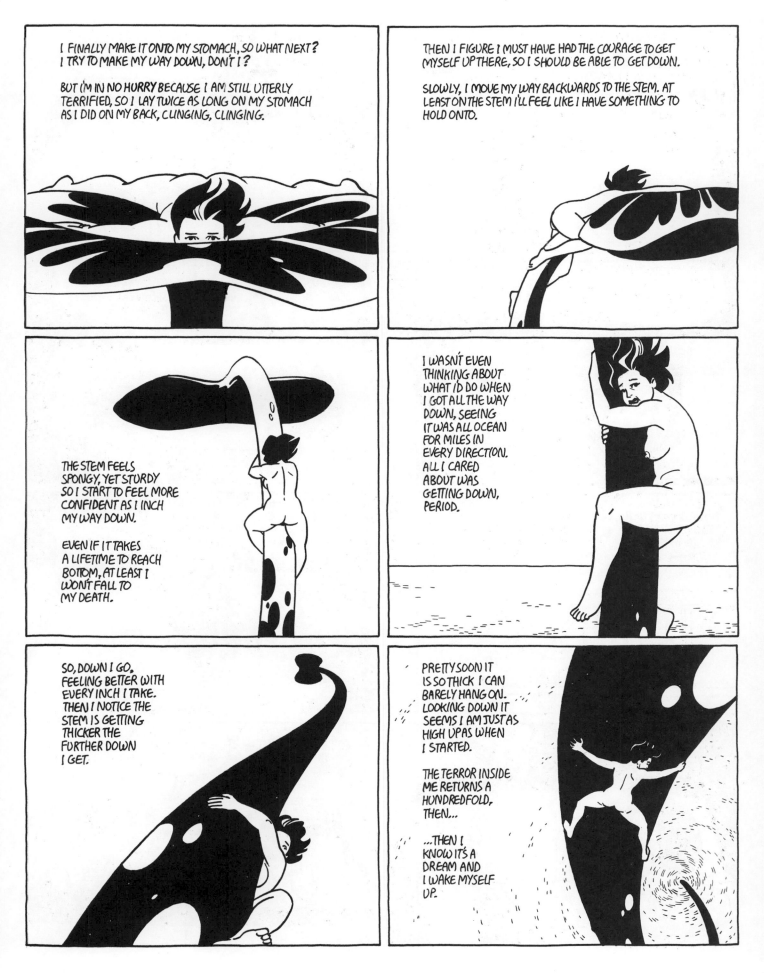

I FINALLY MAKE IT ONTO MY STOMACH, SO WHAT NEXT? I TRY TO MAKE MY WAY DOWN, DON'T I?

BUT I'M IN NO HURRY BECAUSE I AM STILL UTTERLY TERRIFIED, SO I LAY TWICE AS LONG ON MY STOMACH AS I DID ON MY BACK, CLINGING, CLINGING.

THEN I FIGURE I MUST HAVE HAD THE COURAGE TO GET MYSELF UP THERE, SO I SHOULD BE ABLE TO GET DOWN.

SLOWLY, I MOVE MY WAY BACKWARDS TO THE STEM. AT LEAST ON THE STEM I'LL FEEL LIKE I HAVE SOMETHING TO HOLD ONTO.

THE STEM FEELS SPONGY, YET STURDY SO I START TO FEEL MORE CONFIDENT AS I INCH MY WAY DOWN.

EVEN IF IT TAKES A LIFETIME TO REACH BOTTOM, AT LEAST I WON'T FALL TO MY DEATH.

I WASN'T EVEN THINKING ABOUT WHAT I'D DO WHEN I GOT ALL THE WAY DOWN, SEEING IT WAS ALL OCEAN FOR MILES IN EVERY DIRECTION. ALL I CARED ABOUT WAS GETTING DOWN, PERIOD.

SO, DOWN I GO, FEELING BETTER WITH EVERY INCH I TAKE. THEN I NOTICE THE STEM IS GETTING THICKER THE FURTHER DOWN I GET.

PRETTY SOON IT IS SO THICK I CAN BARELY HANG ON. LOOKING DOWN IT SEEMS I AM JUST AS HIGH UP AS WHEN I STARTED.

THE TERROR INSIDE ME RETURNS A HUNDREDFOLD, THEN...

...THEN I KNOW IT'S A DREAM AND I WAKE MYSELF UP.

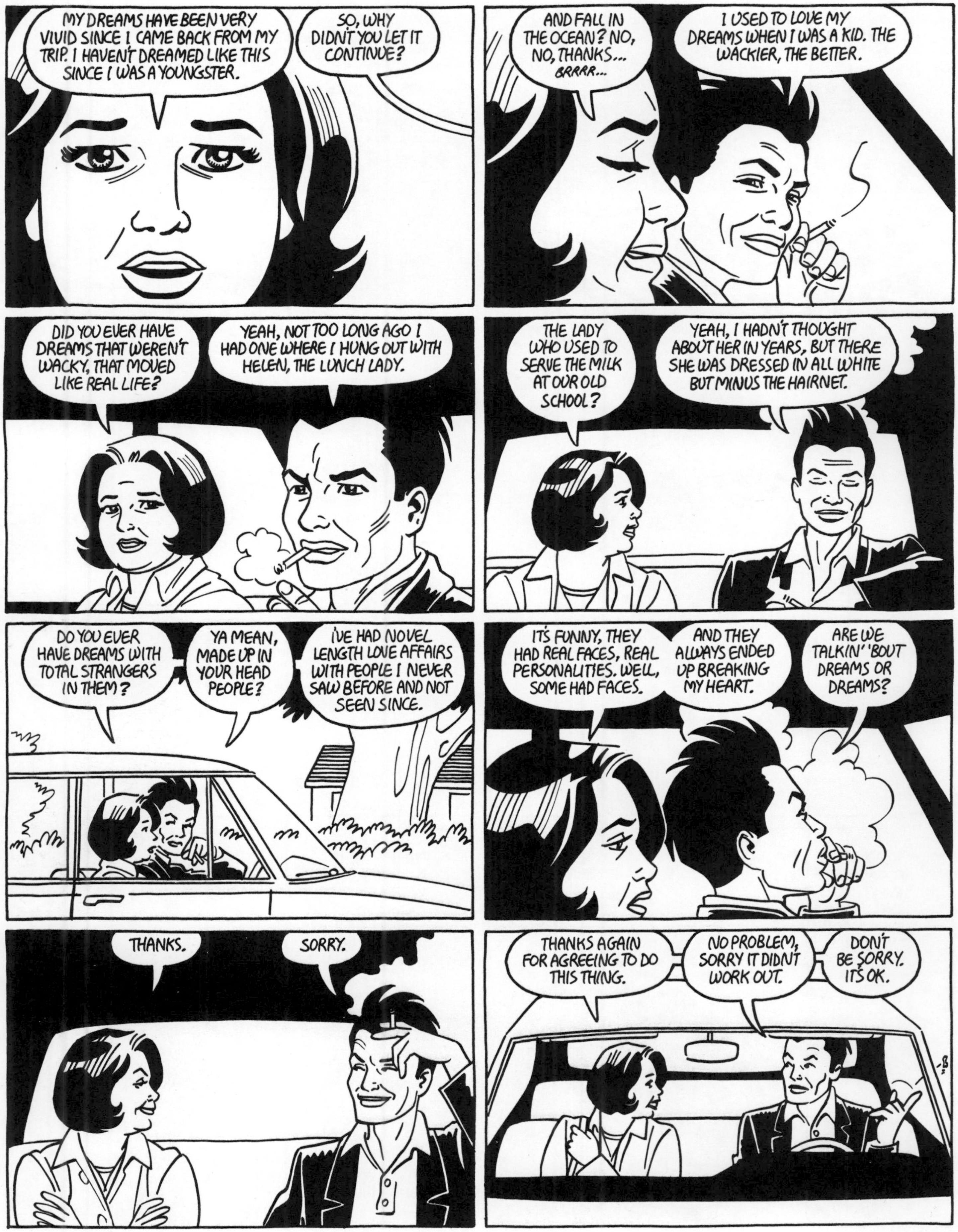
MY DREAMS HAVE BEEN VERY VIVID SINCE I CAME BACK FROM MY TRIP. I HAVEN'T DREAMED LIKE THIS SINCE I WAS A YOUNGSTER.
SO, WHY DIDN'T YOU LET IT CONTINUE?
AND FALL IN THE OCEAN? NO, NO, THANKS... BRRRR...
I USED TO LOVE MY DREAMS WHEN I WAS A KID. THE WACKIER, THE BETTER.
DID YOU EVER HAVE DREAMS THAT WEREN'T WACKY, THAT MOVED LIKE REAL LIFE?
YEAH, NOT TOO LONG AGO I HAD ONE WHERE I HUNG OUT WITH HELEN, THE LUNCH LADY.
THE LADY WHO USED TO SERVE THE MILK AT OUR OLD SCHOOL?
YEAH, I HADN'T THOUGHT ABOUT HER IN YEARS, BUT THERE SHE WAS DRESSED IN ALL WHITE BUT MINUS THE HAIRNET.
DO YOU EVER HAVE DREAMS WITH TOTAL STRANGERS IN THEM?
YA MEAN, MADE UP IN YOUR HEAD PEOPLE?
I'VE HAD NOVEL LENGTH LOVE AFFAIRS WITH PEOPLE I NEVER SAW BEFORE AND NOT SEEN SINCE.
IT'S FUNNY, THEY HAD REAL FACES, REAL PERSONALITIES. WELL, SOME HAD FACES.
AND THEY ALWAYS ENDED UP BREAKING MY HEART.
ARE WE TALKIN' 'BOUT DREAMS OR DREAMS?
THANKS.
SORRY.
THANKS AGAIN FOR AGREEING TO DO THIS THING.
NO PROBLEM, SORRY IT DIDN'T WORK OUT.
DON'T BE SORRY. IT'S OK.

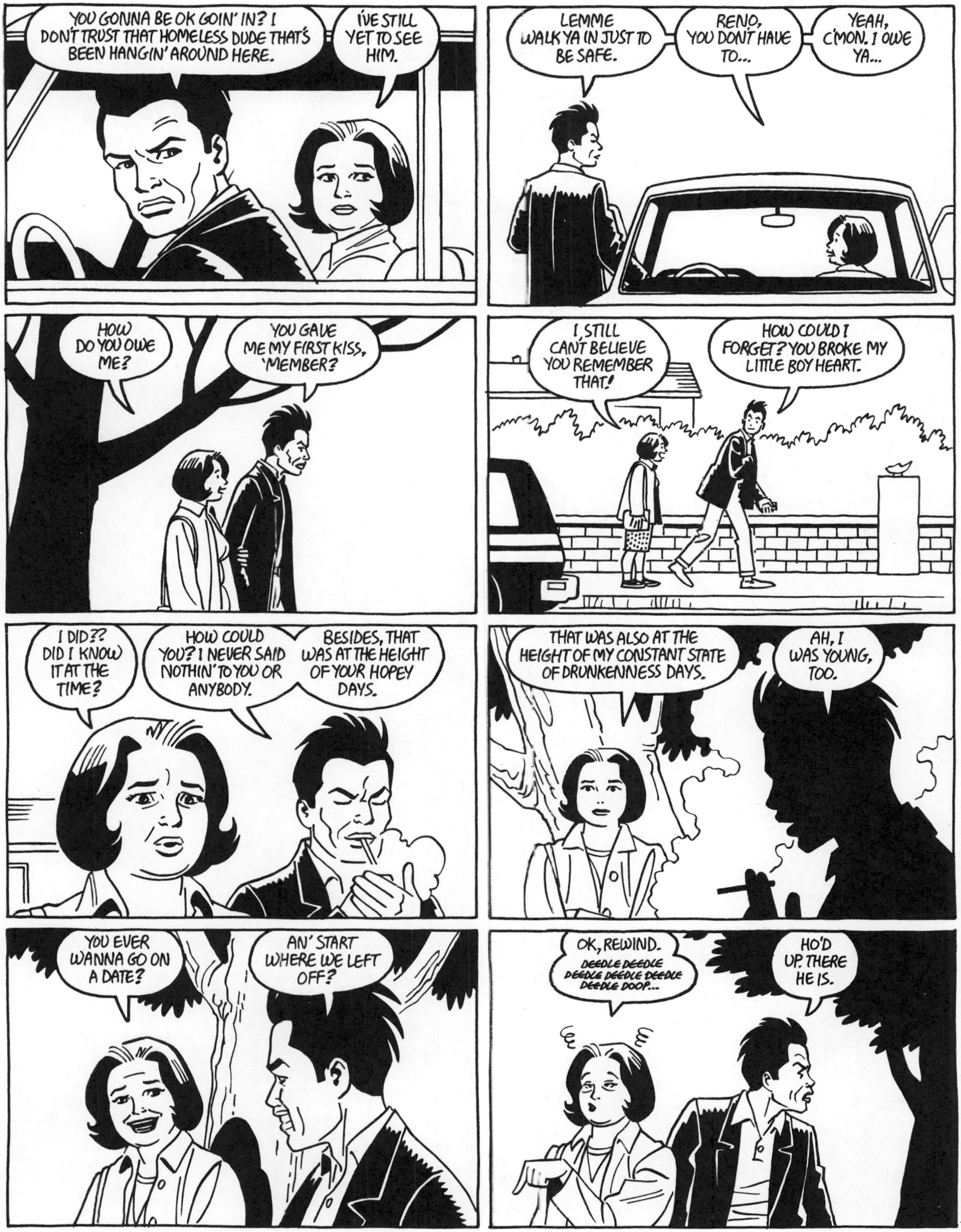
YOU GONNA BE OK GOIN' IN? I DON'T TRUST THAT HOMELESS DUDE THAT'S BEEN HANGIN' AROUND HERE.
I'VE STILL YET TO SEE HIM.
LEMME WALK YA IN JUST TO BE SAFE.
RENO, YOU DON'T HAVE TO...
YEAH, C'MON. I OWE YA...
HOW DO YOU OWE ME?
YOU GAVE ME MY FIRST KISS, 'MEMBER?
I STILL CAN'T BELIEVE YOU REMEMBER THAT!
HOW COULD I FORGET? YOU BROKE MY LITTLE BOY HEART.
I DID?? DID I KNOW IT AT THE TIME?
HOW COULD YOU? I NEVER SAID NOTHIN' TO YOU OR ANYBODY.
BESIDES, THAT WAS AT THE HEIGHT OF YOUR HOPEY DAYS.
THAT WAS ALSO AT THE HEIGHT OF MY CONSTANT STATE OF DRUNKENNESS DAYS.
AH, I WAS YOUNG, TOO.
YOU EVER WANNA GO ON A DATE?
AN' START WHERE WE LEFT OFF?
OK, REWIND.
DEEDLE DEEDLE DEEDLE DEEDLE DEEDLE DEEDLE DOOP...
HO'D UP. THERE HE IS.

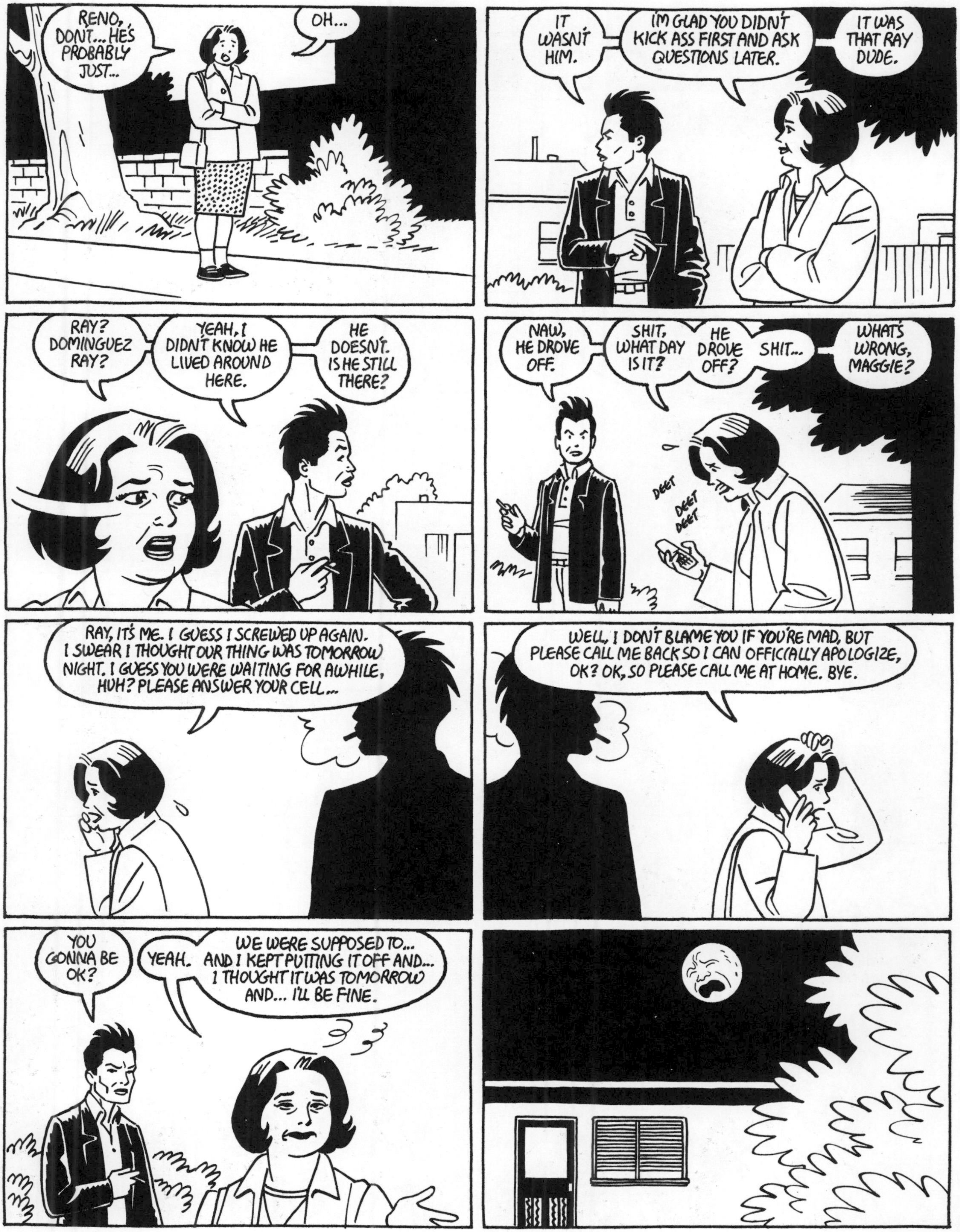
RENO, DONT... HE'S PROBABLY JUST...
OH...
IT WASN'T HIM.
I'M GLAD YOU DIDN'T KICK ASS FIRST AND ASK QUESTIONS LATER.
IT WAS THAT RAY DUDE.
RAY? DOMINGUEZ RAY?
YEAH, I DIDN'T KNOW HE LIVED AROUND HERE.
HE DOESN'T. IS HE STILL THERE?
NAW, HE DROVE OFF.
SHIT, WHAT DAY IS IT?
HE DROVE OFF?
SHIT...
WHAT'S WRONG, MAGGIE?
DEET
DEET DEET
RAY, IT'S ME. I GUESS I SCREWED UP AGAIN. I SWEAR I THOUGHT OUR THING WAS TOMORROW NIGHT. I GUESS YOU WERE WAITING FOR AWHILE, HUH? PLEASE ANSWER YOUR CELL...
WELL, I DON'T BLAME YOU IF YOU'RE MAD, BUT PLEASE CALL ME BACK SO I CAN OFFICIALLY APOLOGIZE, OK? OK, SO PLEASE CALL ME AT HOME. BYE.
YOU GONNA BE OK?
YEAH.
WE WERE SUPPOSED TO... AND I KEPT PUTTING IT OFF AND... I THOUGHT IT WAS TOMORROW AND... I'LL BE FINE.

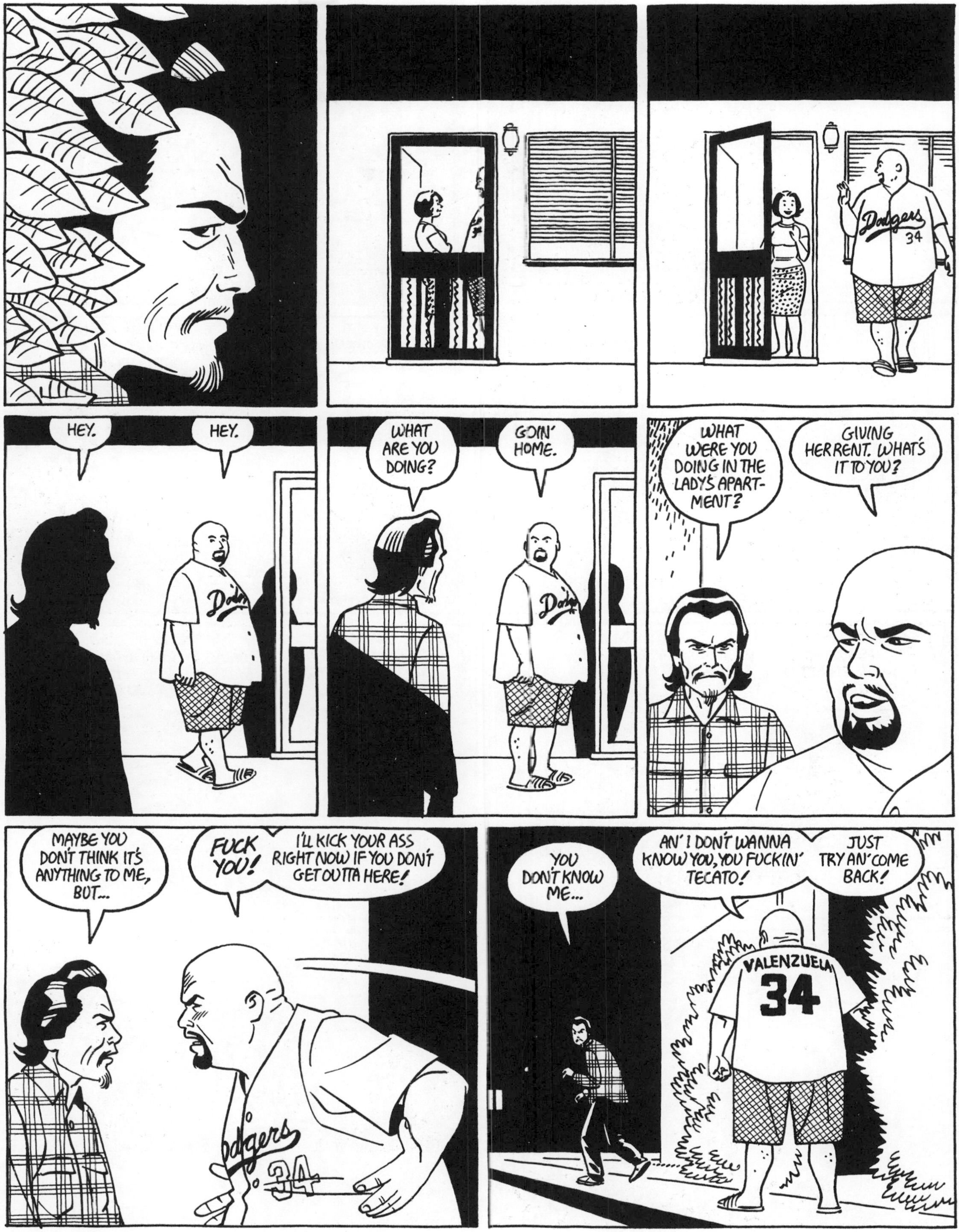

Dodgers
34
HEY.
HEY.
WHAT ARE YOU DOING?
GOIN' HOME.
WHAT WERE YOU DOING IN THE LADY'S APARTMENT?
GIVING HER RENT. WHAT'S IT TO YOU?
MAYBE YOU DON'T THINK IT'S ANYTHING TO ME, BUT...
FUCK YOU!
I'LL KICK YOUR ASS RIGHT NOW IF YOU DON'T GET OUTTA HERE!
YOU DON'T KNOW ME...
AN' I DON'T WANNA KNOW YOU, YOU FUCKIN' TECATO!
JUST TRY AN' COME BACK!
VALENZUELA
34

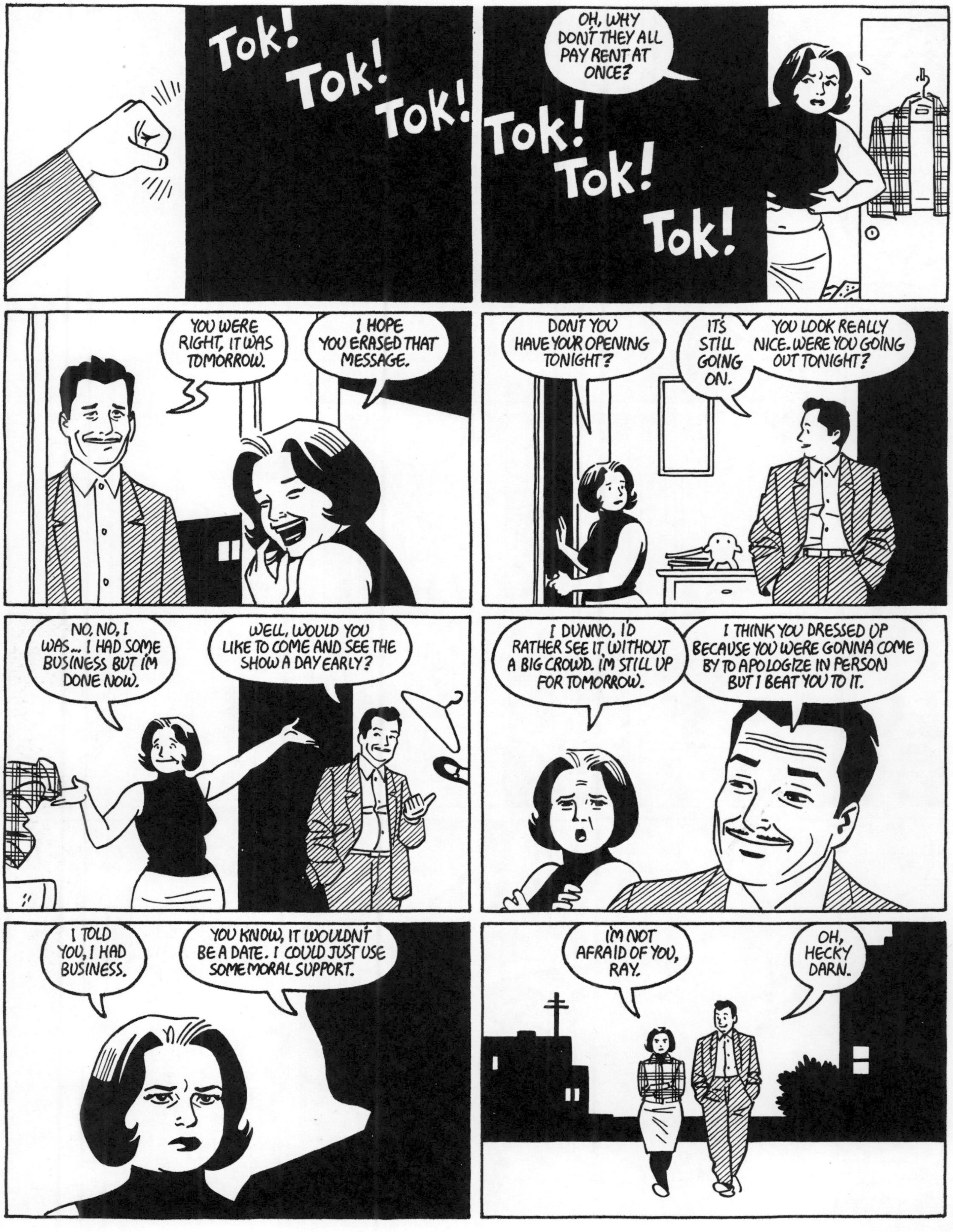
Tok!
Tok!
Tok!
Tok!
Tok!
Tok!
OH, WHY DON'T THEY ALL PAY RENT AT ONCE?
YOU WERE RIGHT, IT WAS TOMORROW.
I HOPE YOU ERASED THAT MESSAGE.
DON'T YOU HAVE YOUR OPENING TONIGHT?
IT'S STILL GOING ON.
YOU LOOK REALLY NICE. WERE YOU GOING OUT TONIGHT?
NO, NO, I WAS... I HAD SOME BUSINESS BUT I'M DONE NOW.
WELL, WOULD YOU LIKE TO COME AND SEE THE SHOW A DAY EARLY?
I DUNNO, I'D RATHER SEE IT WITHOUT A BIG CROWD. I'M STILL UP FOR TOMORROW.
I THINK YOU DRESSED UP BECAUSE YOU WERE GONNA COME BY TO APOLOGIZE IN PERSON BUT I BEAT YOU TO IT.
I TOLD YOU, I HAD BUSINESS.
YOU KNOW, IT WOULDN'T BE A DATE. I COULD JUST USE SOME MORAL SUPPORT.
I'M NOT AFRAID OF YOU, RAY.
OH, HECKY DARN.

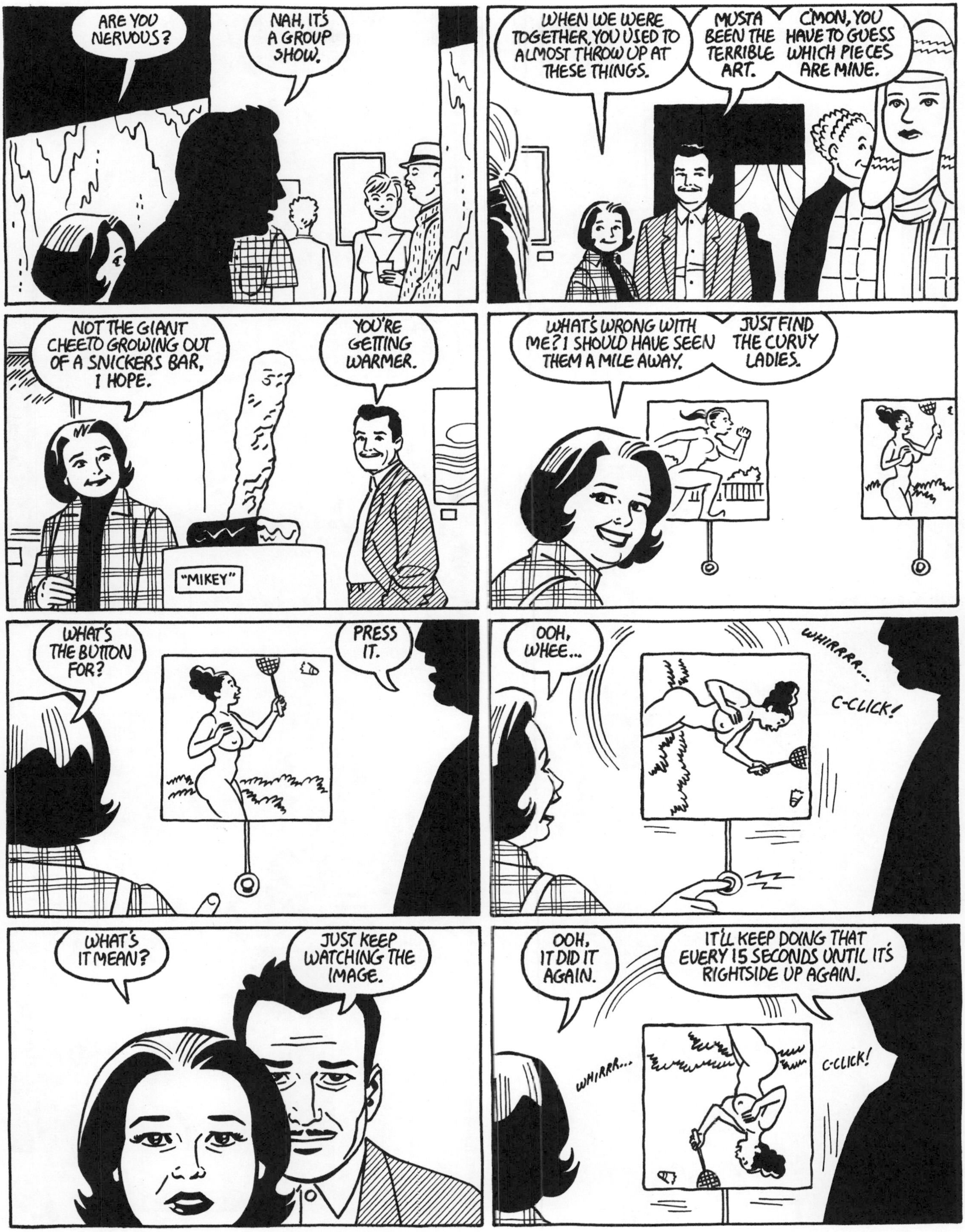
ARE YOU NERVOUS?
NAH, IT'S A GROUP SHOW.
WHEN WE WERE TOGETHER, YOU USED TO ALMOST THROW UP AT THESE THINGS.
MUSTA BEEN THE TERRIBLE ART.
C'MON, YOU HAVE TO GUESS WHICH PIECES ARE MINE.
NOT THE GIANT CHEETO GROWING OUT OF A SNICKERS BAR, I HOPE.
"MIKEY"
YOU'RE GETTING WARMER.
WHAT'S WRONG WITH ME? I SHOULD HAVE SEEN THEM A MILE AWAY.
JUST FIND THE CURVY LADIES.
WHAT'S THE BUTTON FOR?
PRESS IT.
OOH, WHEE...
WHIRRRR...
C-CLICK!
WHAT'S IT MEAN?
JUST KEEP WATCHING THE IMAGE.
OOH, IT DID IT AGAIN.
IT'LL KEEP DOING THAT EVERY 15 SECONDS UNTIL IT'S RIGHTSIDE UP AGAIN.
WHIRRR...
C-CLICK!

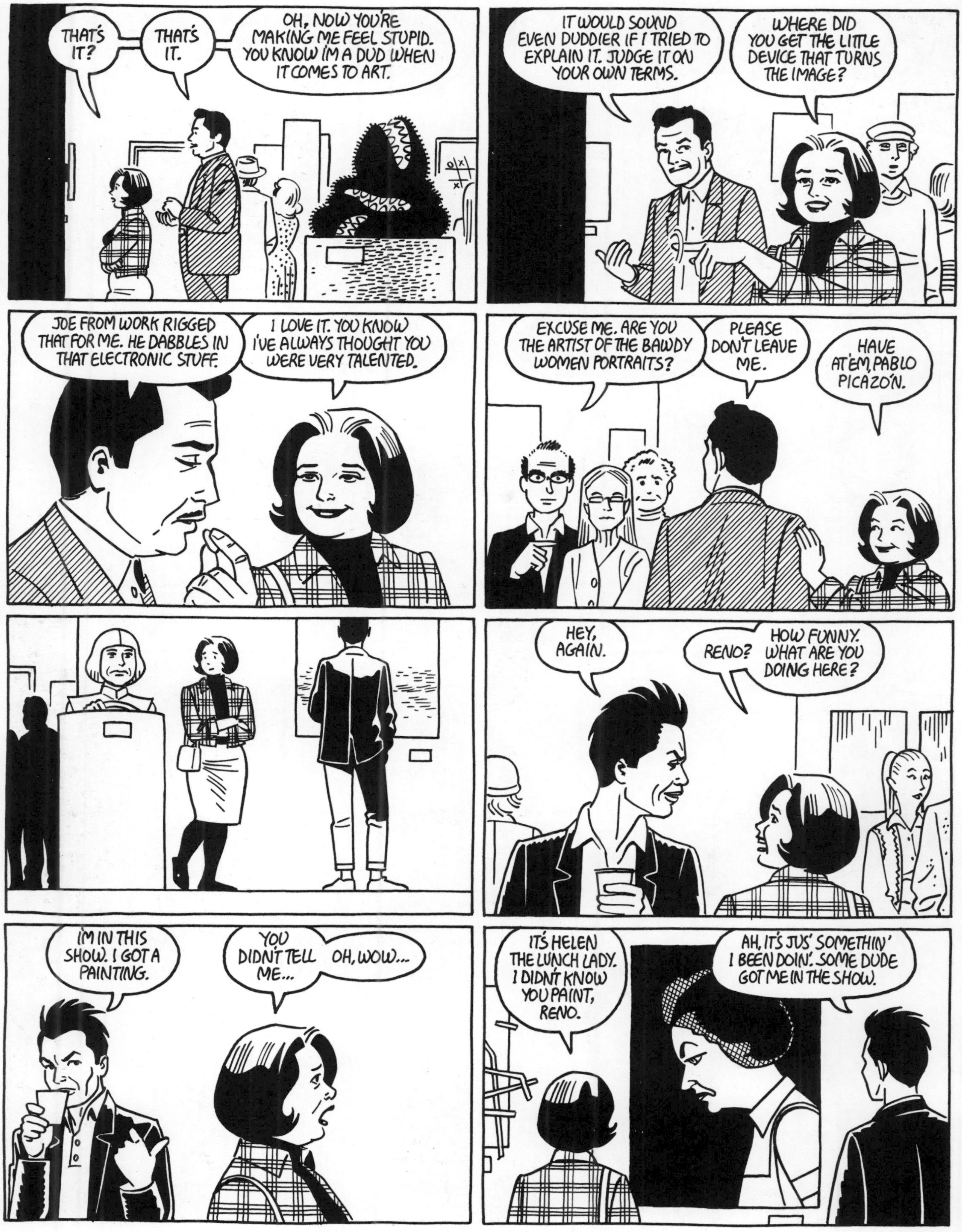
THAT'S IT?
THAT'S IT.
OH, NOW YOU'RE MAKING ME FEEL STUPID. YOU KNOW I'M A DUD WHEN IT COMES TO ART.
IT WOULD SOUND EVEN DUDDIER IF I TRIED TO EXPLAIN IT. JUDGE IT ON YOUR OWN TERMS.
WHERE DID YOU GET THE LITTLE DEVICE THAT TURNS THE IMAGE?
JOE FROM WORK RIGGED THAT FOR ME. HE DABBLES IN THAT ELECTRONIC STUFF.
I LOVE IT. YOU KNOW I'VE ALWAYS THOUGHT YOU WERE VERY TALENTED.
EXCUSE ME. ARE YOU THE ARTIST OF THE BAWDY WOMEN PORTRAITS?
PLEASE DON'T LEAVE ME.
HAVE AT'EM, PABLO PICAZO'N.
HEY, AGAIN.
RENO?
HOW FUNNY. WHAT ARE YOU DOING HERE?
I'M IN THIS SHOW. I GOT A PAINTING.
YOU DIDN'T TELL ME...
OH, WOW...
IT'S HELEN THE LUNCH LADY. I DIDN'T KNOW YOU PAINT, RENO.
AH, IT'S JUS' SOMETHIN' I BEEN DOIN'. SOME DUDE GOT ME IN THE SHOW.

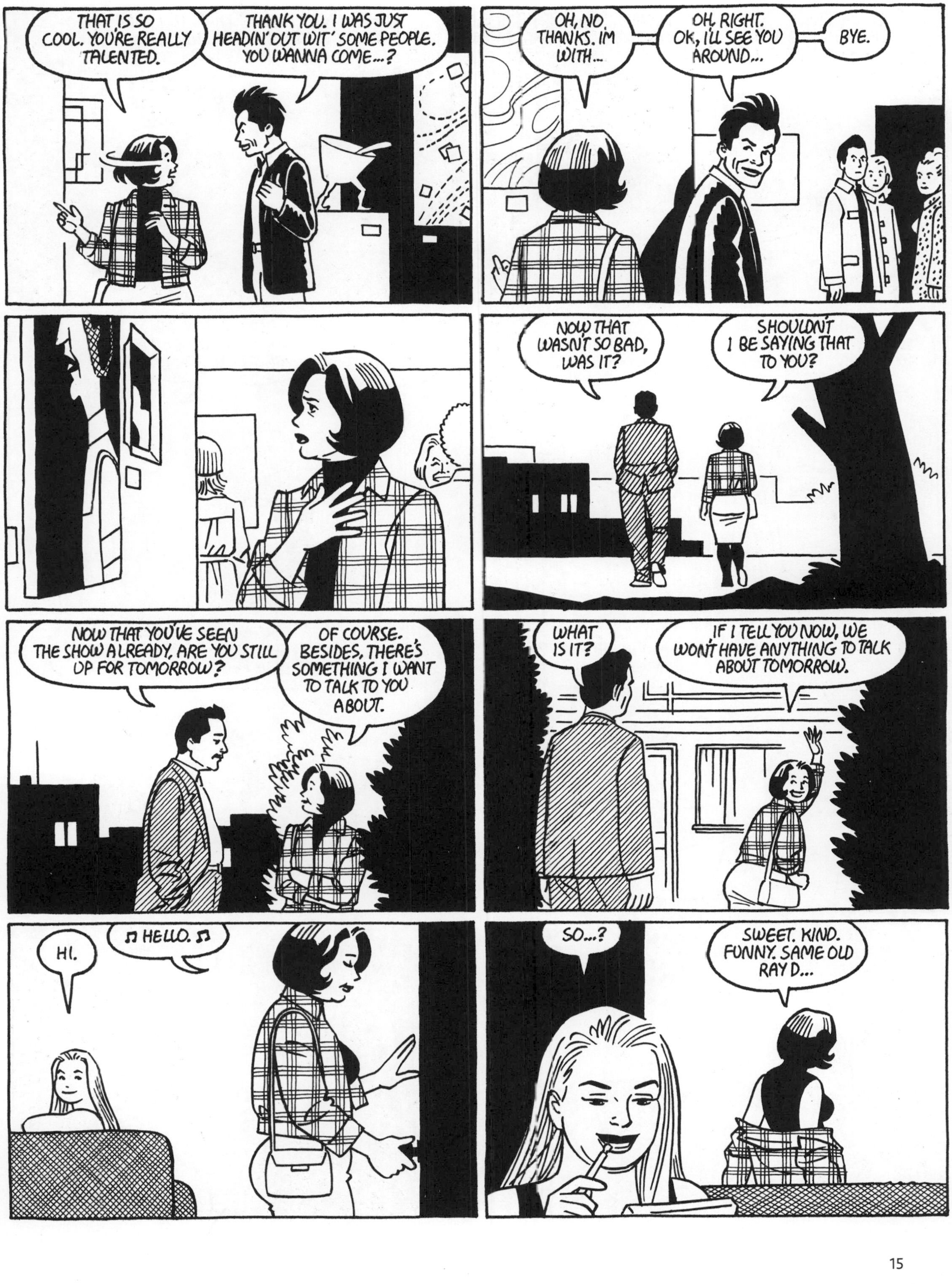
THAT IS SO COOL. YOU'RE REALLY TALENTED.
THANK YOU. I WAS JUST HEADIN' OUT WIT' SOME PEOPLE. YOU WANNA COME...?
OH, NO THANKS. I'M WITH...
OH, RIGHT. OK, I'LL SEE YOU AROUND...
BYE.
NOW THAT WASN'T SO BAD, WAS IT?
SHOULDN'T I BE SAYING THAT TO YOU?
NOW THAT YOU'VE SEEN THE SHOW ALREADY, ARE YOU STILL UP FOR TOMORROW?
OF COURSE. BESIDES, THERE'S SOMETHING I WANT TO TALK TO YOU ABOUT.
WHAT IS IT?
IF I TELL YOU NOW, WE WON'T HAVE ANYTHING TO TALK ABOUT TOMORROW.
HI.
♫ HELLO. ♫
SO...?
SWEET. KIND. FUNNY. SAME OLD RAY D...

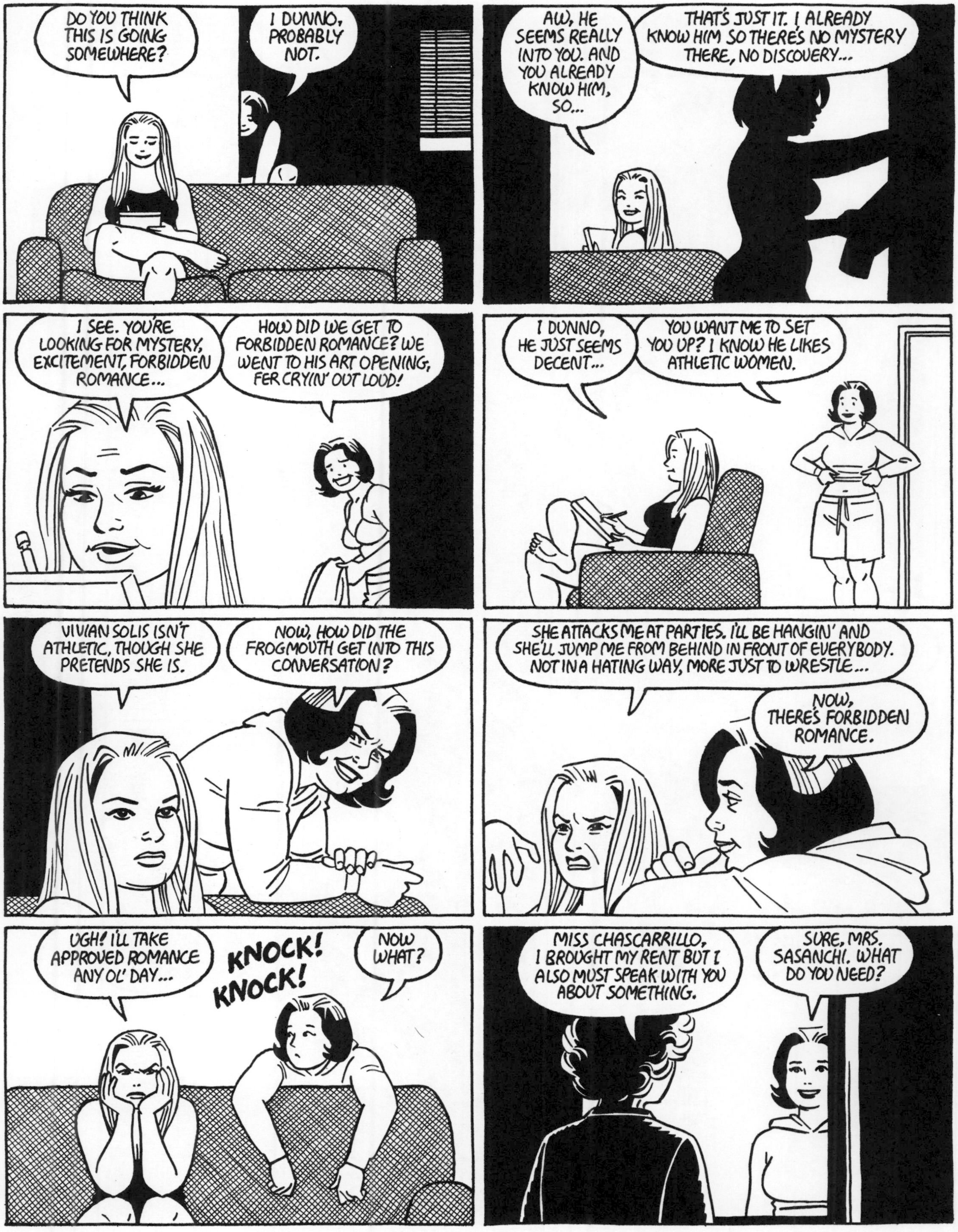
DO YOU THINK THIS IS GOING SOMEWHERE?
I DUNNO, PROBABLY NOT.
AW, HE SEEMS REALLY INTO YOU. AND YOU ALREADY KNOW HIM, SO...
THAT'S JUST IT. I ALREADY KNOW HIM SO THERE'S NO MYSTERY THERE, NO DISCOVERY...
I SEE. YOU'RE LOOKING FOR MYSTERY, EXCITEMENT, FORBIDDEN ROMANCE...
HOW DID WE GET TO FORBIDDEN ROMANCE? WE WENT TO HIS ART OPENING, FER CRYIN' OUT LOUD!
I DUNNO, HE JUST SEEMS DECENT...
YOU WANT ME TO SET YOU UP? I KNOW HE LIKES ATHLETIC WOMEN.
VIVIAN SOLIS ISN'T ATHLETIC, THOUGH SHE PRETENDS SHE IS.
NOW, HOW DID THE FROGMOUTH GET INTO THIS CONVERSATION?
SHE ATTACKS ME AT PARTIES. I'LL BE HANGIN' AND SHE'LL JUMP ME FROM BEHIND IN FRONT OF EVERYBODY. NOT IN A HATING WAY, MORE JUST TO WRESTLE...
NOW, THERE'S FORBIDDEN ROMANCE.
UGH! I'LL TAKE APPROVED ROMANCE ANY OL' DAY...
KNOCK! KNOCK!
NOW WHAT?
MISS CHASCARRILLO, I BROUGHT MY RENT BUT I ALSO MUST SPEAK WITH YOU ABOUT SOMETHING.
SURE, MRS. SASANCHI. WHAT DO YOU NEED?

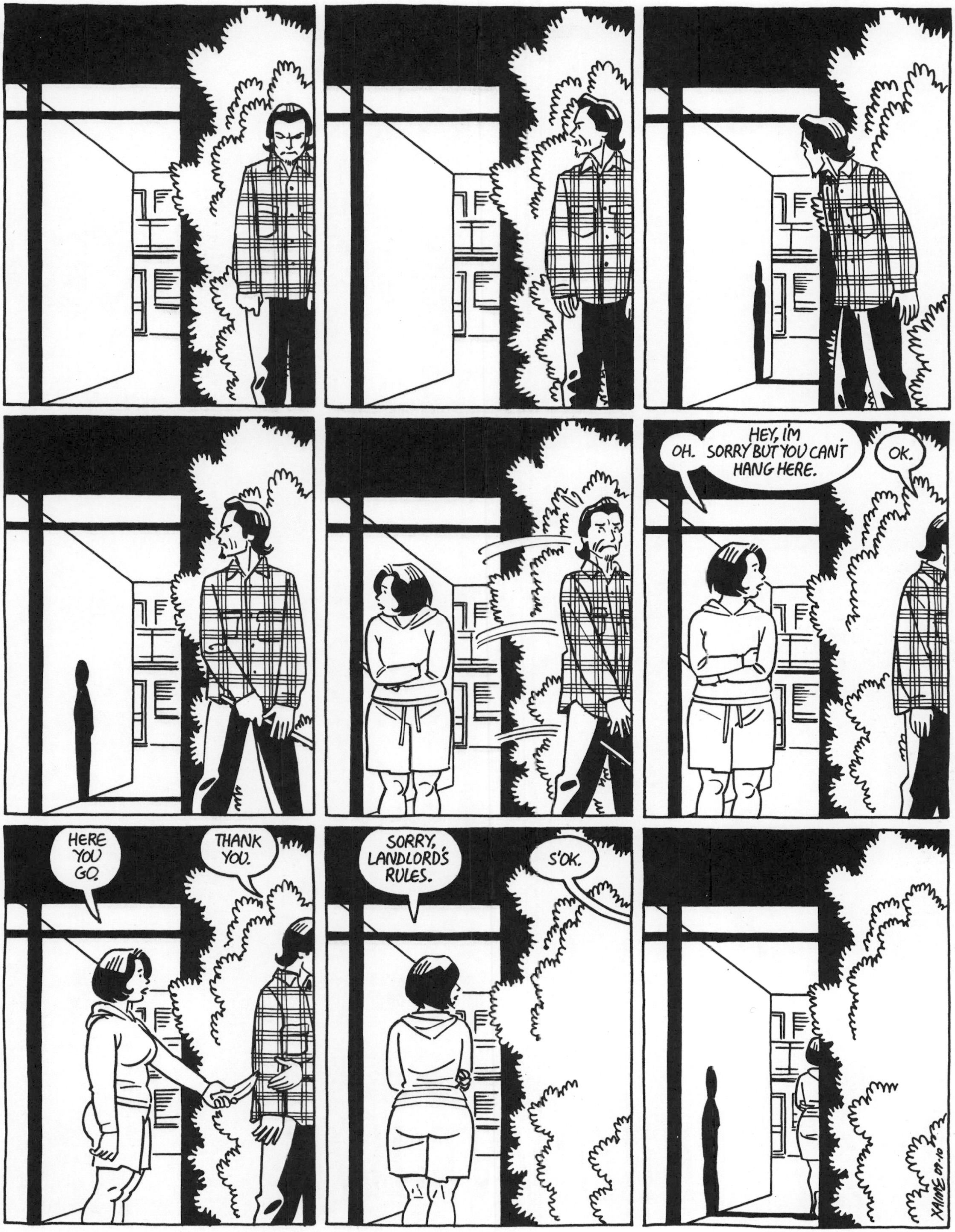

OH.
HEY, I'M SORRY BUT YOU CAN'T HANG HERE.
OK.
HERE YOU GO.
THANK YOU.
SORRY, LANDLORD'S RULES.
S'OK.
XAIME 09.10

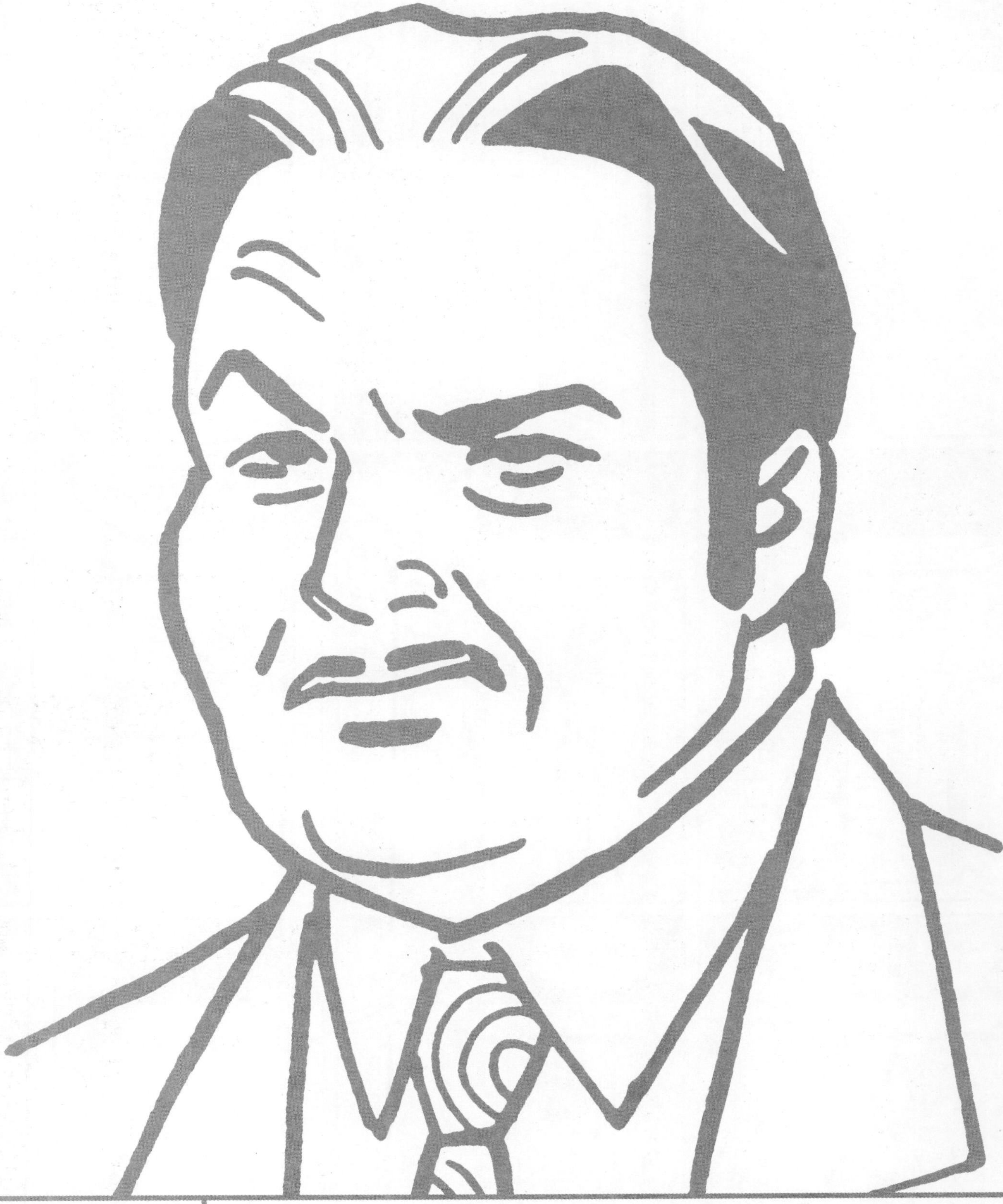

2 BROWNTOWN

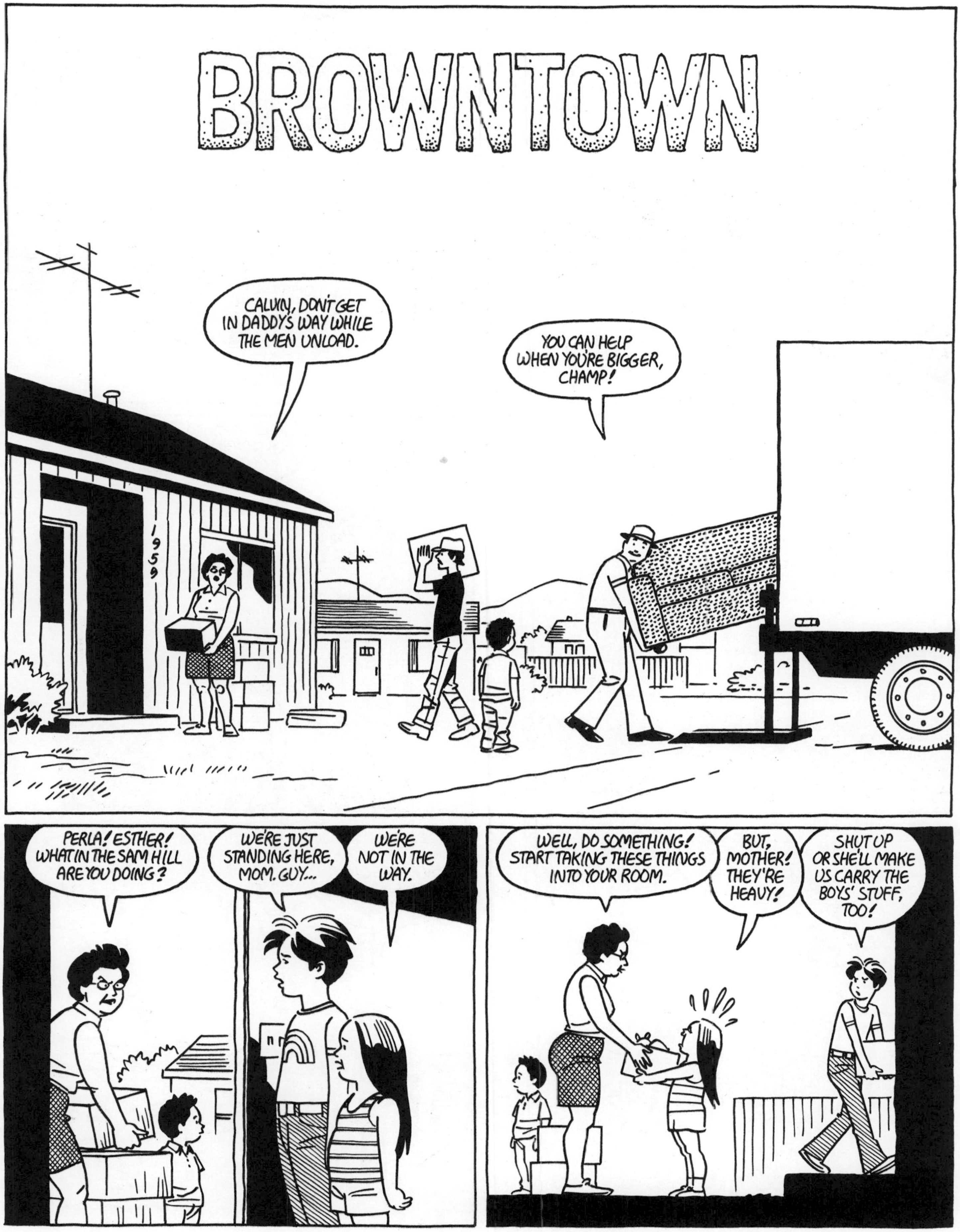
BROWNTOWN
CALVIN, DON'T GET IN DADDY'S WAY WHILE THE MEN UNLOAD.
YOU CAN HELP WHEN YOU'RE BIGGER, CHAMP!
1959
PERLA! ESTHER! WHAT IN THE SAM HILL ARE YOU DOING?
WE'RE JUST STANDING HERE, MOM. GUY...
WE'RE NOT IN THE WAY.
WELL, DO SOMETHING! START TAKING THESE THINGS INTO YOUR ROOM.
BUT, MOTHER! THEY'RE HEAVY!
SHUT UP OR SHE'LL MAKE US CARRY THE BOYS' STUFF, TOO!

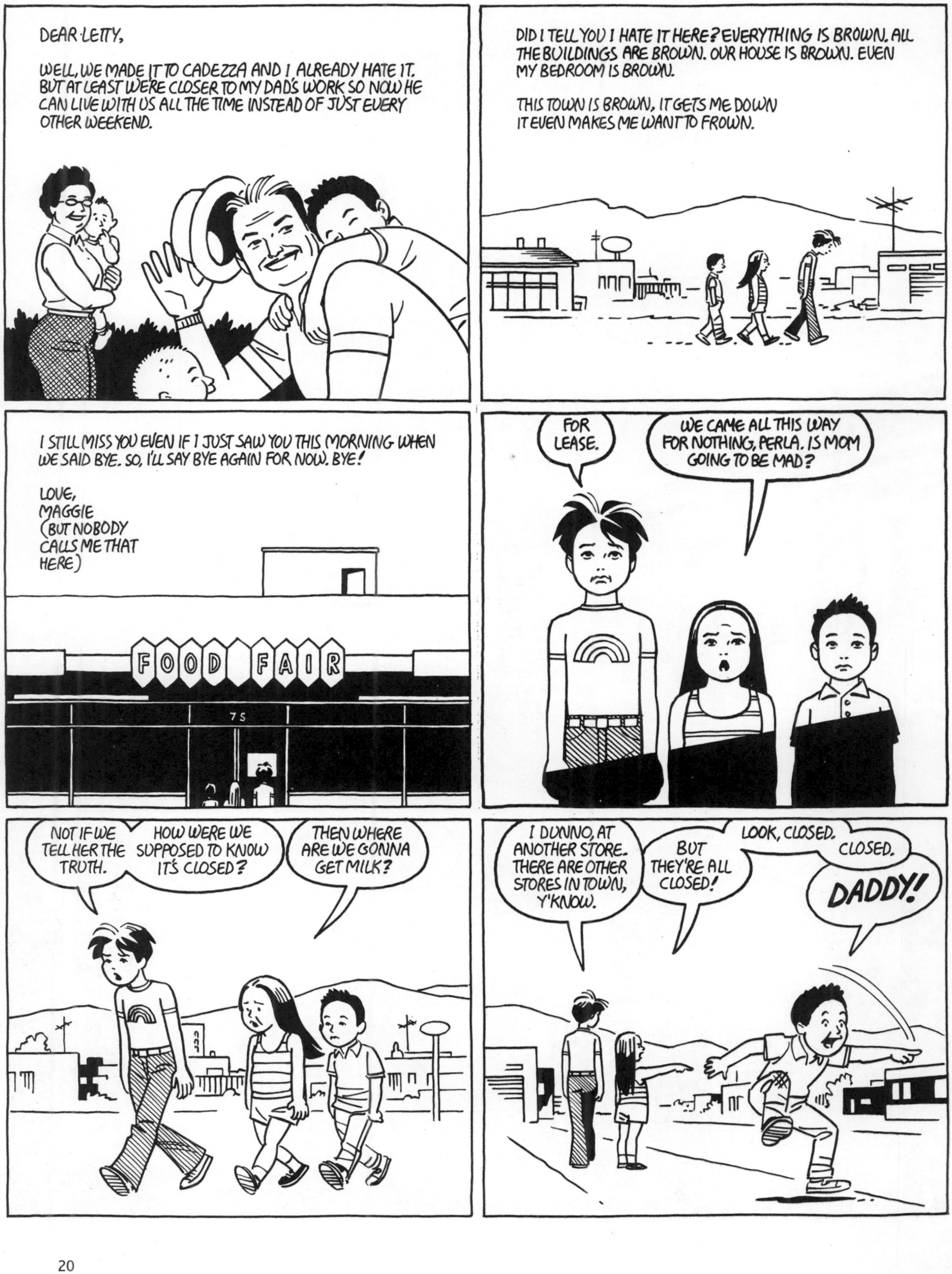
DEAR LETTY,
WELL, WE MADE IT TO CADEZZA AND I ALREADY HATE IT. BUT AT LEAST WE'RE CLOSER TO MY DAD'S WORK SO NOW HE CAN LIVE WITH US ALL THE TIME INSTEAD OF JUST EVERY OTHER WEEKEND.
DID I TELL YOU I HATE IT HERE? EVERYTHING IS BROWN. ALL THE BUILDINGS ARE BROWN. OUR HOUSE IS BROWN. EVEN MY BEDROOM IS BROWN.
THIS TOWN IS BROWN, IT GETS ME DOWN
IT EVEN MAKES ME WANT TO FROWN.
I STILL MISS YOU EVEN IF I JUST SAW YOU THIS MORNING WHEN WE SAID BYE. SO, I'LL SAY BYE AGAIN FOR NOW. BYE!
LOVE,
MAGGIE
(BUT NOBODY CALLS ME THAT HERE)
FOOD FAIR
75
FOR LEASE.
WE CAME ALL THIS WAY FOR NOTHING, PERLA. IS MOM GOING TO BE MAD?
NOT IF WE TELL HER THE TRUTH.
HOW WERE WE SUPPOSED TO KNOW IT'S CLOSED?
THEN WHERE ARE WE GONNA GET MILK?
I DUNNO, AT ANOTHER STORE. THERE ARE OTHER STORES IN TOWN, Y'KNOW.
BUT THEY'RE ALL CLOSED!
LOOK, CLOSED.
CLOSED.
DADDY!

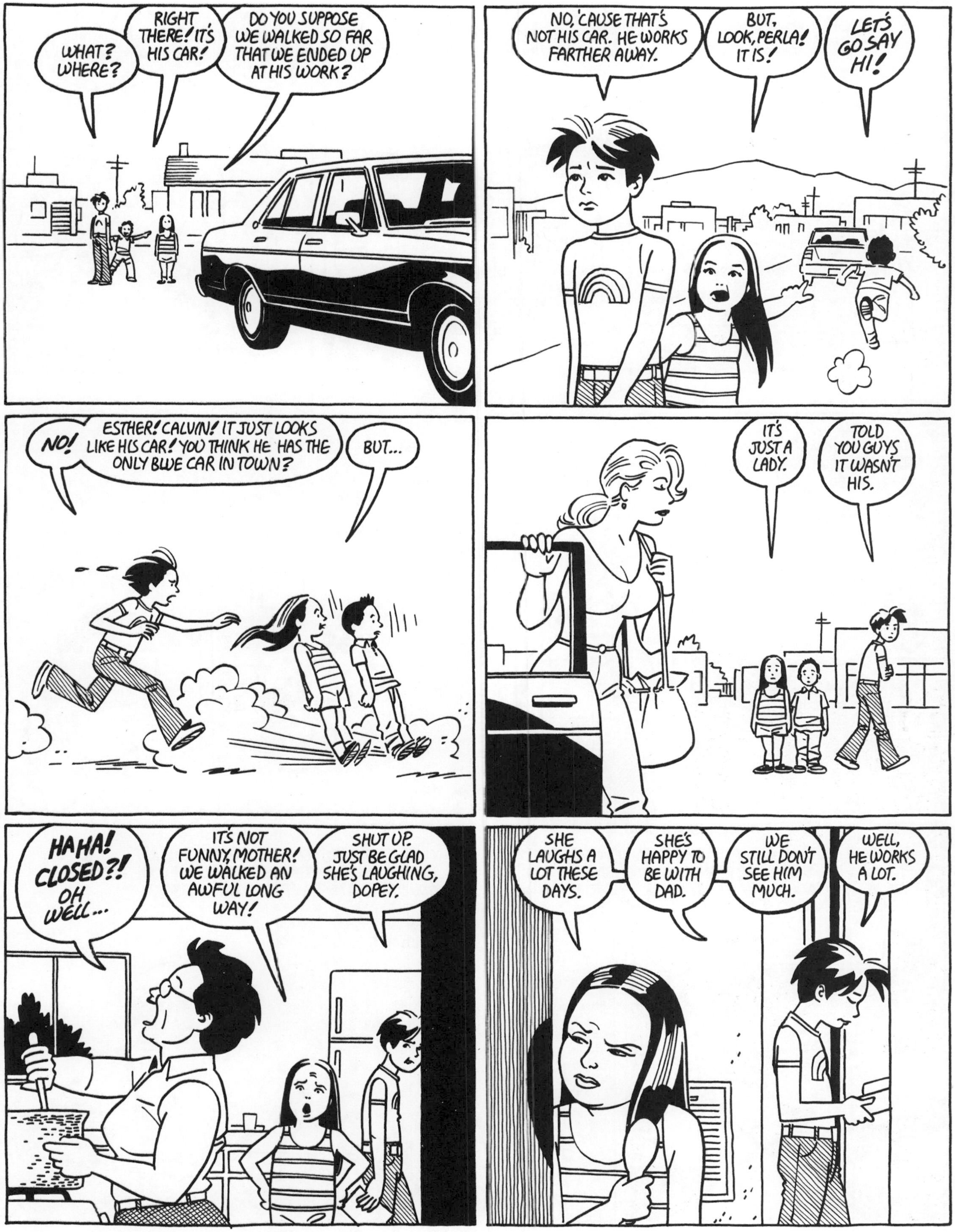
WHAT? WHERE?
RIGHT THERE! IT'S HIS CAR!
DO YOU SUPPOSE WE WALKED SO FAR THAT WE ENDED UP AT HIS WORK?
NO, 'CAUSE THAT'S NOT HIS CAR. HE WORKS FARTHER AWAY.
BUT, LOOK, PERLA! IT IS!
LET'S GO SAY HI!
NO!
ESTHER! CALVIN! IT JUST LOOKS LIKE HIS CAR! YOU THINK HE HAS THE ONLY BLUE CAR IN TOWN?
BUT...
IT'S JUST A LADY.
TOLD YOU GUYS IT WASN'T HIS.
HAHA! CLOSED?! OH WELL...
IT'S NOT FUNNY, MOTHER! WE WALKED AN AWFUL LONG WAY!
SHUT UP. JUST BE GLAD SHE'S LAUGHING, DOPEY.
SHE LAUGHS A LOT THESE DAYS.
SHE'S HAPPY TO BE WITH DAD.
WE STILL DON'T SEE HIM MUCH.
WELL, HE WORKS A LOT.

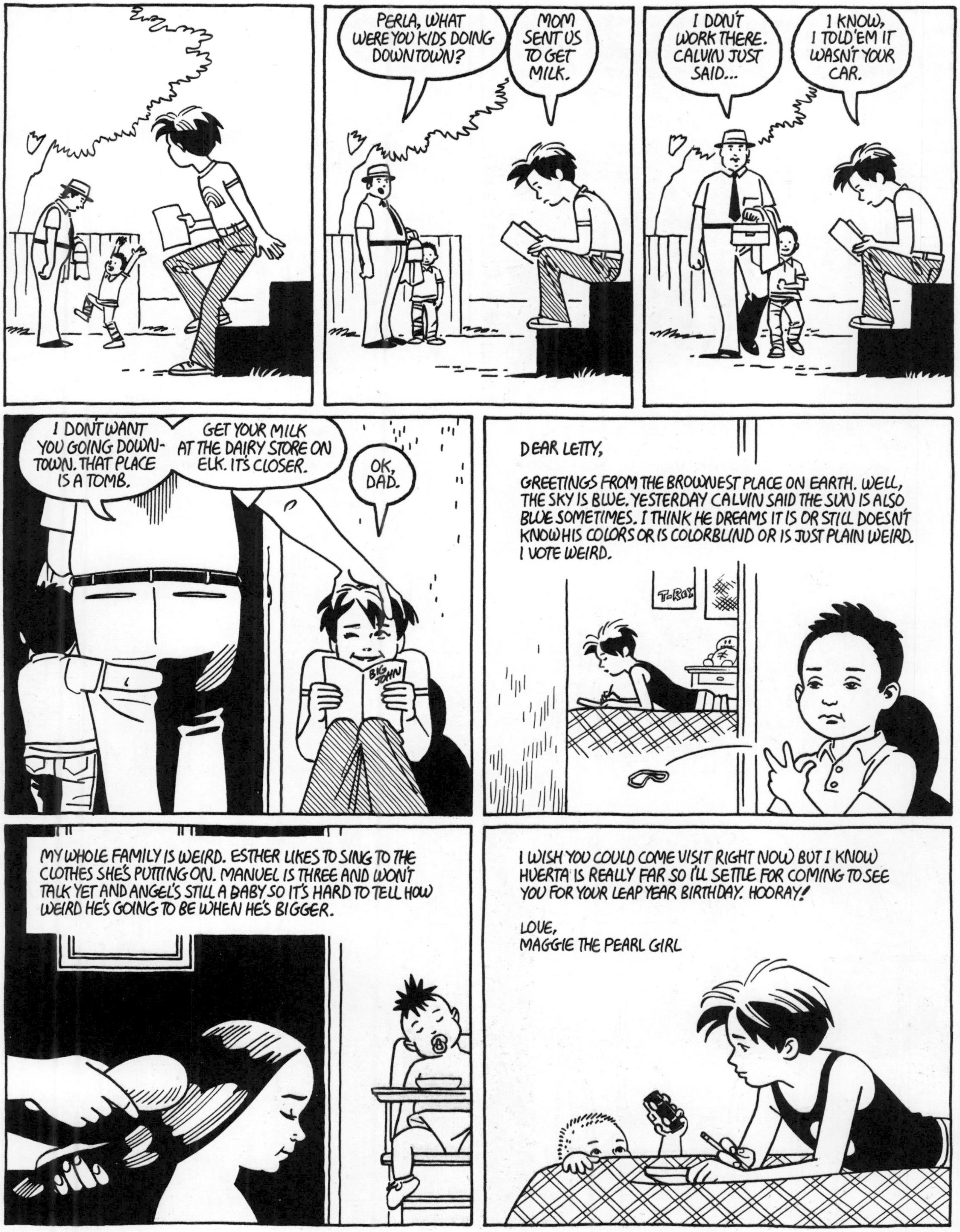
PERLA, WHAT WERE YOU KIDS DOING DOWNTOWN?
MOM SENT US TO GET MILK.
I DON'T WORK THERE. CALVIN JUST SAID...
I KNOW, I TOLD'EM IT WASN'T YOUR CAR.
I DON'T WANT YOU GOING DOWNTOWN. THAT PLACE IS A TOMB.
GET YOUR MILK AT THE DAIRY STORE ON ELK. IT'S CLOSER.
OK, DAD.
BIG JOHN
DEAR LETTY,
GREETINGS FROM THE BROWNEST PLACE ON EARTH. WELL, THE SKY IS BLUE. YESTERDAY CALVIN SAID THE SUN IS ALSO BLUE SOMETIMES. I THINK HE DREAMS IT IS OR STILL DOESN'T KNOW HIS COLORS OR IS COLORBLIND OR IS JUST PLAIN WEIRD. I VOTE WEIRD.
T-ROY
MY WHOLE FAMILY IS WEIRD. ESTHER LIKES TO SING TO THE CLOTHES SHE'S PUTTING ON. MANUEL IS THREE AND WON'T TALK YET AND ANGEL'S STILL A BABY SO IT'S HARD TO TELL HOW WEIRD HE'S GOING TO BE WHEN HE'S BIGGER.
I WISH YOU COULD COME VISIT RIGHT NOW BUT I KNOW HUERTA IS REALLY FAR SO I'LL SETTLE FOR COMING TO SEE YOU FOR YOUR LEAP YEAR BIRTHDAY. HOORAY!
LOVE,
MAGGIE THE PEARL GIRL

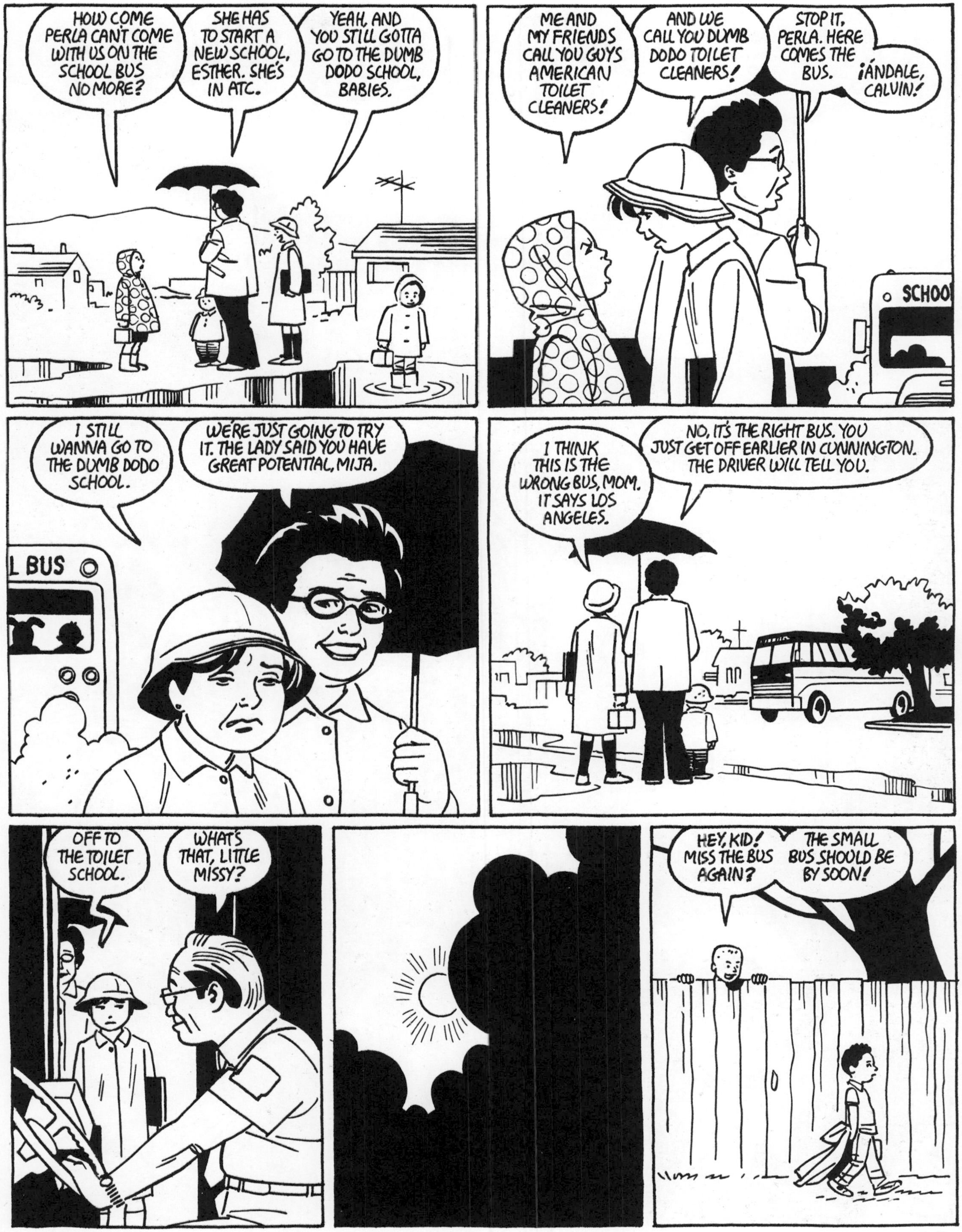
HOW COME PERLA CAN'T COME WITH US ON THE SCHOOL BUS NO MORE?
SHE HAS TO START A NEW SCHOOL, ESTHER. SHE'S IN ATC.
YEAH, AND YOU STILL GOTTA GO TO THE DUMB DODO SCHOOL, BABIES.
ME AND MY FRIENDS CALL YOU GUYS AMERICAN TOILET CLEANERS!
AND WE CALL YOU DUMB DODO TOILET CLEANERS!
STOP IT, PERLA. HERE COMES THE BUS.
¡ÁNDALE, CALVIN!
SCHOO
I STILL WANNA GO TO THE DUMB DODO SCHOOL.
WE'RE JUST GOING TO TRY IT. THE LADY SAID YOU HAVE GREAT POTENTIAL, MIJA.
L BUS
I THINK THIS IS THE WRONG BUS, MOM. IT SAYS LOS ANGELES.
NO, IT'S THE RIGHT BUS. YOU JUST GET OFF EARLIER IN CUNNINGTON. THE DRIVER WILL TELL YOU.
OFF TO THE TOILET SCHOOL.
WHAT'S THAT, LITTLE MISSY?
HEY, KID! MISS THE BUS AGAIN?
THE SMALL BUS SHOULD BE BY SOON!

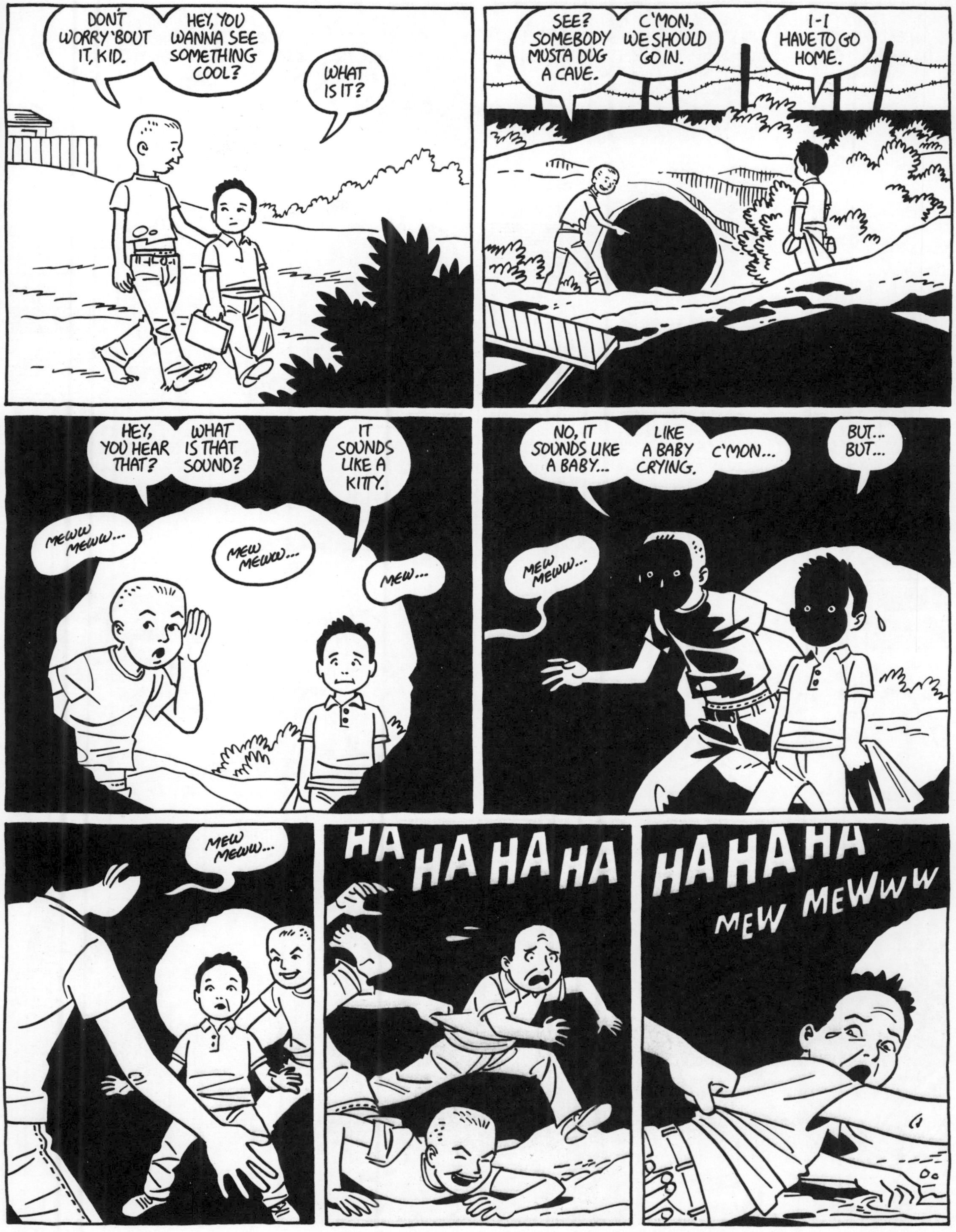
DON'T WORRY 'BOUT IT, KID.
HEY, YOU WANNA SEE SOMETHING COOL?
WHAT IS IT?
SEE? SOMEBODY MUSTA DUG A CAVE.
C'MON, WE SHOULD GO IN.
I-I HAVE TO GO HOME.
HEY, YOU HEAR THAT?
WHAT IS THAT SOUND?
IT SOUNDS LIKE A KITTY.
MEWW MEWW...
MEW MEWW...
MEW...
NO, IT SOUNDS LIKE A BABY...
LIKE A BABY CRYING.
C'MON...
BUT... BUT...
MEW MEWW...
MEW MEWW...
HA HA HA HA
HA HA HA HA
MEW MEWWW

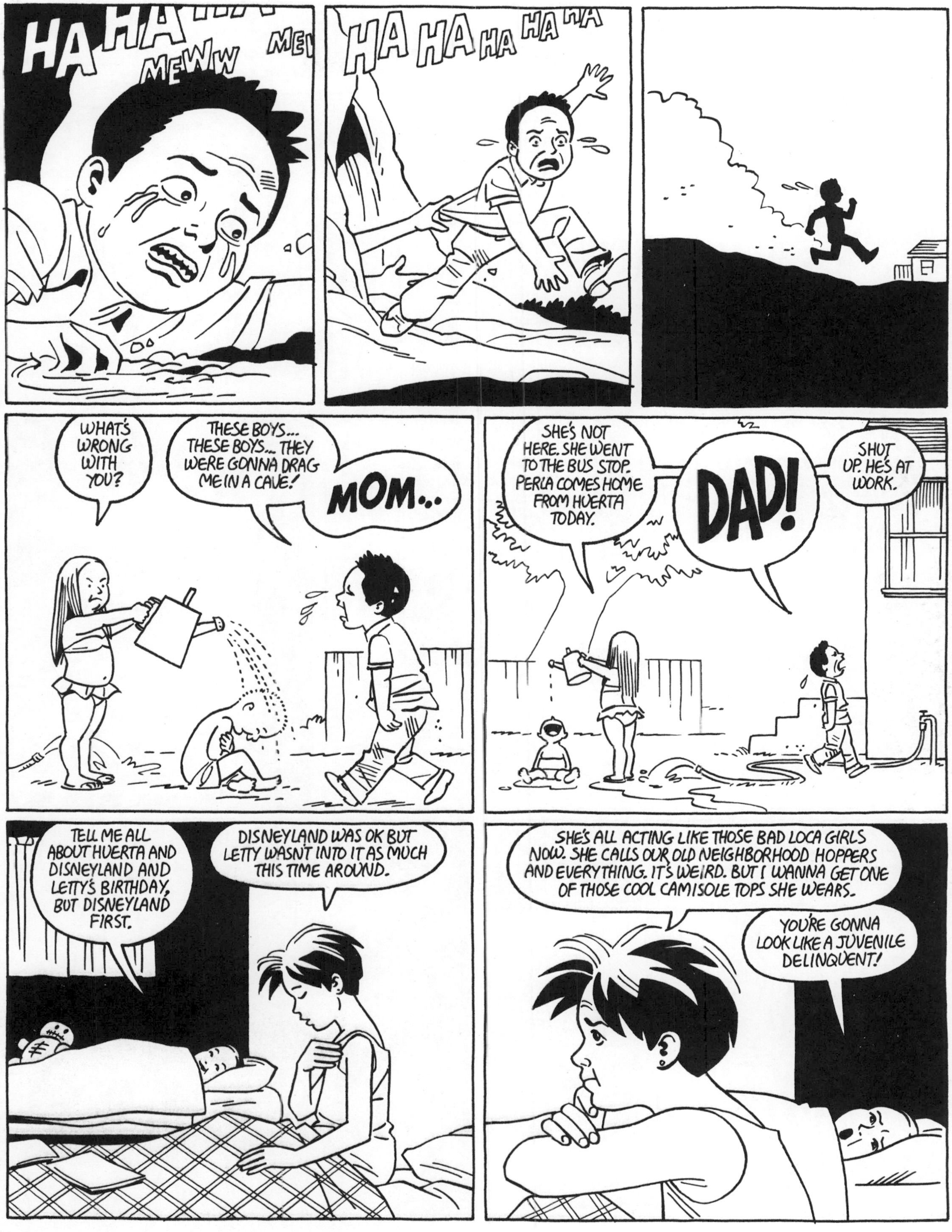
HA HA
MEWW
MEW
HA HA HA HA HA
WHAT'S WRONG WITH YOU?
THESE BOYS... THESE BOYS... THEY WERE GONNA DRAG ME IN A CAVE!
MOM...
SHE'S NOT HERE. SHE WENT TO THE BUS STOP. PERLA COMES HOME FROM HUERTA TODAY.
DAD!
SHUT UP. HE'S AT WORK.
TELL ME ALL ABOUT HUERTA AND DISNEYLAND AND LETTY'S BIRTHDAY, BUT DISNEYLAND FIRST.
DISNEYLAND WAS OK BUT LETTY WASN'T INTO IT AS MUCH THIS TIME AROUND.
SHE'S ALL ACTING LIKE THOSE BAD LOCA GIRLS NOW. SHE CALLS OUR OLD NEIGHBORHOOD HOPPERS AND EVERYTHING. IT'S WEIRD. BUT I WANNA GET ONE OF THOSE COOL CAMISOLE TOPS SHE WEARS.
YOU'RE GONNA LOOK LIKE A JUVENILE DELINQUENT!

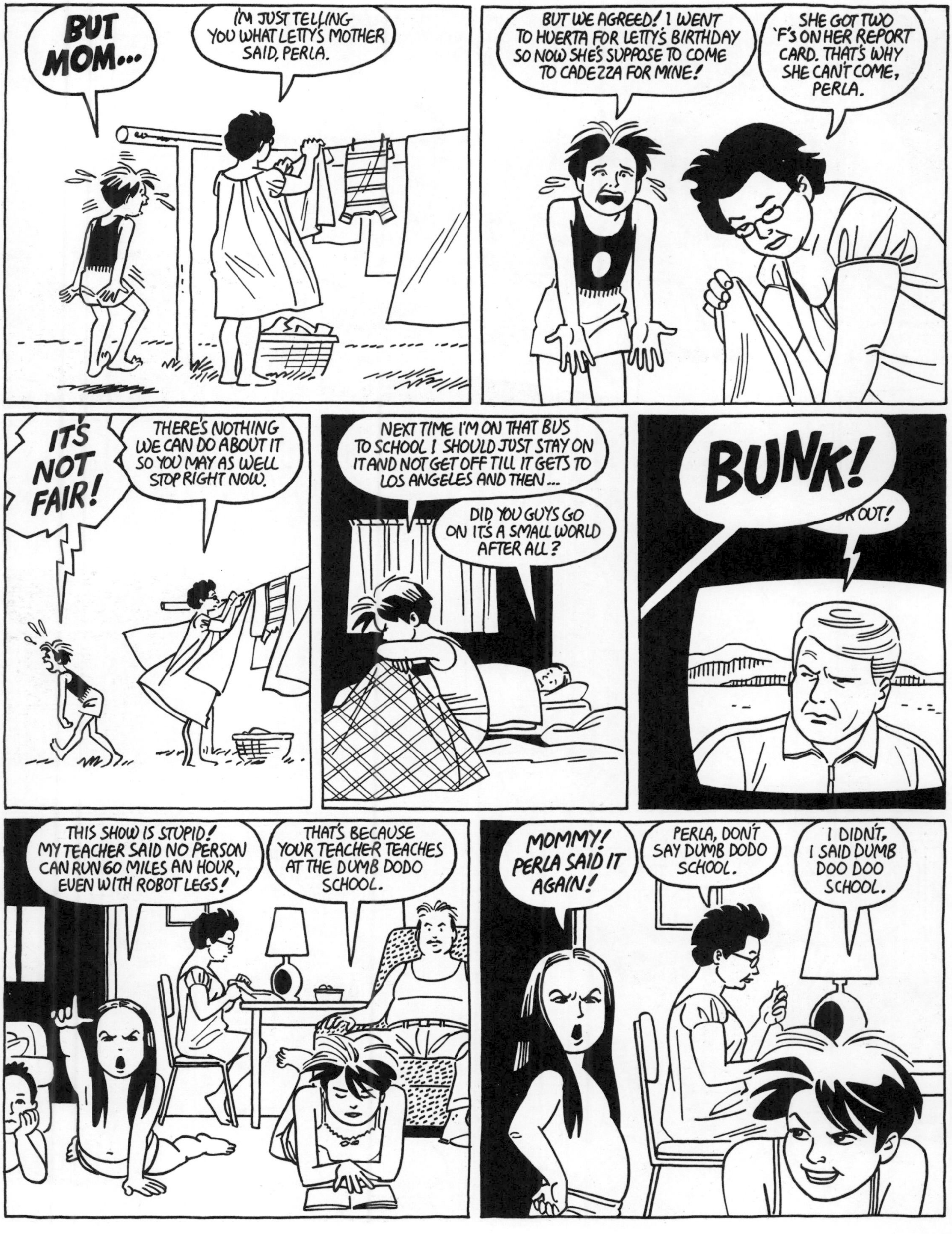
BUT MOM...
I'M JUST TELLING YOU WHAT LETTY'S MOTHER SAID, PERLA.
BUT WE AGREED! I WENT TO HUERTA FOR LETTY'S BIRTHDAY SO NOW SHE'S SUPPOSE TO COME TO CADEZZA FOR MINE!
SHE GOT TWO `F'S ON HER REPORT CARD. THAT'S WHY SHE CAN'T COME, PERLA.
IT'S NOT FAIR!
THERE'S NOTHING WE CAN DO ABOUT IT SO YOU MAY AS WELL STOP RIGHT NOW.
NEXT TIME I'M ON THAT BUS TO SCHOOL I SHOULD JUST STAY ON IT AND NOT GET OFF TILL IT GETS TO LOS ANGELES AND THEN...
DID YOU GUYS GO ON IT'S A SMALL WORLD AFTER ALL?
BUNK!
THIS SHOW IS STUPID! MY TEACHER SAID NO PERSON CAN RUN 60 MILES AN HOUR, EVEN WITH ROBOT LEGS!
THAT'S BECAUSE YOUR TEACHER TEACHES AT THE DUMB DODO SCHOOL.
MOMMY! PERLA SAID IT AGAIN!
PERLA, DON'T SAY DUMB DODO SCHOOL.
I DIDN'T, I SAID DUMB DOO DOO SCHOOL.

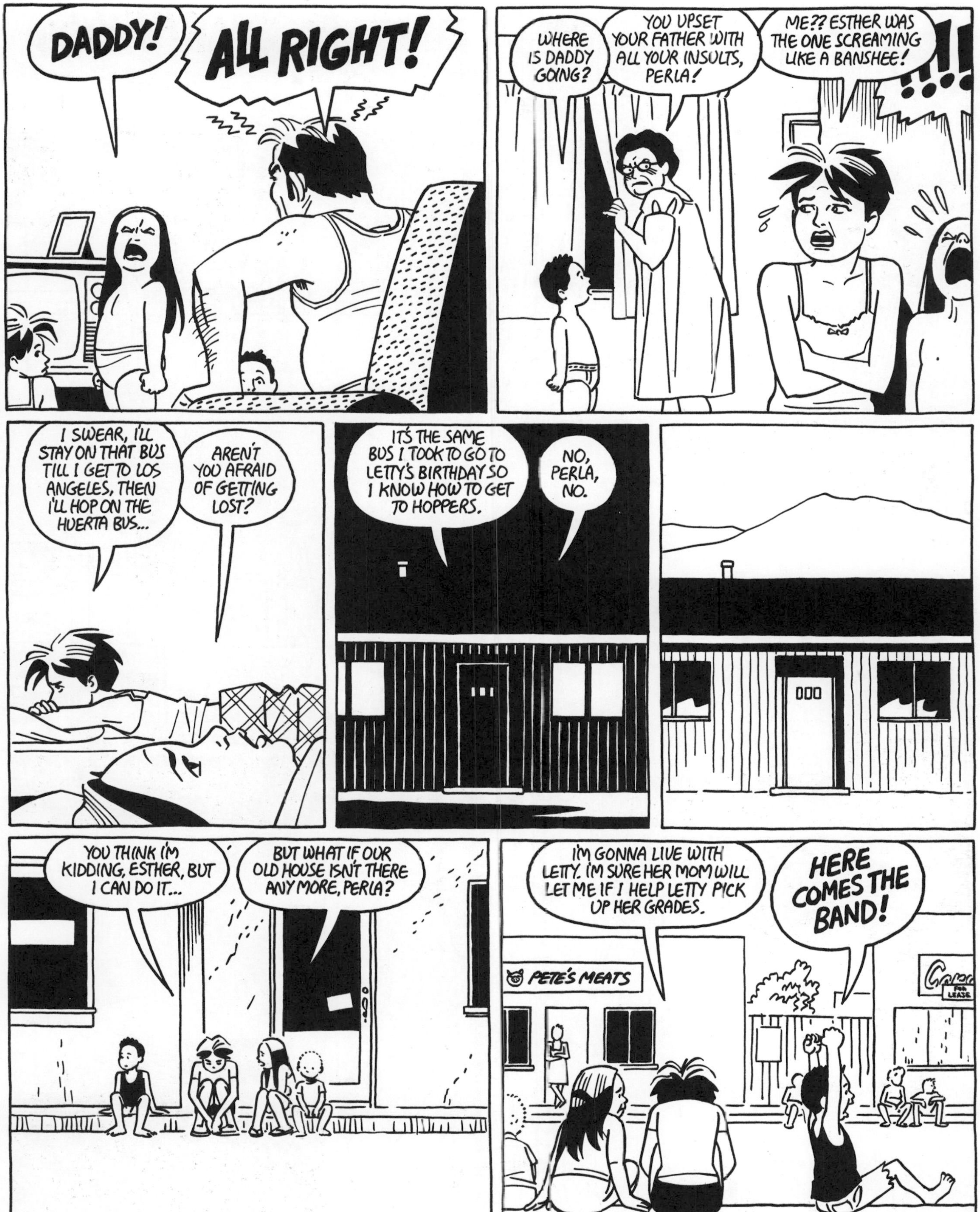
DADDY!
ALL RIGHT!
WHERE IS DADDY GOING?
YOU UPSET YOUR FATHER WITH ALL YOUR INSULTS, PERLA!
ME?? ESTHER WAS THE ONE SCREAMING LIKE A BANSHEE!
I SWEAR, I'LL STAY ON THAT BUS TILL I GET TO LOS ANGELES, THEN I'LL HOP ON THE HUERTA BUS...
AREN'T YOU AFRAID OF GETTING LOST?
IT'S THE SAME BUS I TOOK TO GO TO LETTY'S BIRTHDAY SO I KNOW HOW TO GET TO HOPPERS.
NO, PERLA, NO.
YOU THINK I'M KIDDING, ESTHER, BUT I CAN DO IT...
BUT WHAT IF OUR OLD HOUSE ISN'T THERE ANY MORE, PERLA?
I'M GONNA LIVE WITH LETTY. I'M SURE HER MOM WILL LET ME IF I HELP LETTY PICK UP HER GRADES.
HERE COMES THE BAND!
PETE'S MEATS
FOR LEASE

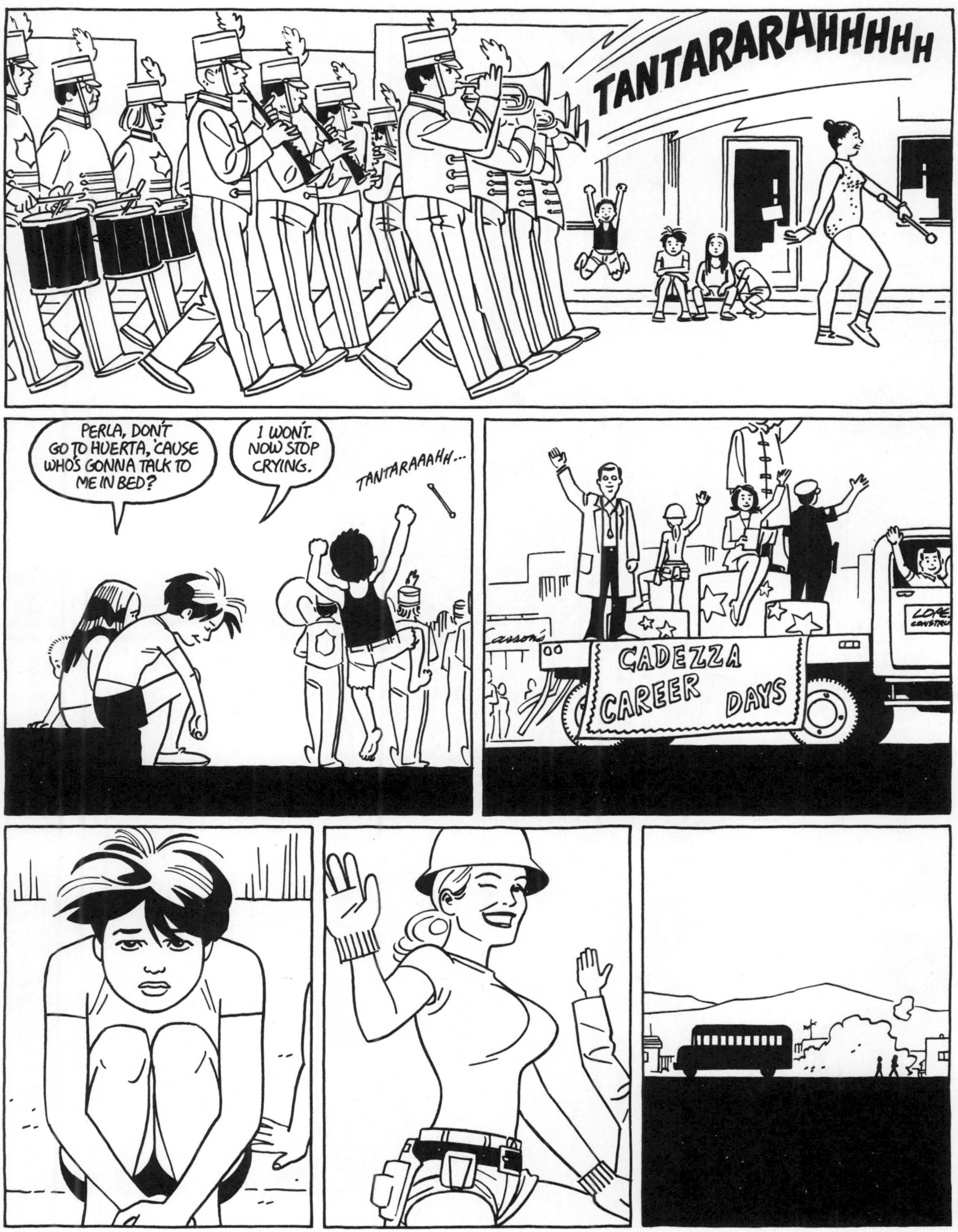
TANTARARAHHHHHH
PERLA, DON'T GO TO HUERTA, 'CAUSE WHO'S GONNA TALK TO ME IN BED?
I WON'T. NOW STOP CRYING.
TANTARAAAHH...
CADEZZA CAREER DAYS

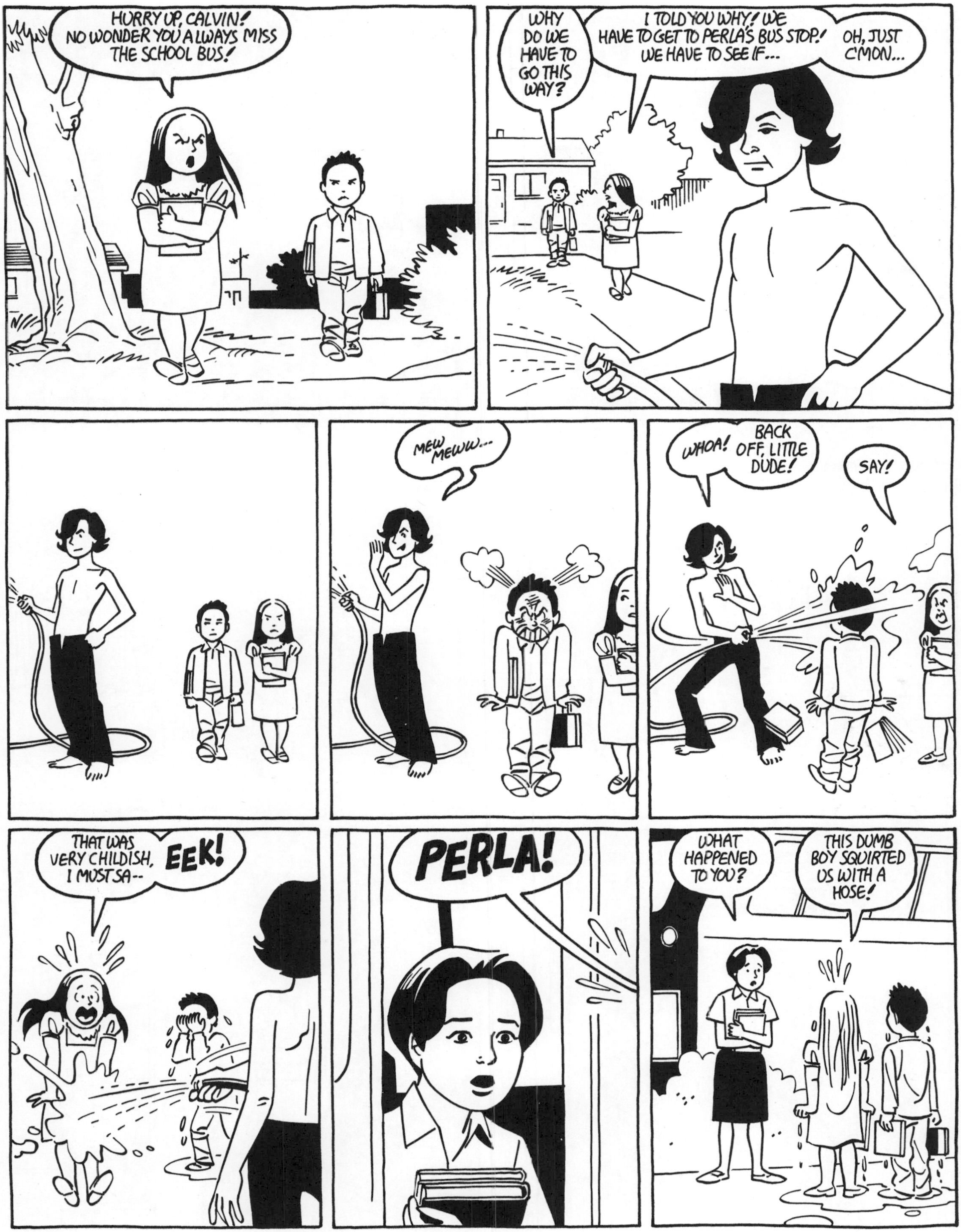
HURRY UP, CALVIN! NO WONDER YOU ALWAYS MISS THE SCHOOL BUS!
WHY DO WE HAVE TO GO THIS WAY?
I TOLD YOU WHY! WE HAVE TO GET TO PERLA'S BUS STOP! WE HAVE TO SEE IF...
OH, JUST C'MON...
MEW MEWW...
WHOA!
BACK OFF, LITTLE DUDE!
SAY!
THAT WAS VERY CHILDISH, I MUST SA--
EEK!
PERLA!
WHAT HAPPENED TO YOU?
THIS DUMB BOY SQUIRTED US WITH A HOSE!

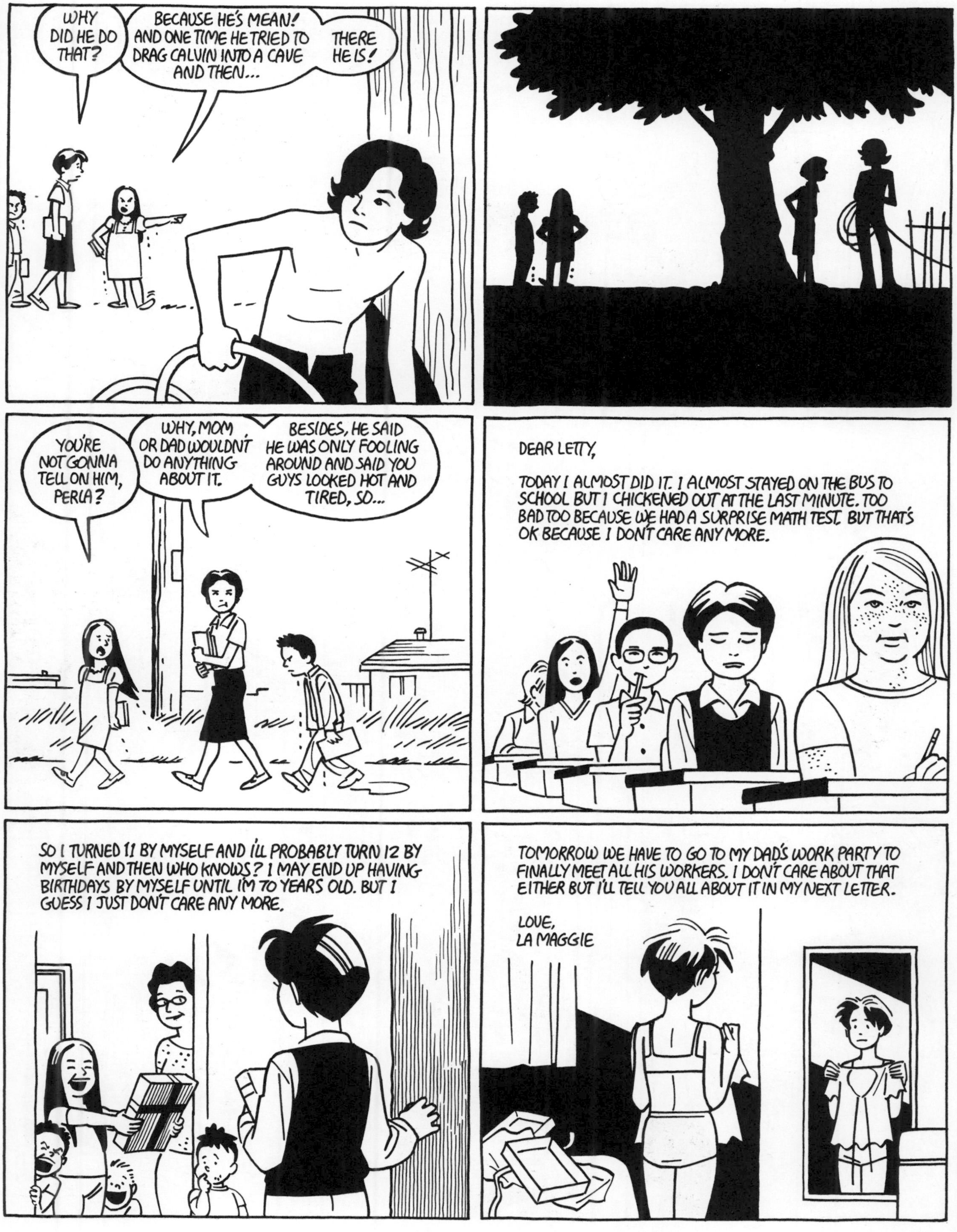
WHY DID HE DO THAT?
BECAUSE HE'S MEAN! AND ONE TIME HE TRIED TO DRAG CALVIN INTO A CAVE AND THEN...
THERE HE IS!
YOU'RE NOT GONNA TELL ON HIM, PERLA?
WHY, MOM OR DAD WOULDN'T DO ANYTHING ABOUT IT.
BESIDES, HE SAID HE WAS ONLY FOOLING AROUND AND SAID YOU GUYS LOOKED HOT AND TIRED, SO...
DEAR LETTY,
TODAY I ALMOST DID IT. I ALMOST STAYED ON THE BUS TO SCHOOL BUT I CHICKENED OUT AT THE LAST MINUTE. TOO BAD TOO BECAUSE WE HAD A SURPRISE MATH TEST. BUT THAT'S OK BECAUSE I DON'T CARE ANY MORE.
SO I TURNED 11 BY MYSELF AND I'LL PROBABLY TURN 12 BY MYSELF AND THEN WHO KNOWS? I MAY END UP HAVING BIRTHDAYS BY MYSELF UNTIL I'M 70 YEARS OLD. BUT I GUESS I JUST DON'T CARE ANY MORE.
TOMORROW WE HAVE TO GO TO MY DAD'S WORK PARTY TO FINALLY MEET ALL HIS WORKERS. I DON'T CARE ABOUT THAT EITHER BUT I'LL TELL YOU ALL ABOUT IT IN MY NEXT LETTER.
LOVE,
LA MAGGIE

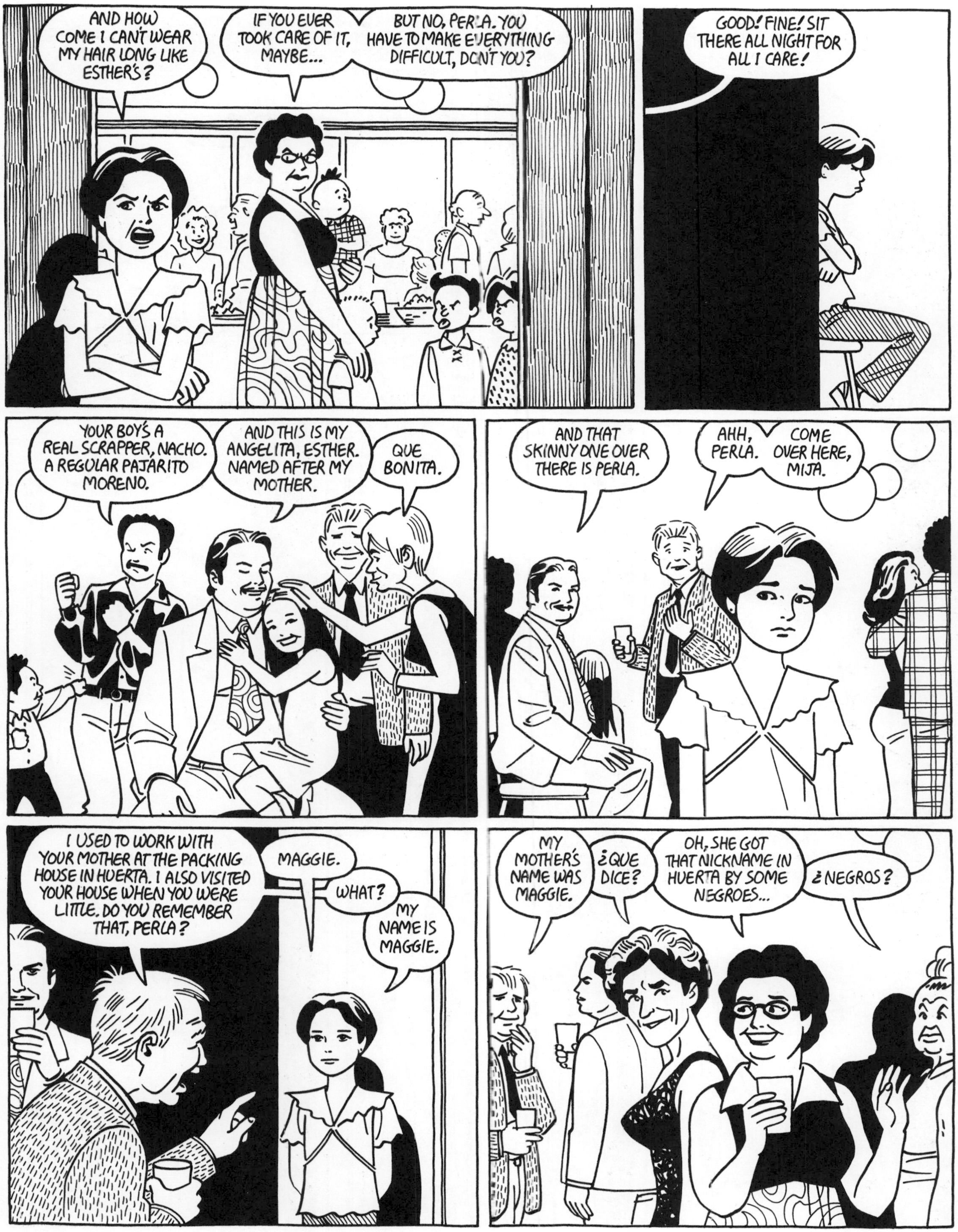
AND HOW COME I CAN'T WEAR MY HAIR LONG LIKE ESTHER'S?
IF YOU EVER TOOK CARE OF IT, MAYBE...
BUT NO, PERLA. YOU HAVE TO MAKE EVERYTHING DIFFICULT, DON'T YOU?
GOOD! FINE! SIT THERE ALL NIGHT FOR ALL I CARE!
YOUR BOY'S A REAL SCRAPPER, NACHO. A REGULAR PAJARITO MORENO.
AND THIS IS MY ANGELITA, ESTHER. NAMED AFTER MY MOTHER.
QUE BONITA.
AND THAT SKINNY ONE OVER THERE IS PERLA.
AHH, PERLA.
COME OVER HERE, MIJA.
I USED TO WORK WITH YOUR MOTHER AT THE PACKING HOUSE IN HUERTA. I ALSO VISITED YOUR HOUSE WHEN YOU WERE LITTLE. DO YOU REMEMBER THAT, PERLA?
MAGGIE.
WHAT?
MY NAME IS MAGGIE.
MY MOTHER'S NAME WAS MAGGIE.
¿QUE DICE?
OH, SHE GOT THAT NICKNAME IN HUERTA BY SOME NEGROES...
¿NEGROS?

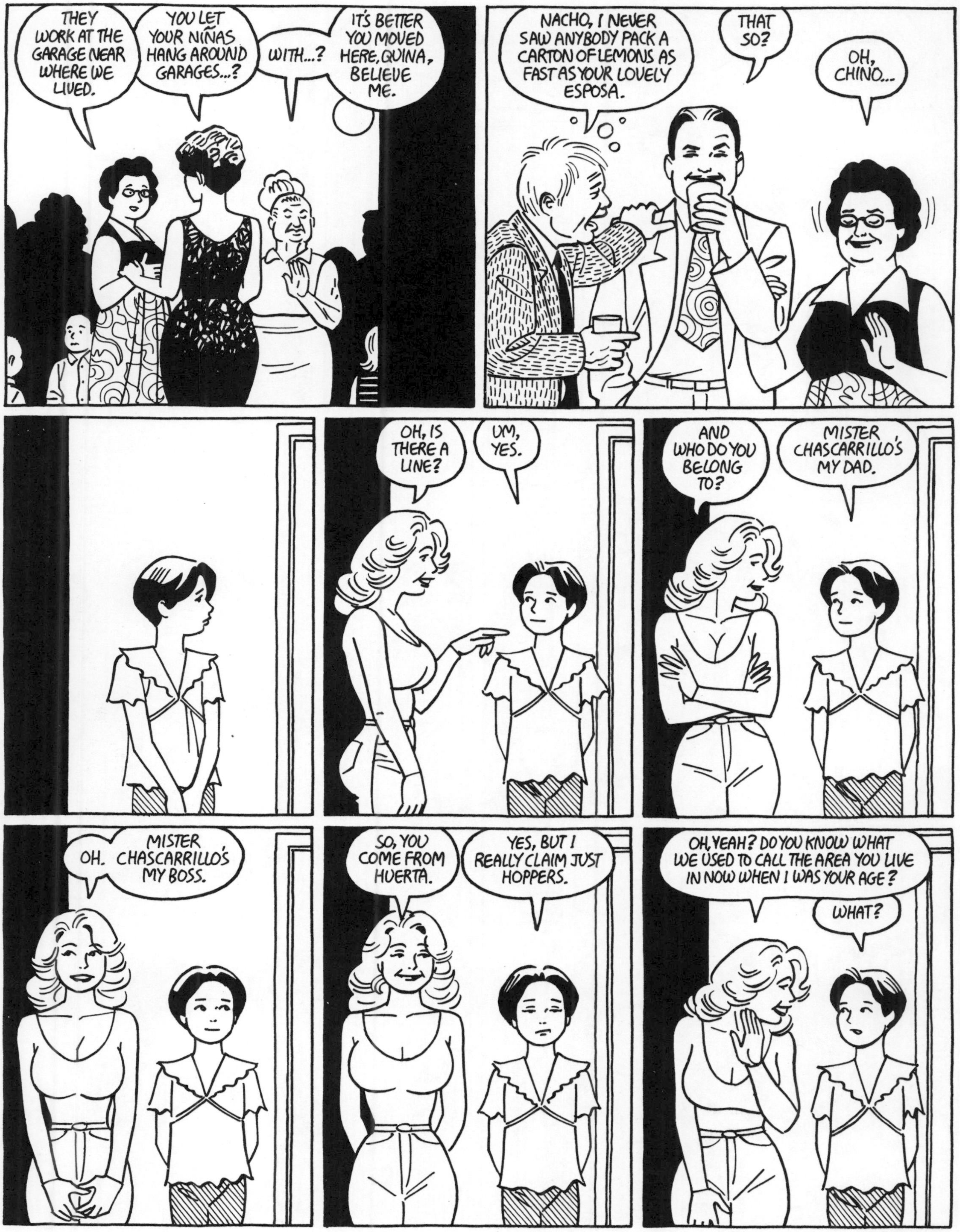
THEY WORK AT THE GARAGE NEAR WHERE WE LIVED.
YOU LET YOUR NIÑAS HANG AROUND GARAGES...?
WITH...?
IT'S BETTER YOU MOVED HERE, QUINA, BELIEVE ME.
NACHO, I NEVER SAW ANYBODY PACK A CARTON OF LEMONS AS FAST AS YOUR LOVELY ESPOSA.
THAT SO?
OH, CHINO...
OH, IS THERE A LINE?
UM, YES.
AND WHO DO YOU BELONG TO?
MISTER CHASCARRILLO'S MY DAD.
OH.
MISTER CHASCARRILLO'S MY BOSS.
SO, YOU COME FROM HUERTA.
YES, BUT I REALLY CLAIM JUST HOPPERS.
OH, YEAH? DO YOU KNOW WHAT WE USED TO CALL THE AREA YOU LIVE IN NOW WHEN I WAS YOUR AGE?
WHAT?

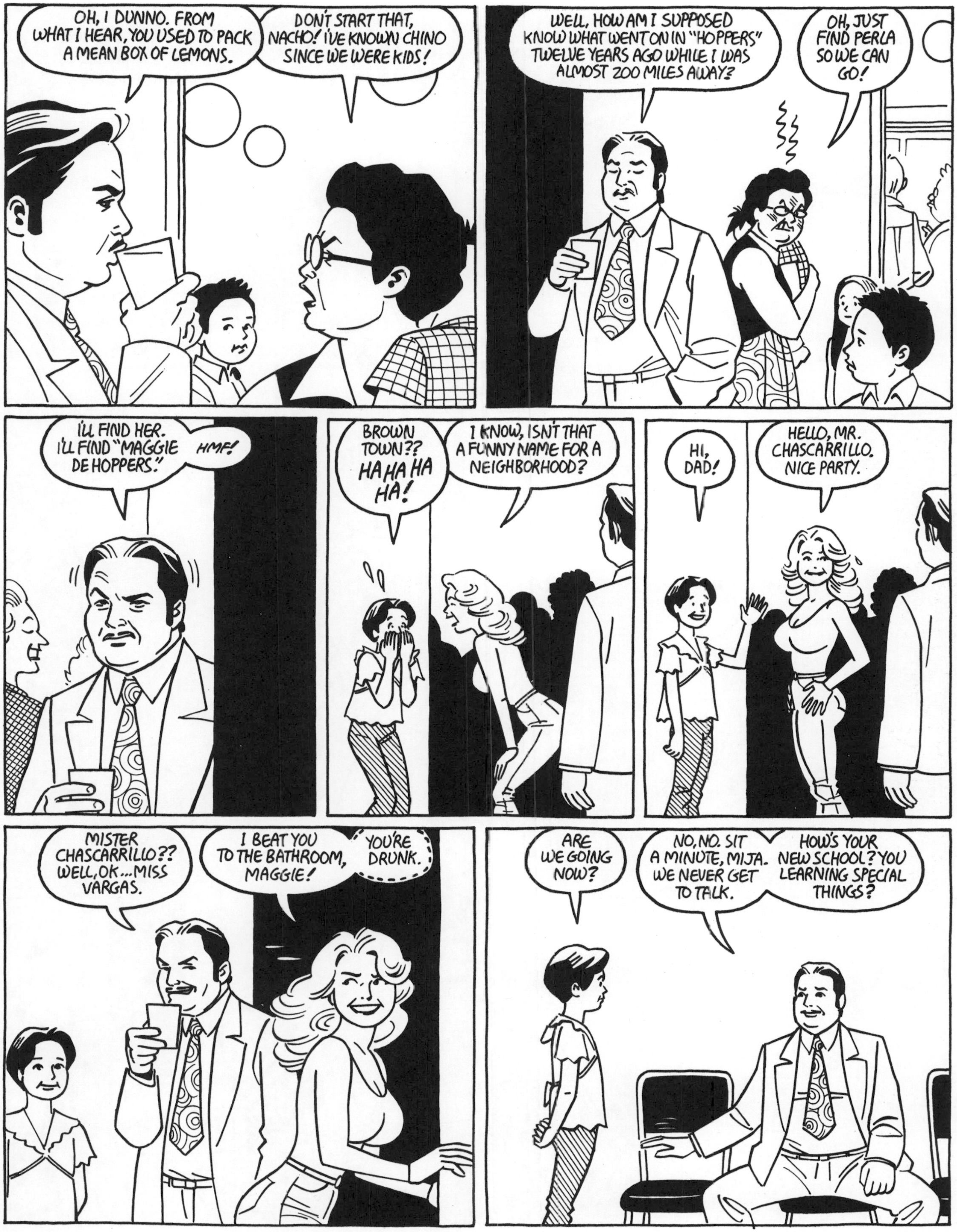
OH, I DUNNO. FROM WHAT I HEAR, YOU USED TO PACK A MEAN BOX OF LEMONS.
DON'T START THAT, NACHO! I'VE KNOWN CHINO SINCE WE WERE KIDS!
WELL, HOW AM I SUPPOSED KNOW WHAT WENT ON IN "HOPPERS" TWELVE YEARS AGO WHILE I WAS ALMOST 200 MILES AWAY?
OH, JUST FIND PERLA SO WE CAN GO!
I'LL FIND HER. I'LL FIND "MAGGIE DE HOPPERS."
HMF!
BROWN TOWN?? HA HA HA HA!
I KNOW, ISN'T THAT A FUNNY NAME FOR A NEIGHBORHOOD?
HI, DAD!
HELLO, MR. CHASCARRILLO. NICE PARTY.
MISTER CHASCARRILLO?? WELL, OK... MISS VARGAS.
I BEAT YOU TO THE BATHROOM, MAGGIE!
YOU'RE DRUNK.
ARE WE GOING NOW?
NO, NO. SIT A MINUTE, MIJA. WE NEVER GET TO TALK.
HOW'S YOUR NEW SCHOOL? YOU LEARNING SPECIAL THINGS?

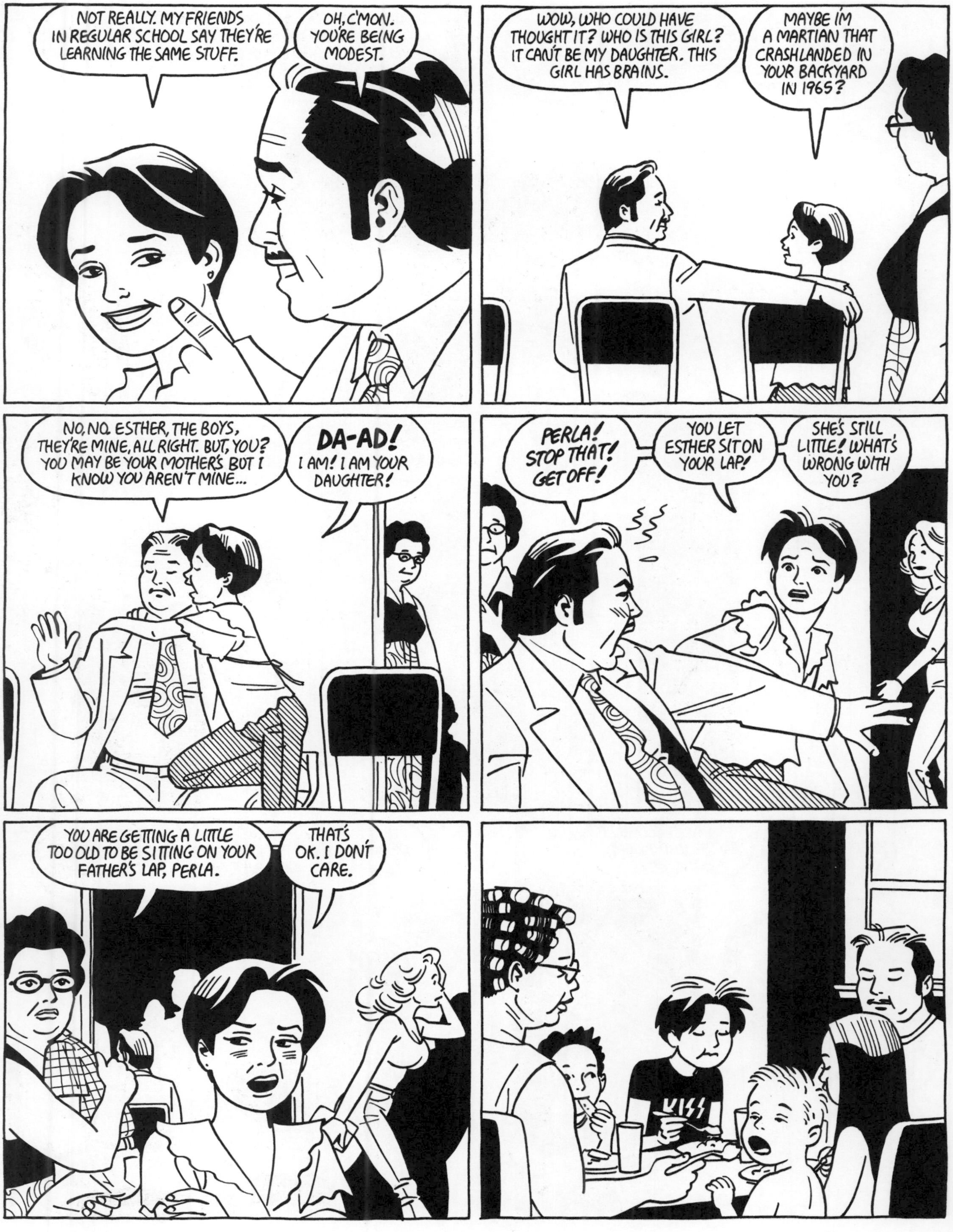
NOT REALLY. MY FRIENDS IN REGULAR SCHOOL SAY THEY'RE LEARNING THE SAME STUFF.
OH, C'MON. YOU'RE BEING MODEST.
WOW, WHO COULD HAVE THOUGHT IT? WHO IS THIS GIRL? IT CAN'T BE MY DAUGHTER. THIS GIRL HAS BRAINS.
MAYBE I'M A MARTIAN THAT CRASHLANDED IN YOUR BACKYARD IN 1965?
NO, NO. ESTHER, THE BOYS, THEY'RE MINE, ALL RIGHT. BUT, YOU? YOU MAY BE YOUR MOTHER'S BUT I KNOW YOU AREN'T MINE...
DA-AD! I AM! I AM YOUR DAUGHTER!
PERLA! STOP THAT! GET OFF!
YOU LET ESTHER SIT ON YOUR LAP!
SHE'S STILL LITTLE! WHAT'S WRONG WITH YOU?
YOU ARE GETTING A LITTLE TOO OLD TO BE SITTING ON YOUR FATHER'S LAP, PERLA.
THAT'S OK. I DON'T CARE.
KISS

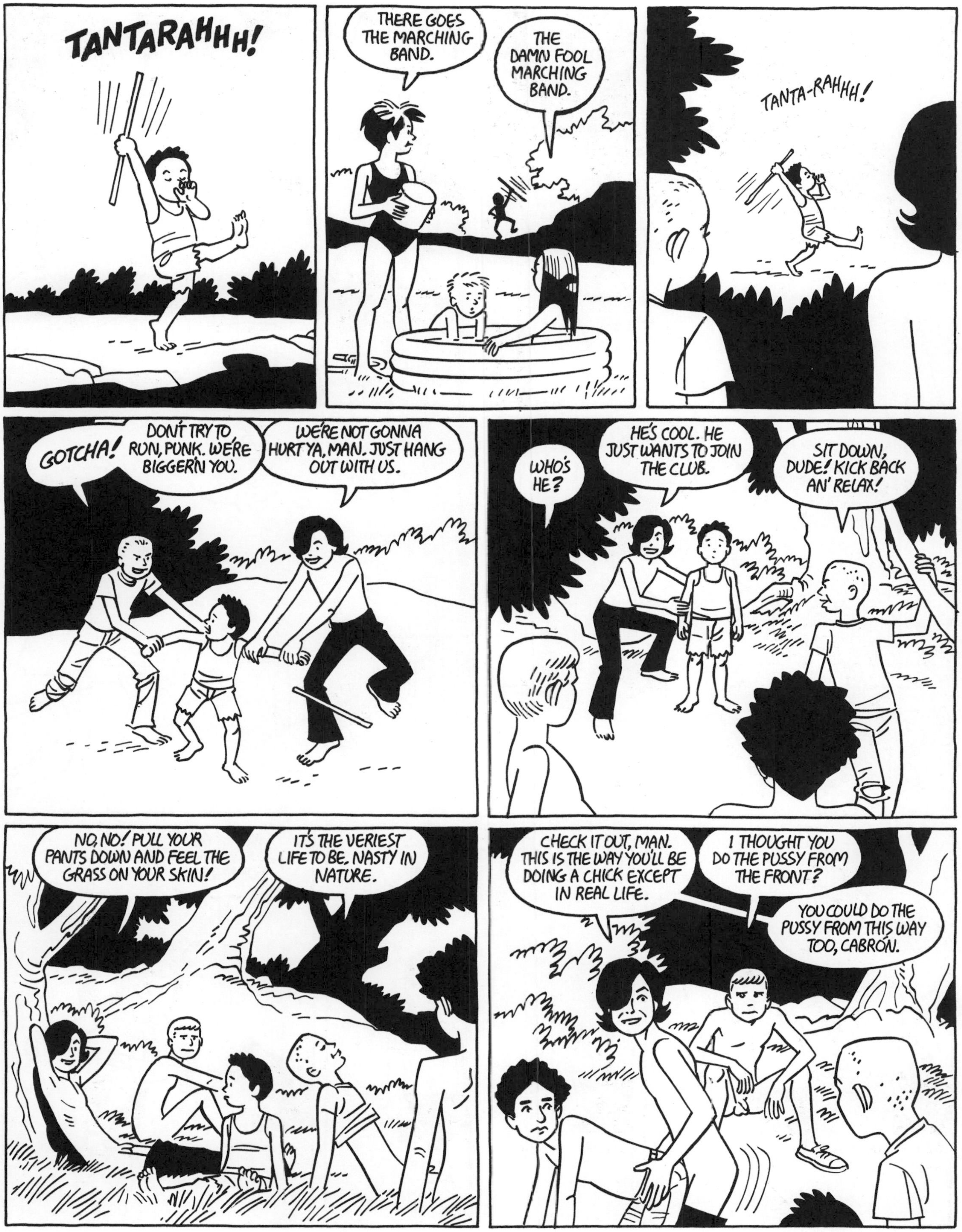
TANTARAHHH!
THERE GOES THE MARCHING BAND.
THE DAMN FOOL MARCHING BAND.
TANTA-RAHHH!
GOTCHA!
DON'T TRY TO RUN, PUNK. WE'RE BIGGER'N YOU.
WE'RE NOT GONNA HURT YA, MAN. JUST HANG OUT WITH US.
WHO'S HE?
HE'S COOL. HE JUST WANTS TO JOIN THE CLUB.
SIT DOWN, DUDE! KICK BACK AN' RELAX!
NO, NO! PULL YOUR PANTS DOWN AND FEEL THE GRASS ON YOUR SKIN!
IT'S THE VERIEST LIFE TO BE. NASTY IN NATURE.
CHECK IT OUT, MAN. THIS IS THE WAY YOU'LL BE DOING A CHICK EXCEPT IN REAL LIFE.
I THOUGHT YOU DO THE PUSSY FROM THE FRONT?
YOU COULD DO THE PUSSY FROM THIS WAY TOO, CABRÓN.

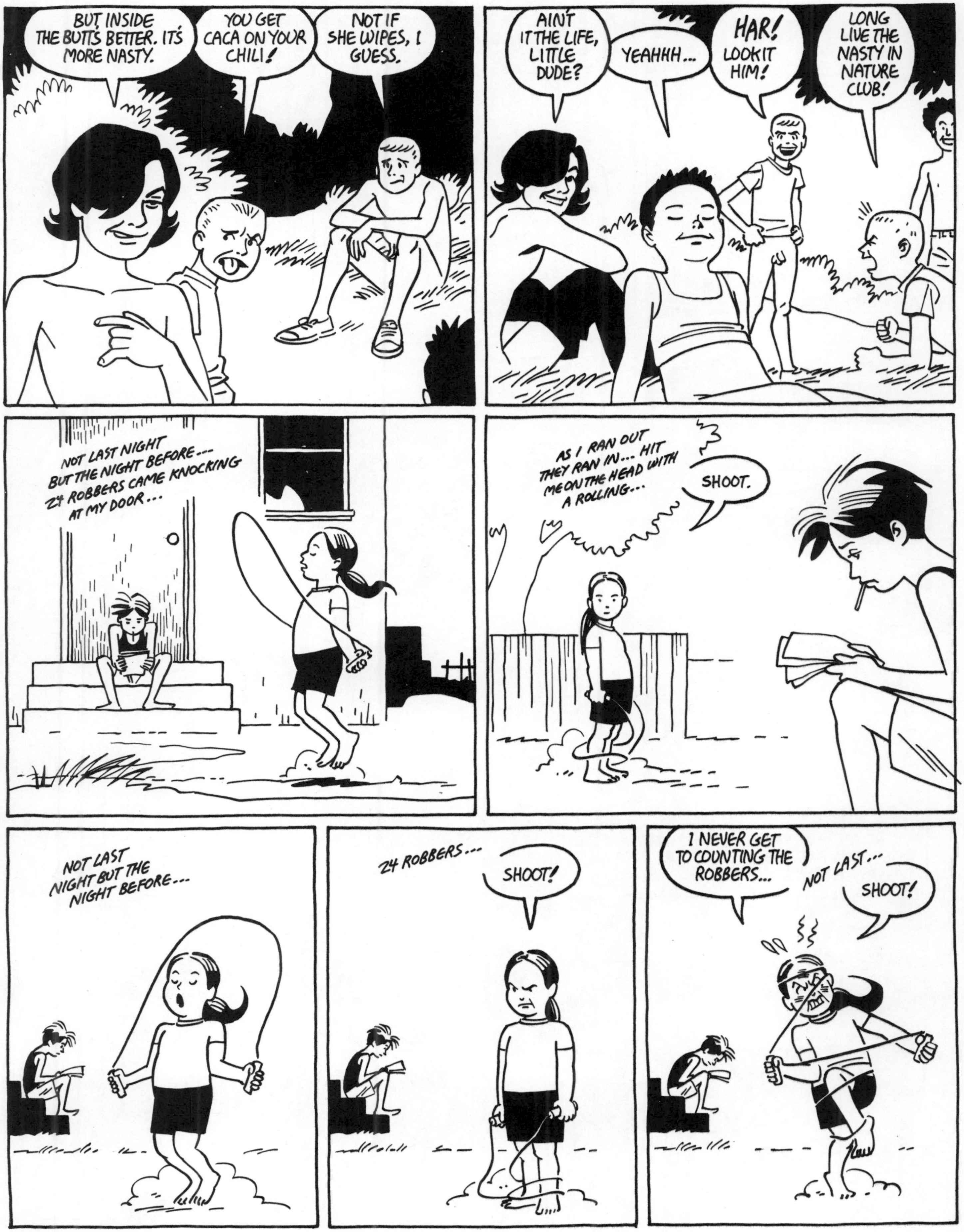
BUT, INSIDE THE BUTT'S BETTER. IT'S MORE NASTY.
YOU GET CACA ON YOUR CHILI!
NOT IF SHE WIPES, I GUESS.
AIN'T IT THE LIFE, LITTLE DUDE?
YEAHHH...
HAR! LOOKIT HIM!
LONG LIVE THE NASTY IN NATURE CLUB!
NOT LAST NIGHT BUT THE NIGHT BEFORE... 24 ROBBERS CAME KNOCKING AT MY DOOR...
AS I RAN OUT THEY RAN IN... HIT ME ON THE HEAD WITH A ROLLING...
SHOOT.
NOT LAST NIGHT BUT THE NIGHT BEFORE...
24 ROBBERS...
SHOOT!
I NEVER GET TO COUNTING THE ROBBERS...
NOT LAST...
SHOOT!

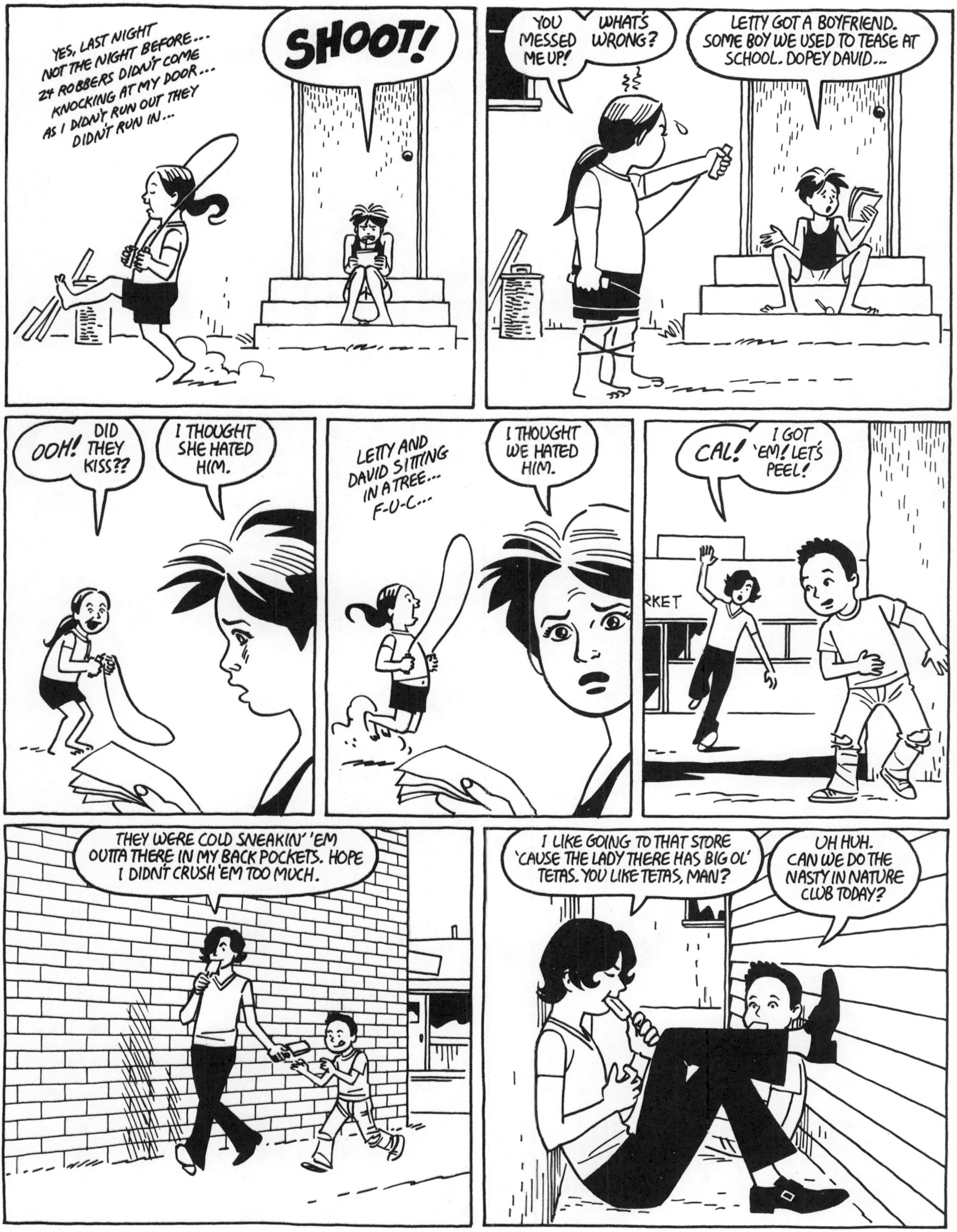

YES, LAST NIGHT NOT THE NIGHT BEFORE... 24 ROBBERS DIDN'T COME KNOCKING AT MY DOOR... AS I DIDN'T RUN OUT THEY DIDN'T RUN IN...
SHOOT!
YOU MESSED ME UP!
WHAT'S WRONG?
LETTY GOT A BOYFRIEND. SOME BOY WE USED TO TEASE AT SCHOOL. DOPEY DAVID...
OOH!
DID THEY KISS??
I THOUGHT SHE HATED HIM.
LETTY AND DAVID SITTING IN A TREE... F-U-C...
I THOUGHT WE HATED HIM.
CAL!
I GOT 'EM! LET'S PEEL!
RKET
THEY WERE COLD SNEAKIN' 'EM OUTTA THERE IN MY BACK POCKETS. HOPE I DIDN'T CRUSH 'EM TOO MUCH.
I LIKE GOING TO THAT STORE 'CAUSE THE LADY THERE HAS BIG OL' TETAS. YOU LIKE TETAS, MAN?
UH HUH. CAN WE DO THE NASTY IN NATURE CLUB TODAY?

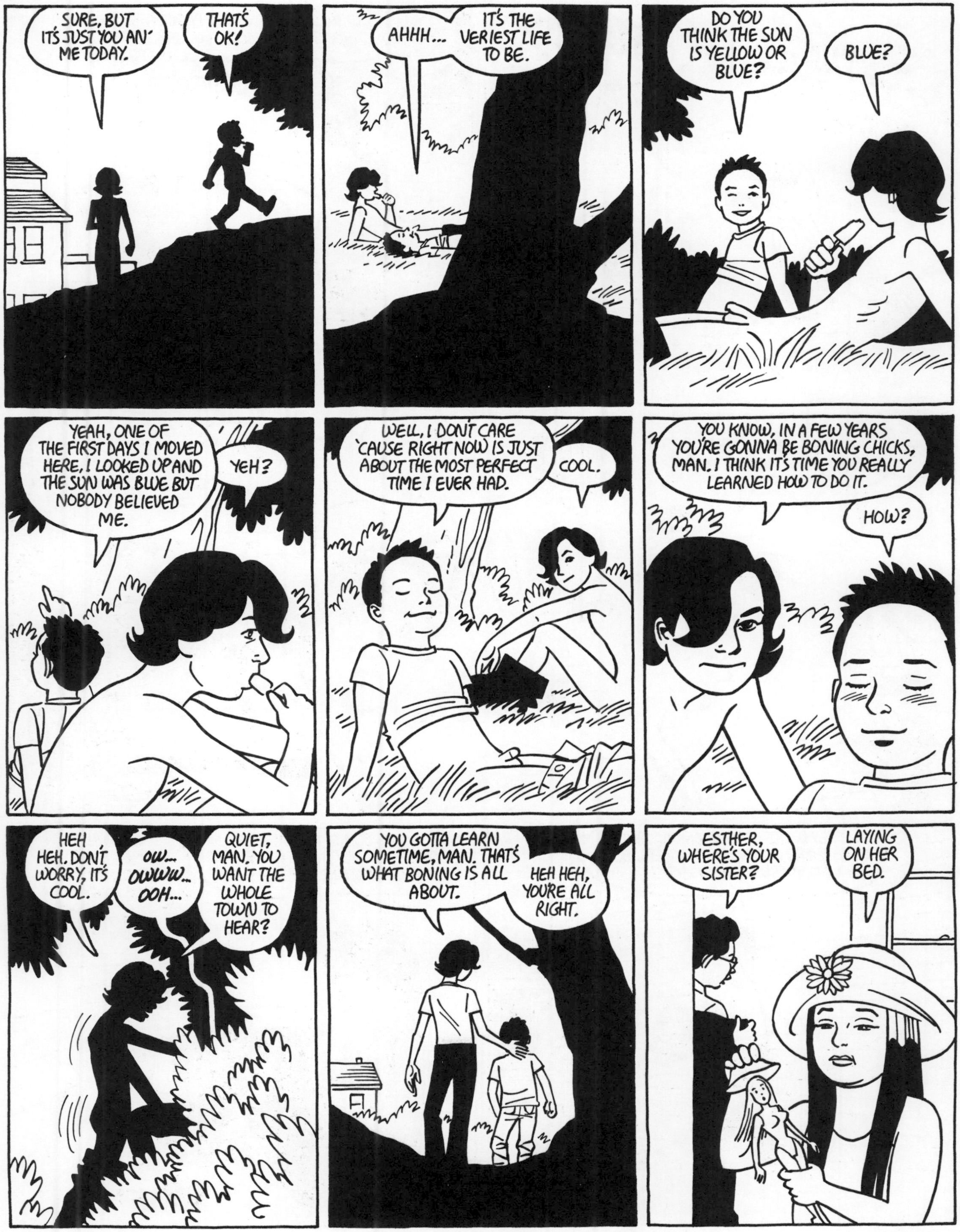
SURE, BUT IT'S JUST YOU AN' ME TODAY.
THAT'S OK!
AHHH...
IT'S THE VERIEST LIFE TO BE.
DO YOU THINK THE SUN IS YELLOW OR BLUE?
BLUE?
YEAH, ONE OF THE FIRST DAYS I MOVED HERE, I LOOKED UP AND THE SUN WAS BLUE BUT NOBODY BELIEVED ME.
YEH?
WELL, I DON'T CARE 'CAUSE RIGHT NOW IS JUST ABOUT THE MOST PERFECT TIME I EVER HAD.
COOL.
YOU KNOW, IN A FEW YEARS YOU'RE GONNA BE BONING CHICKS, MAN. I THINK IT'S TIME YOU REALLY LEARNED HOW TO DO IT.
HOW?
HEH HEH. DON'T WORRY, IT'S COOL.
OW... OWWW... OOH...
QUIET, MAN. YOU WANT THE WHOLE TOWN TO HEAR?
YOU GOTTA LEARN SOMETIME, MAN. THAT'S WHAT BONING IS ALL ABOUT.
HEH HEH, YOU'RE ALL RIGHT.
ESTHER, WHERE'S YOUR SISTER?
LAYING ON HER BED.

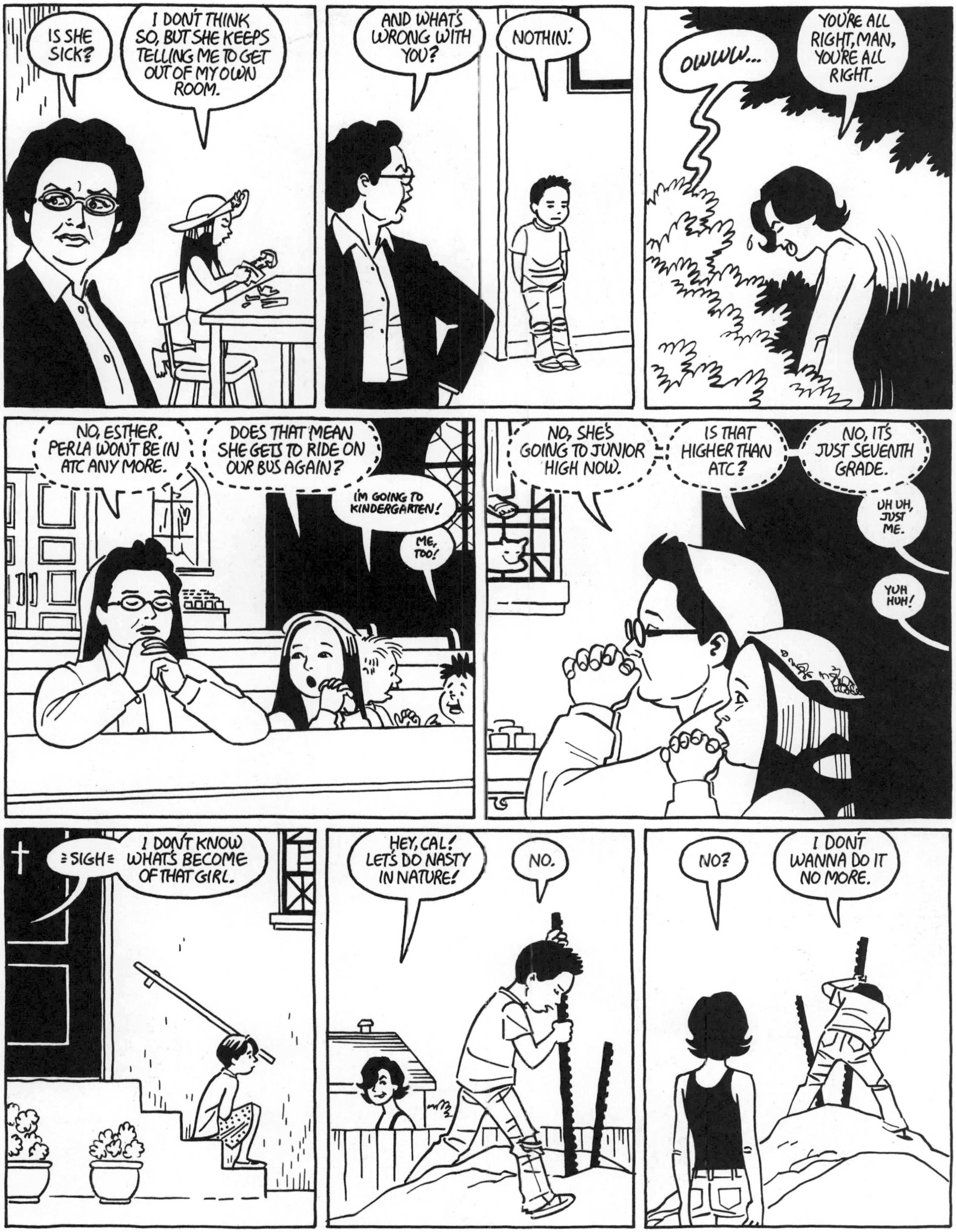
IS SHE SICK?
I DON'T THINK SO, BUT SHE KEEPS TELLING ME TO GET OUT OF MY OWN ROOM.
AND WHAT'S WRONG WITH YOU?
NOTHIN'.
OWWW...
YOU'RE ALL RIGHT, MAN, YOU'RE ALL RIGHT.
NO, ESTHER. PERLA WON'T BE IN ATC ANY MORE.
DOES THAT MEAN SHE GETS TO RIDE ON OUR BUS AGAIN?
I'M GOING TO KINDERGARTEN!
ME, TOO!
NO, SHE'S GOING TO JUNIOR HIGH NOW.
IS THAT HIGHER THAN ATC?
NO, IT'S JUST SEVENTH GRADE.
UH UH, JUST ME.
YUH HUH!
SIGH
I DON'T KNOW WHAT'S BECOME OF THAT GIRL.
HEY, CAL! LET'S DO NASTY IN NATURE!
NO.
NO?
I DON'T WANNA DO IT NO MORE.

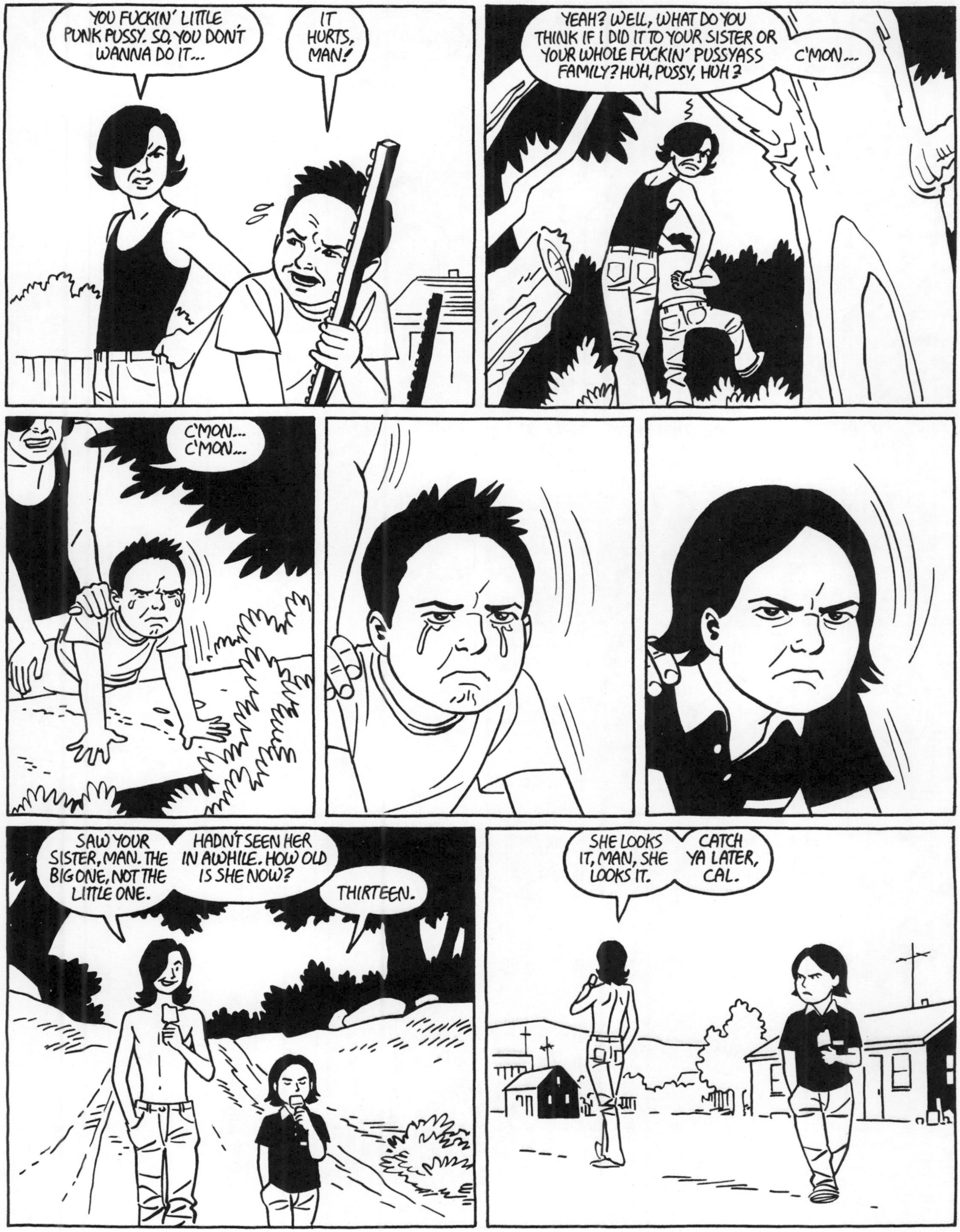
YOU FUCKIN' LITTLE PUNK PUSSY. SO, YOU DON'T WANNA DO IT...
IT HURTS, MAN!
YEAH? WELL, WHAT DO YOU THINK IF I DID IT TO YOUR SISTER OR YOUR WHOLE FUCKIN' PUSSYASS FAMILY? HUH, PUSSY, HUH?
C'MON...
C'MON... C'MON...
SAW YOUR SISTER, MAN. THE BIG ONE, NOT THE LITTLE ONE.
HADN'T SEEN HER IN AWHILE. HOW OLD IS SHE NOW?
THIRTEEN.
SHE LOOKS IT, MAN, SHE LOOKS IT.
CATCH YA LATER, CAL.

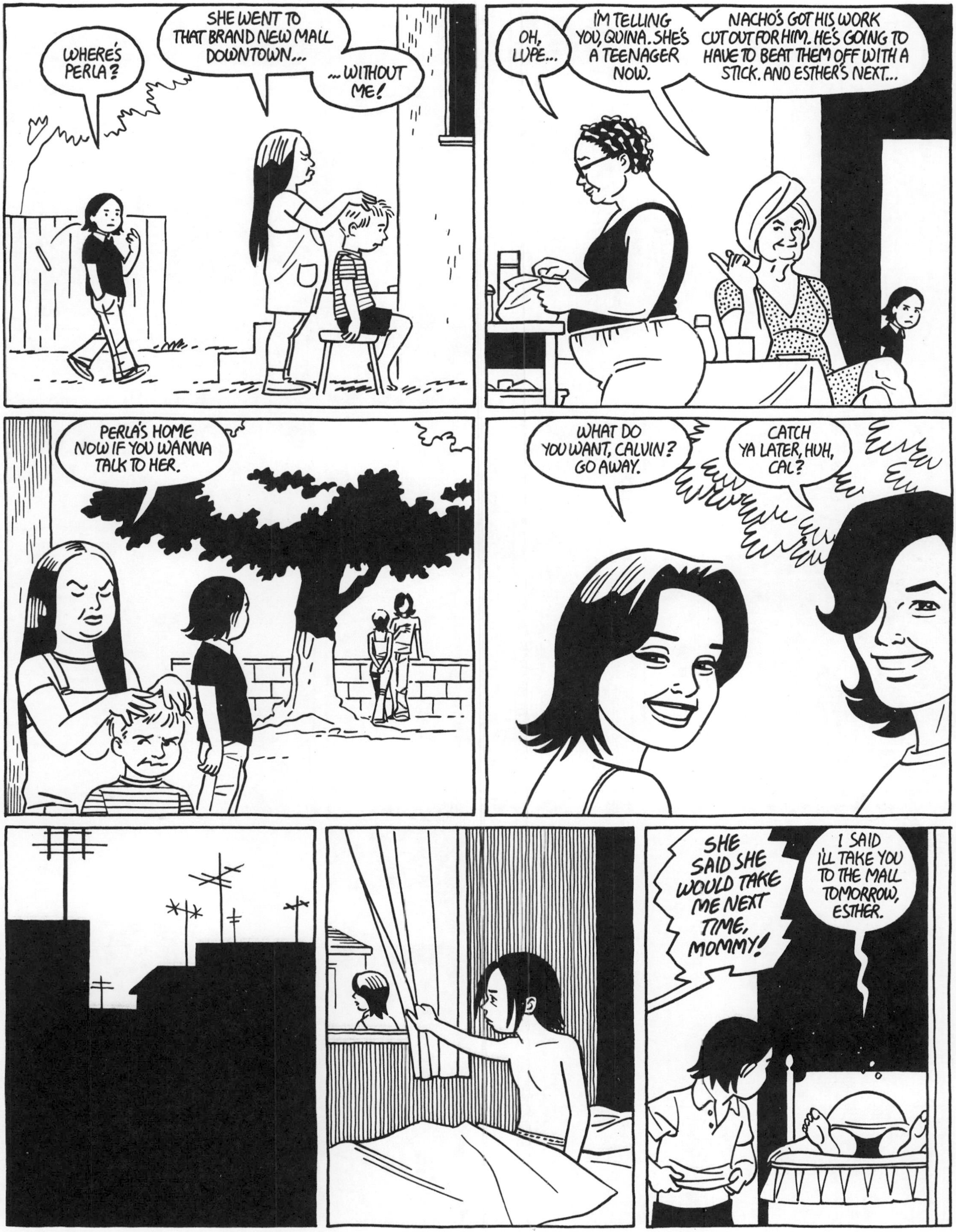
WHERE'S PERLA?
SHE WENT TO THAT BRAND NEW MALL DOWNTOWN...
...WITHOUT ME!
OH, LUPE...
I'M TELLING YOU, QUINA. SHE'S A TEENAGER NOW.
NACHO'S GOT HIS WORK CUT OUT FOR HIM. HE'S GOING TO HAVE TO BEAT THEM OFF WITH A STICK. AND ESTHER'S NEXT...
PERLA'S HOME NOW IF YOU WANNA TALK TO HER.
WHAT DO YOU WANT, CALVIN? GO AWAY.
CATCH YA LATER, HUH, CAL?
SHE SAID SHE WOULD TAKE ME NEXT TIME, MOMMY!
I SAID I'LL TAKE YOU TO THE MALL TOMORROW, ESTHER.

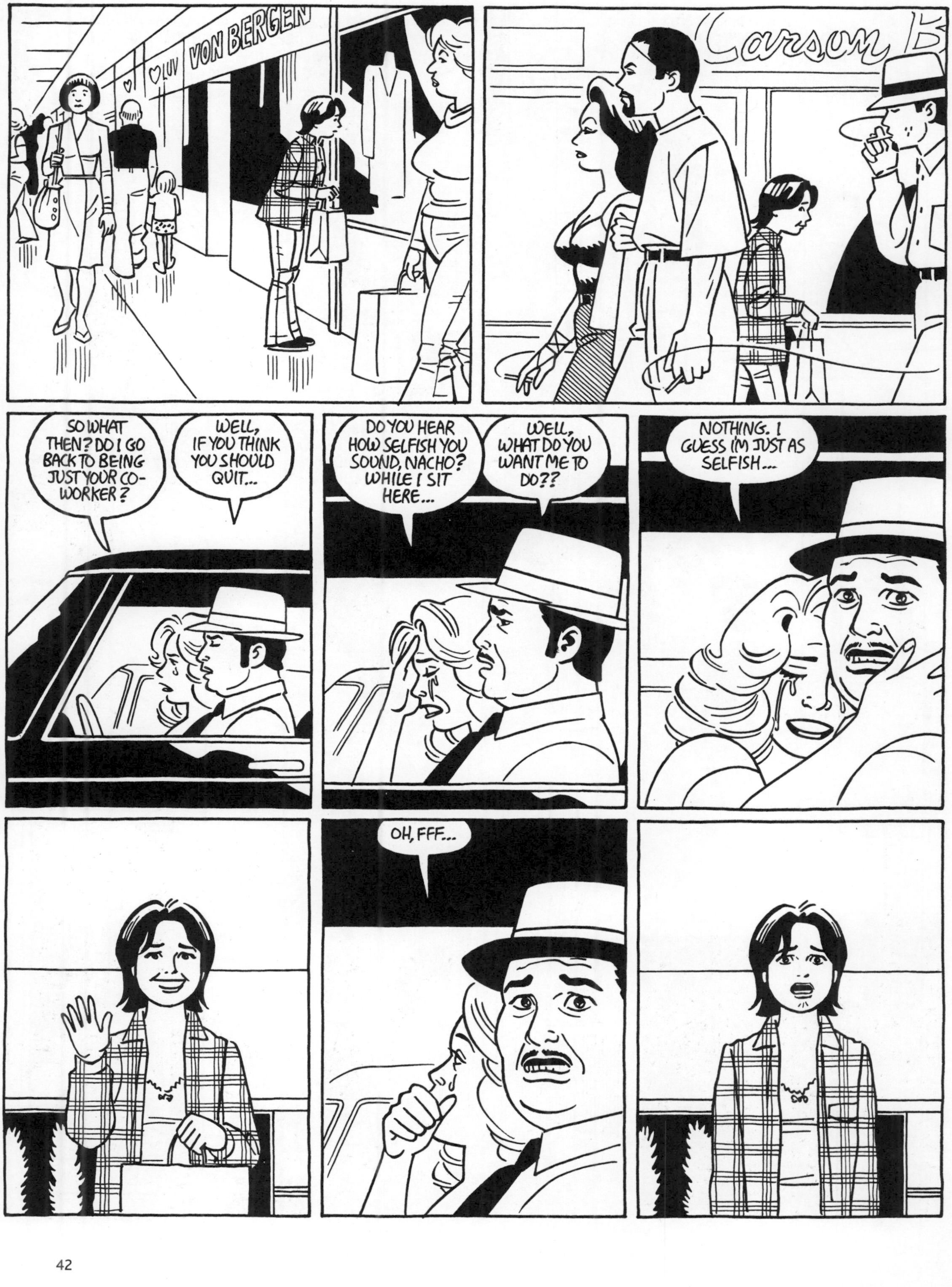
VON BERGEN
LUV
Carson B
SO WHAT THEN? DO I GO BACK TO BEING JUST YOUR CO-WORKER?
WELL, IF YOU THINK YOU SHOULD QUIT...
DO YOU HEAR HOW SELFISH YOU SOUND, NACHO? WHILE I SIT HERE...
WELL, WHAT DO YOU WANT ME TO DO??
NOTHING. I GUESS I'M JUST AS SELFISH...
OH, FFF...

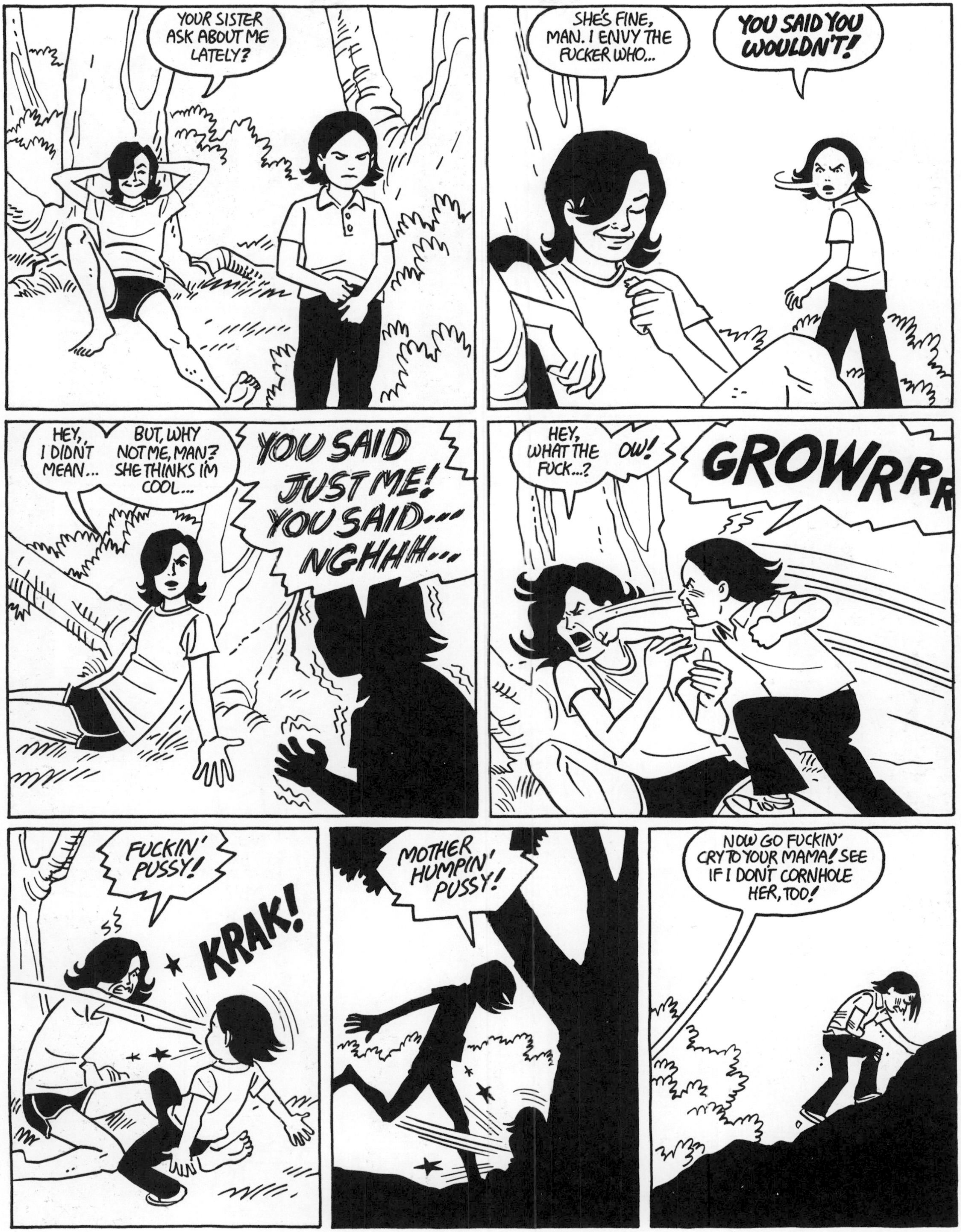
YOUR SISTER ASK ABOUT ME LATELY?
SHE'S FINE, MAN. I ENVY THE FUCKER WHO...
YOU SAID YOU WOULDN'T!
HEY, I DIDN'T MEAN...
BUT, WHY NOT ME, MAN? SHE THINKS I'M COOL...
YOU SAID JUST ME! YOU SAID... NGHHH...
HEY, WHAT THE FUCK...?
OW!
GROWRRR
FUCKIN' PUSSY!
KRAK!
MOTHER HUMPIN' PUSSY!
NOW GO FUCKIN' CRY TO YOUR MAMA! SEE IF I DONT CORNHOLE HER, TOO!

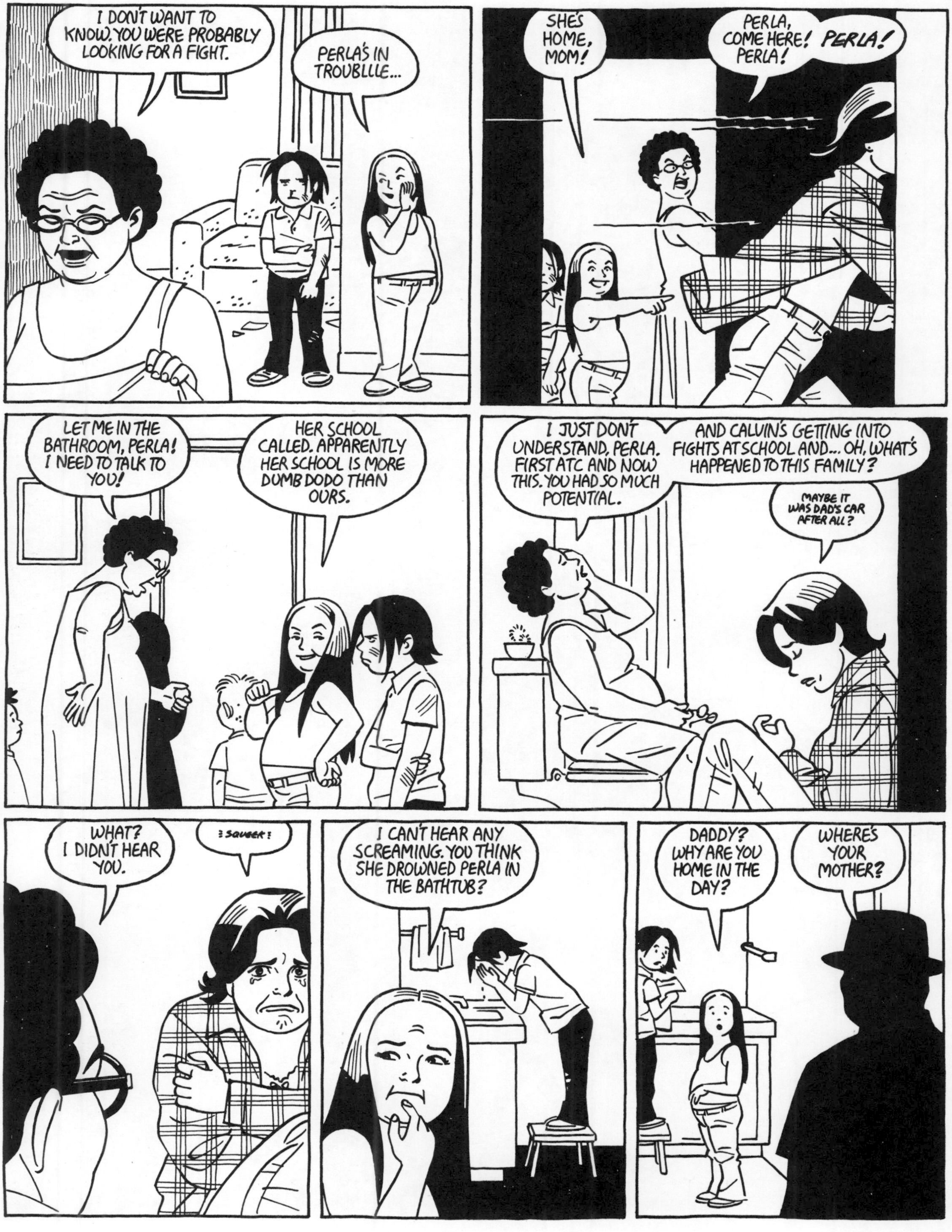
I DON'T WANT TO KNOW. YOU WERE PROBABLY LOOKING FOR A FIGHT.
PERLA'S IN TROUBLLLE...
SHE'S HOME, MOM!
PERLA, COME HERE! PERLA!
PERLA!
LET ME IN THE BATHROOM, PERLA! I NEED TO TALK TO YOU!
HER SCHOOL CALLED. APPARENTLY HER SCHOOL IS MORE DUMB DODO THAN OURS.
I JUST DON'T UNDERSTAND, PERLA. FIRST ATC AND NOW THIS. YOU HAD SO MUCH POTENTIAL.
AND CALVIN'S GETTING INTO FIGHTS AT SCHOOL AND... OH, WHAT'S HAPPENED TO THIS FAMILY?
MAYBE IT WAS DAD'S CAR AFTER ALL?
WHAT? I DIDN'T HEAR YOU.
: SQUEEK :
I CAN'T HEAR ANY SCREAMING. YOU THINK SHE DROWNED PERLA IN THE BATHTUB?
DADDY? WHY ARE YOU HOME IN THE DAY?
WHERE'S YOUR MOTHER?

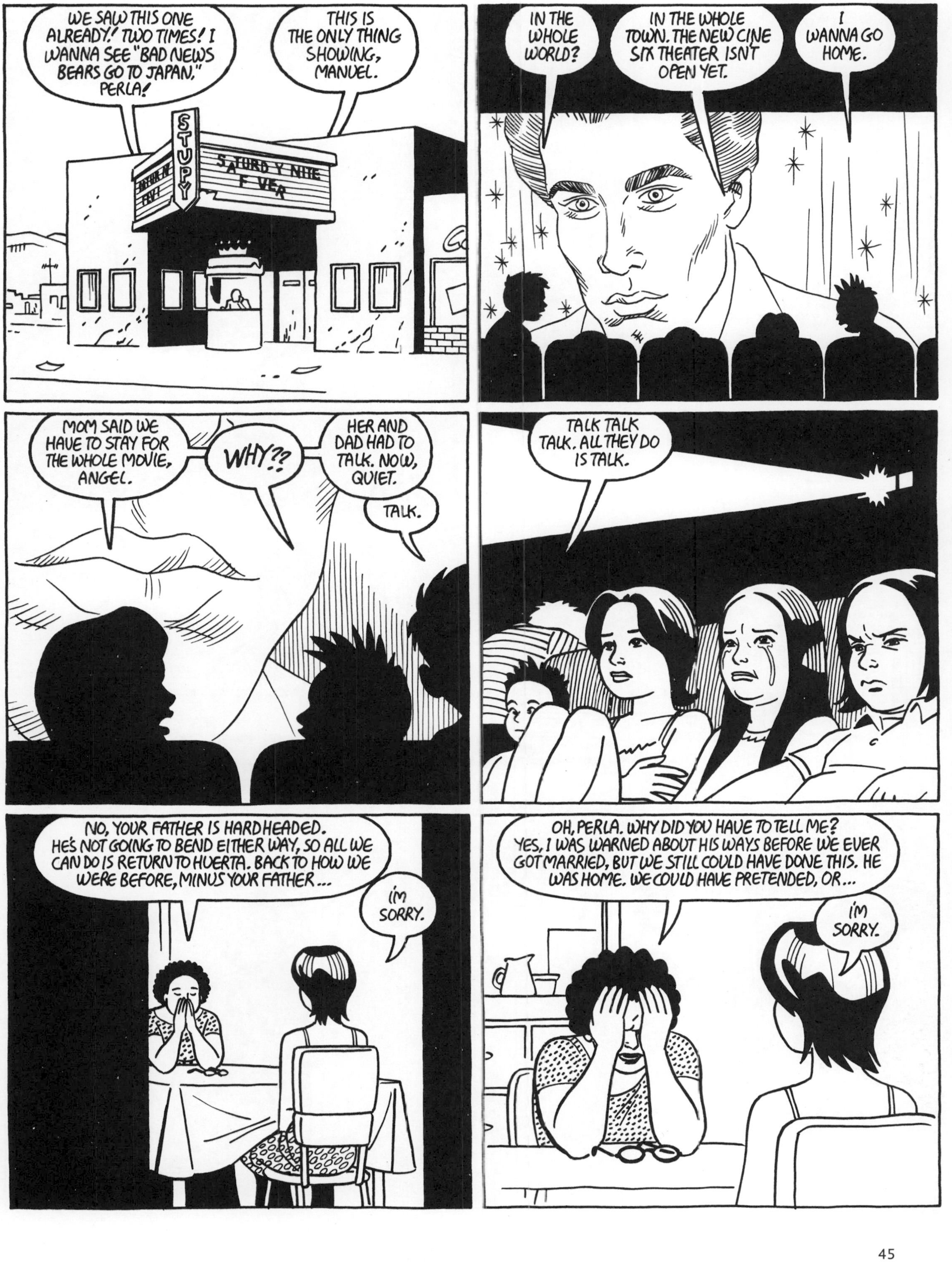
WE SAW THIS ONE ALREADY! TWO TIMES! I WANNA SEE "BAD NEWS BEARS GO TO JAPAN," PERLA!
THIS IS THE ONLY THING SHOWING, MANUEL.
STUPY
SATURDY NITE F VER
IN THE WHOLE WORLD?
IN THE WHOLE TOWN. THE NEW CINE SIX THEATER ISN'T OPEN YET.
I WANNA GO HOME.
MOM SAID WE HAVE TO STAY FOR THE WHOLE MOVIE, ANGEL.
WHY??
HER AND DAD HAD TO TALK. NOW, QUIET.
TALK.
TALK TALK TALK. ALL THEY DO IS TALK.
NO, YOUR FATHER IS HARD HEADED. HE'S NOT GOING TO BEND EITHER WAY, SO ALL WE CAN DO IS RETURN TO HUERTA. BACK TO HOW WE WERE BEFORE, MINUS YOUR FATHER...
I'M SORRY.
OH, PERLA. WHY DID YOU HAVE TO TELL ME? YES, I WAS WARNED ABOUT HIS WAYS BEFORE WE EVER GOT MARRIED, BUT WE STILL COULD HAVE DONE THIS. HE WAS HOME. WE COULD HAVE PRETENDED, OR...
I'M SORRY.

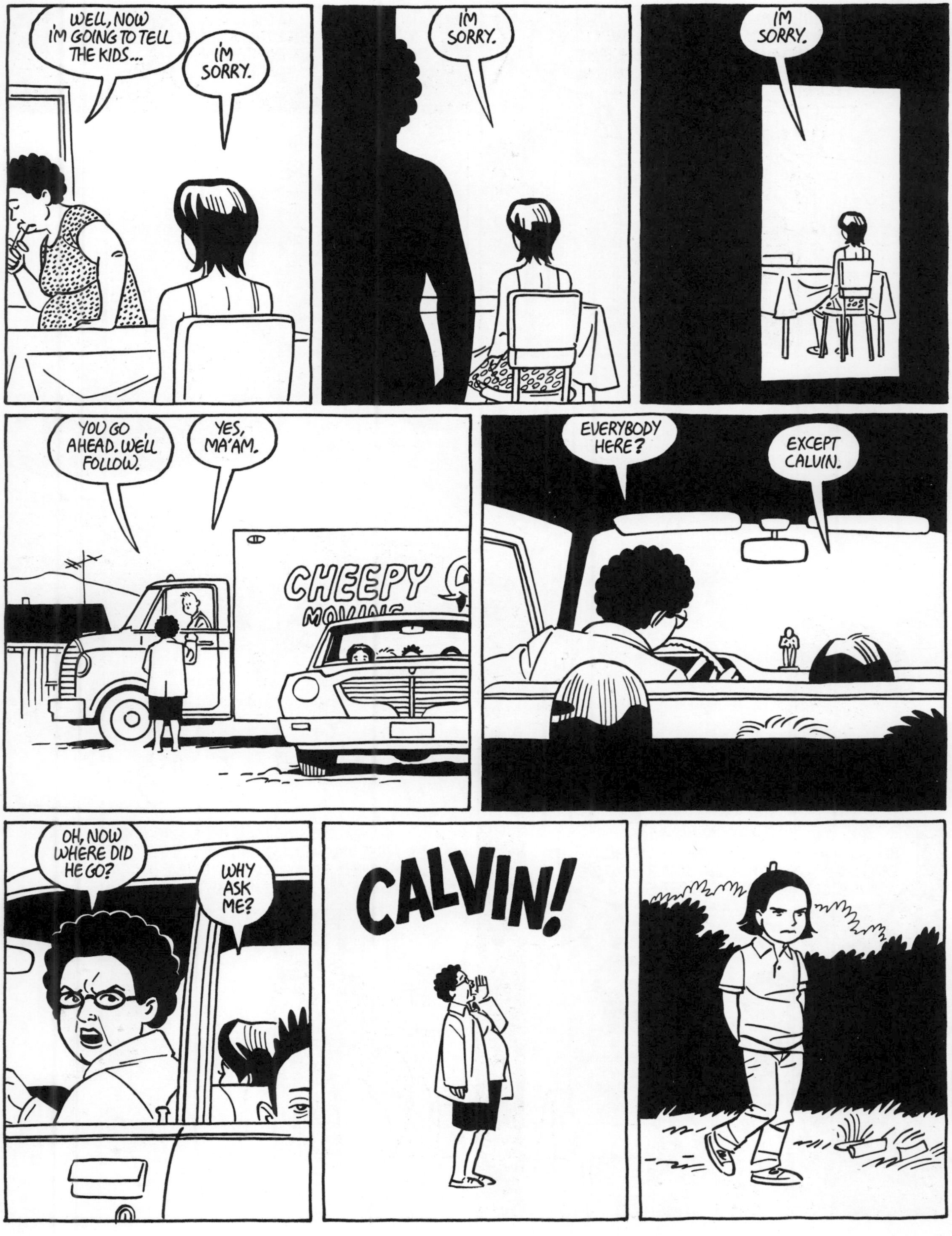
WELL, NOW I'M GOING TO TELL THE KIDS...
I'M SORRY.
I'M SORRY.
I'M SORRY.
YOU GO AHEAD. WE'LL FOLLOW.
YES, MA'AM.
CHEEPY
EVERYBODY HERE?
EXCEPT CALVIN.
OH, NOW WHERE DID HE GO?
WHY ASK ME?
CALVIN!

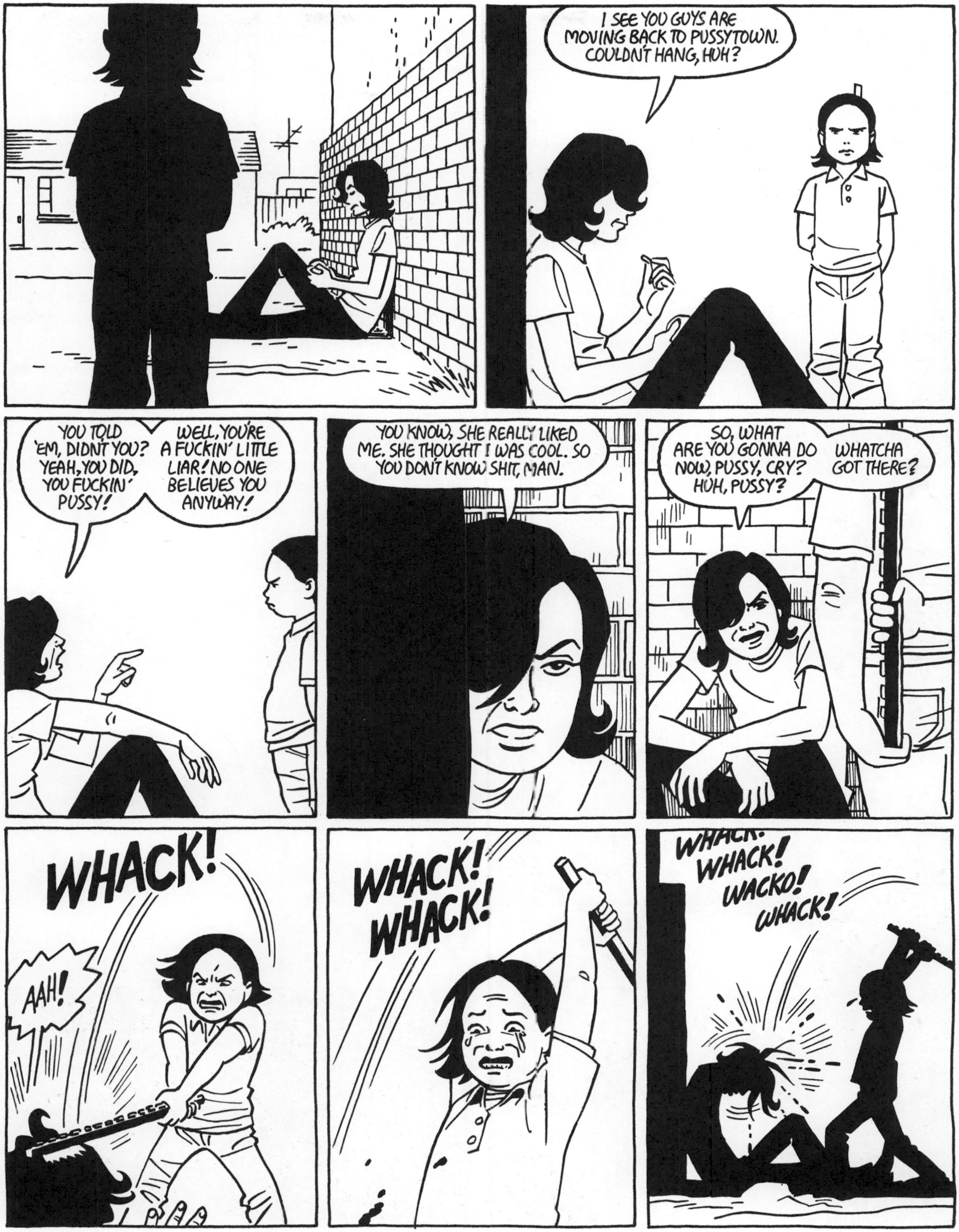
I SEE YOU GUYS ARE MOVING BACK TO PUSSYTOWN. COULDN'T HANG, HUH?
YOU TOLD 'EM, DIDN'T YOU? YEAH, YOU DID, YOU FUCKIN' PUSSY!
WELL, YOU'RE A FUCKIN' LITTLE LIAR! NO ONE BELIEVES YOU ANYWAY!
YOU KNOW, SHE REALLY LIKED ME. SHE THOUGHT I WAS COOL. SO YOU DON'T KNOW SHIT, MAN.
SO, WHAT ARE YOU GONNA DO NOW, PUSSY, CRY? HUH, PUSSY?
WHATCHA GOT THERE?
WHACK!
AAH!
WHACK! WHACK!
WHACK! WACKO! WHACK!

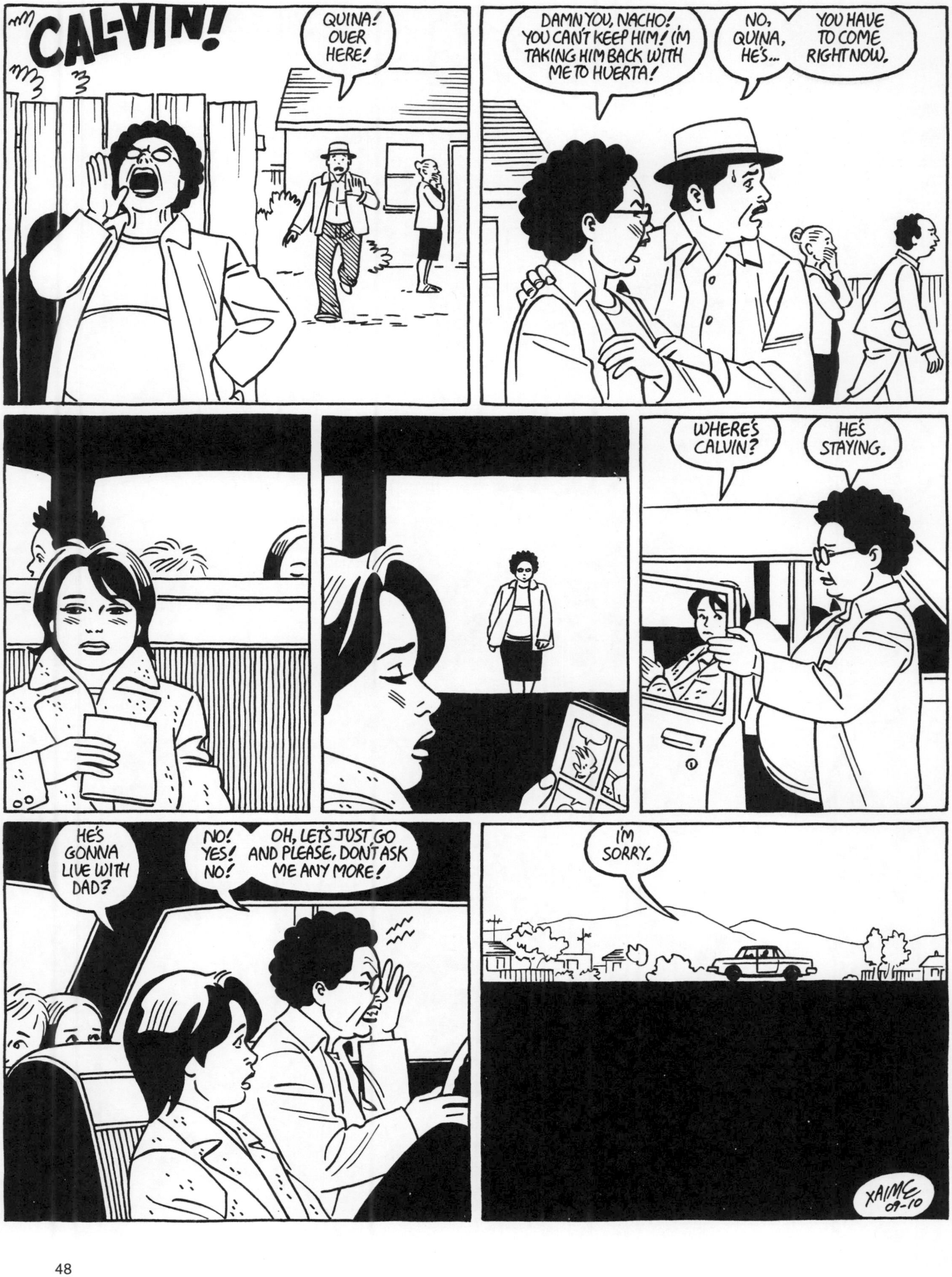
CAL-VIN!
QUINA! OVER HERE!
DAMN YOU, NACHO! YOU CAN'T KEEP HIM! I'M TAKING HIM BACK WITH ME TO HUERTA!
NO, QUINA, HE'S...
YOU HAVE TO COME RIGHT NOW.
WHERE'S CALVIN?
HE'S STAYING.
HE'S GONNA LIVE WITH DAD?
NO! YES! NO!
OH, LET'S JUST GO AND PLEASE, DON'T ASK ME ANY MORE!
I'M SORRY.
XAIME 09-10

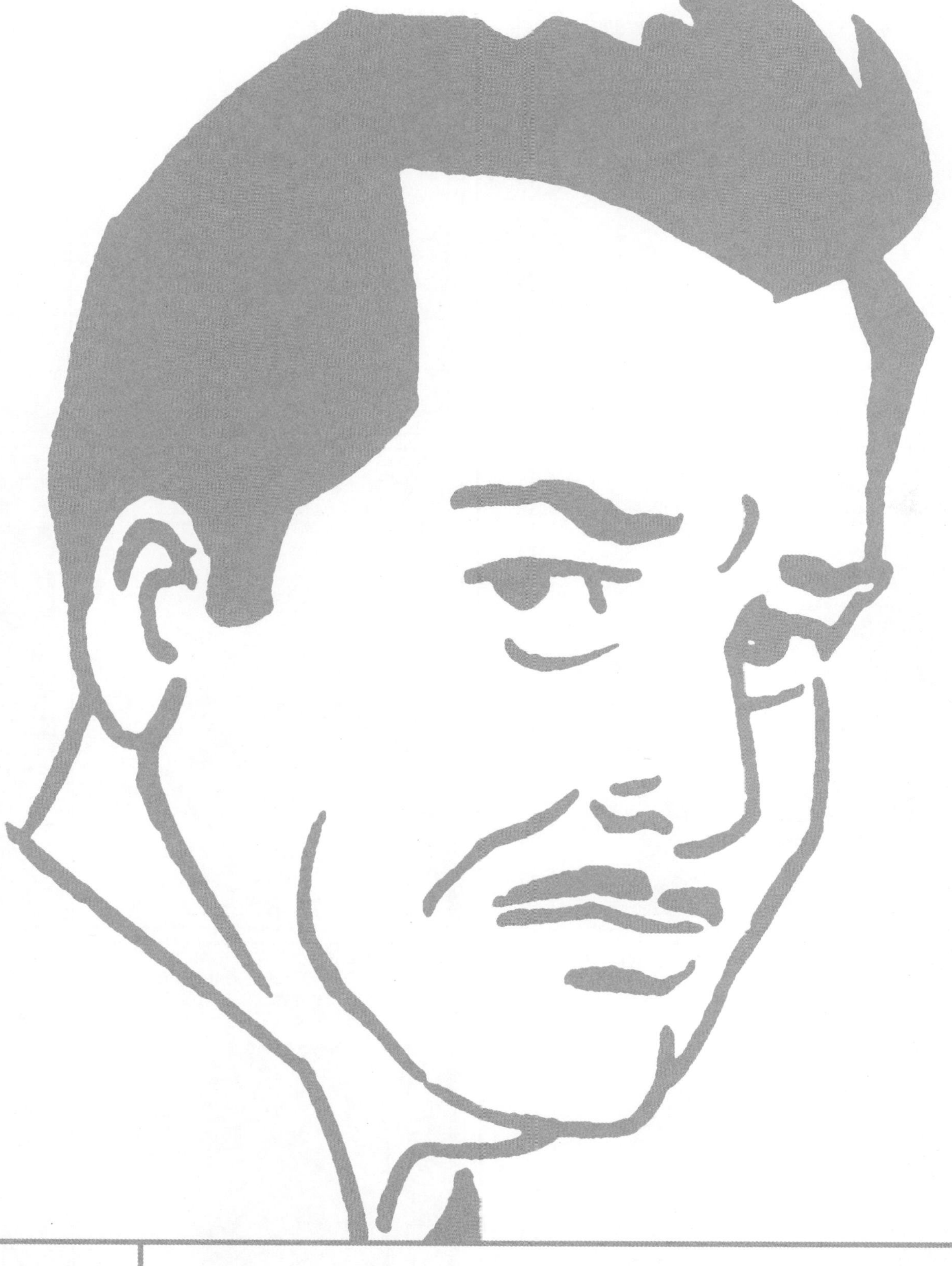

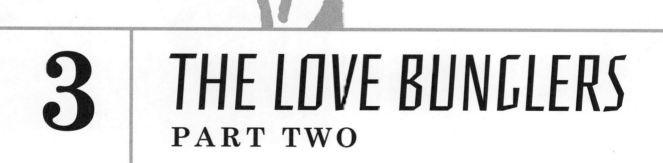

3 THE LOVE BUNGLERS

PART TWO

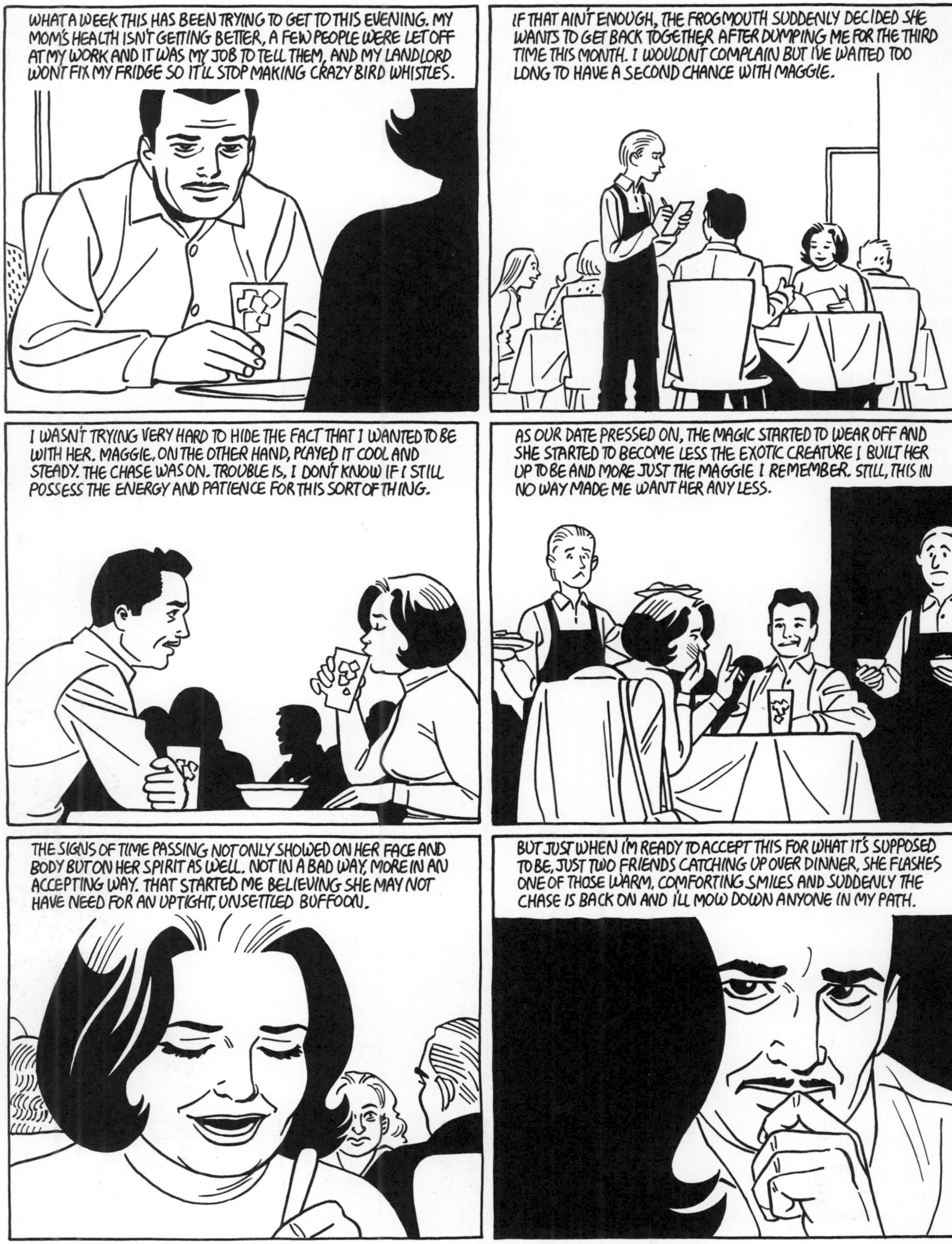
WHAT A WEEK THIS HAS BEEN TRYING TO GET TO THIS EVENING. MY MOM'S HEALTH ISN'T GETTING BETTER, A FEW PEOPLE WERE LET OFF AT MY WORK AND IT WAS MY JOB TO TELL THEM, AND MY LANDLORD WON'T FIX MY FRIDGE SO IT'LL STOP MAKING CRAZY BIRD WHISTLES.
IF THAT AIN'T ENOUGH, THE FROGMOUTH SUDDENLY DECIDED SHE WANTS TO GET BACK TOGETHER AFTER DUMPING ME FOR THE THIRD TIME THIS MONTH. I WOULDN'T COMPLAIN BUT I'VE WAITED TOO LONG TO HAVE A SECOND CHANCE WITH MAGGIE.
I WASN'T TRYING VERY HARD TO HIDE THE FACT THAT I WANTED TO BE WITH HER. MAGGIE, ON THE OTHER HAND, PLAYED IT COOL AND STEADY. THE CHASE WAS ON. TROUBLE IS, I DON'T KNOW IF I STILL POSSESS THE ENERGY AND PATIENCE FOR THIS SORT OF THING.
AS OUR DATE PRESSED ON, THE MAGIC STARTED TO WEAR OFF AND SHE STARTED TO BECOME LESS THE EXOTIC CREATURE I BUILT HER UP TO BE AND MORE JUST THE MAGGIE I REMEMBER. STILL, THIS IN NO WAY MADE ME WANT HER ANY LESS.
THE SIGNS OF TIME PASSING NOT ONLY SHOWED ON HER FACE AND BODY BUT ON HER SPIRIT AS WELL. NOT IN A BAD WAY, MORE IN AN ACCEPTING WAY. THAT STARTED ME BELIEVING SHE MAY NOT HAVE NEED FOR AN UPTIGHT, UNSETTLED BUFFOON.
BUT JUST WHEN I'M READY TO ACCEPT THIS FOR WHAT IT'S SUPPOSED TO BE, JUST TWO FRIENDS CATCHING UP OVER DINNER, SHE FLASHES ONE OF THOSE WARM, COMFORTING SMILES AND SUDDENLY THE CHASE IS BACK ON AND I'LL MOW DOWN ANYONE IN MY PATH.

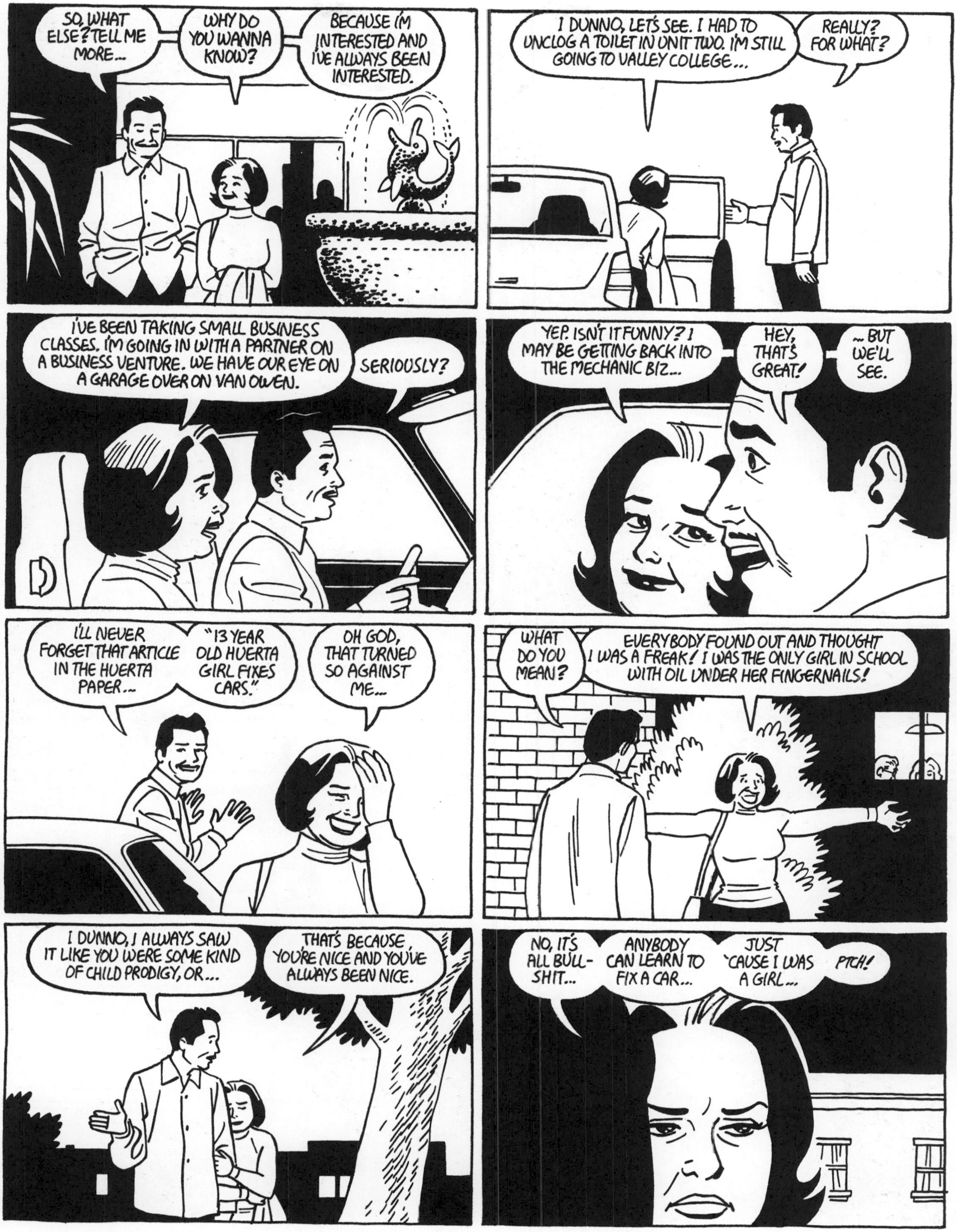
SO, WHAT ELSE? TELL ME MORE...
WHY DO YOU WANNA KNOW?
BECAUSE I'M INTERESTED AND I'VE ALWAYS BEEN INTERESTED.
I DUNNO, LET'S SEE. I HAD TO UNCLOG A TOILET IN UNIT TWO. I'M STILL GOING TO VALLEY COLLEGE...
REALLY? FOR WHAT?
I'VE BEEN TAKING SMALL BUSINESS CLASSES. I'M GOING IN WITH A PARTNER ON A BUSINESS VENTURE. WE HAVE OUR EYE ON A GARAGE OVER ON VAN OWEN.
SERIOUSLY?
YEP. ISN'T IT FUNNY? I MAY BE GETTING BACK INTO THE MECHANIC BIZ...
HEY, THAT'S GREAT!
...BUT WE'LL SEE.
I'LL NEVER FORGET THAT ARTICLE IN THE HUERTA PAPER...
"13 YEAR OLD HUERTA GIRL FIXES CARS."
OH GOD, THAT TURNED SO AGAINST ME...
WHAT DO YOU MEAN?
EVERYBODY FOUND OUT AND THOUGHT I WAS A FREAK! I WAS THE ONLY GIRL IN SCHOOL WITH OIL UNDER HER FINGERNAILS!
I DUNNO, I ALWAYS SAW IT LIKE YOU WERE SOME KIND OF CHILD PRODIGY, OR...
THAT'S BECAUSE, YOU'RE NICE AND YOU'VE ALWAYS BEEN NICE.
NO, IT'S ALL BULL-SHIT...
ANYBODY CAN LEARN TO FIX A CAR...
JUST 'CAUSE I WAS A GIRL...
PTCH!

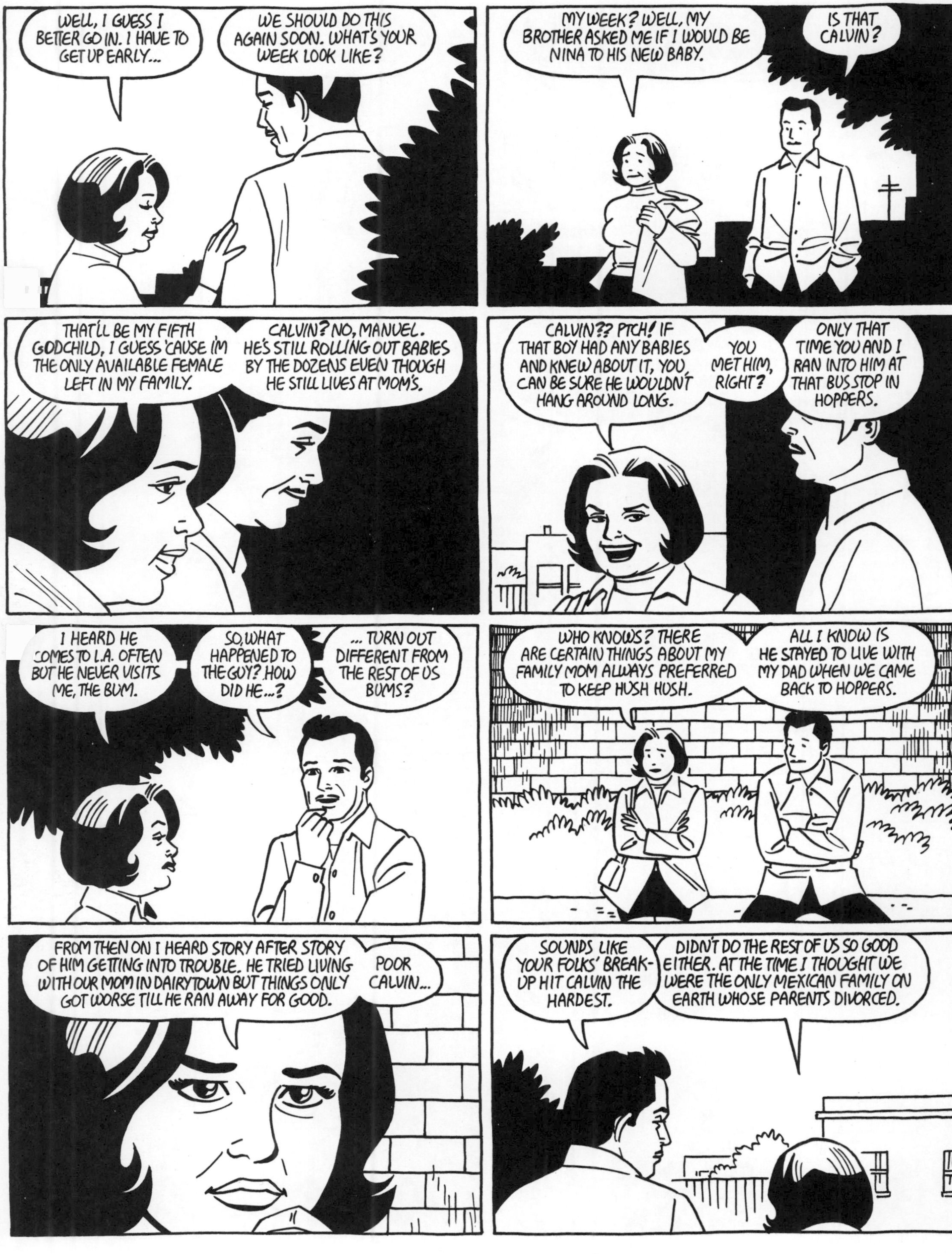
WELL, I GUESS I BETTER GO IN. I HAVE TO GET UP EARLY...
WE SHOULD DO THIS AGAIN SOON. WHAT'S YOUR WEEK LOOK LIKE?
MY WEEK? WELL, MY BROTHER ASKED ME IF I WOULD BE NINA TO HIS NEW BABY.
IS THAT CALVIN?
THAT'LL BE MY FIFTH GODCHILD, I GUESS 'CAUSE I'M THE ONLY AVAILABLE FEMALE LEFT IN MY FAMILY.
CALVIN? NO, MANUEL. HE'S STILL ROLLING OUT BABIES BY THE DOZENS EVEN THOUGH HE STILL LIVES AT MOM'S.
CALVIN?? PTCH! IF THAT BOY HAD ANY BABIES AND KNEW ABOUT IT, YOU CAN BE SURE HE WOULDN'T HANG AROUND LONG.
YOU MET HIM, RIGHT?
ONLY THAT TIME YOU AND I RAN INTO HIM AT THAT BUS STOP IN HOPPERS.
I HEARD HE COMES TO L.A. OFTEN BUT HE NEVER VISITS ME, THE BUM.
SO, WHAT HAPPENED TO THE GUY? HOW DID HE...?
...TURN OUT DIFFERENT FROM THE REST OF US BUMS?
WHO KNOWS? THERE ARE CERTAIN THINGS ABOUT MY FAMILY MOM ALWAYS PREFERRED TO KEEP HUSH HUSH.
ALL I KNOW IS HE STAYED TO LIVE WITH MY DAD WHEN WE CAME BACK TO HOPPERS.
FROM THEN ON I HEARD STORY AFTER STORY OF HIM GETTING INTO TROUBLE. HE TRIED LIVING WITH OUR MOM IN DAIRYTOWN BUT THINGS ONLY GOT WORSE TILL HE RAN AWAY FOR GOOD.
POOR CALVIN...
SOUNDS LIKE YOUR FOLKS' BREAK-UP HIT CALVIN THE HARDEST.
DIDN'T DO THE REST OF US SO GOOD EITHER. AT THE TIME I THOUGHT WE WERE THE ONLY MEXICAN FAMILY ON EARTH WHOSE PARENTS DIVORCED.

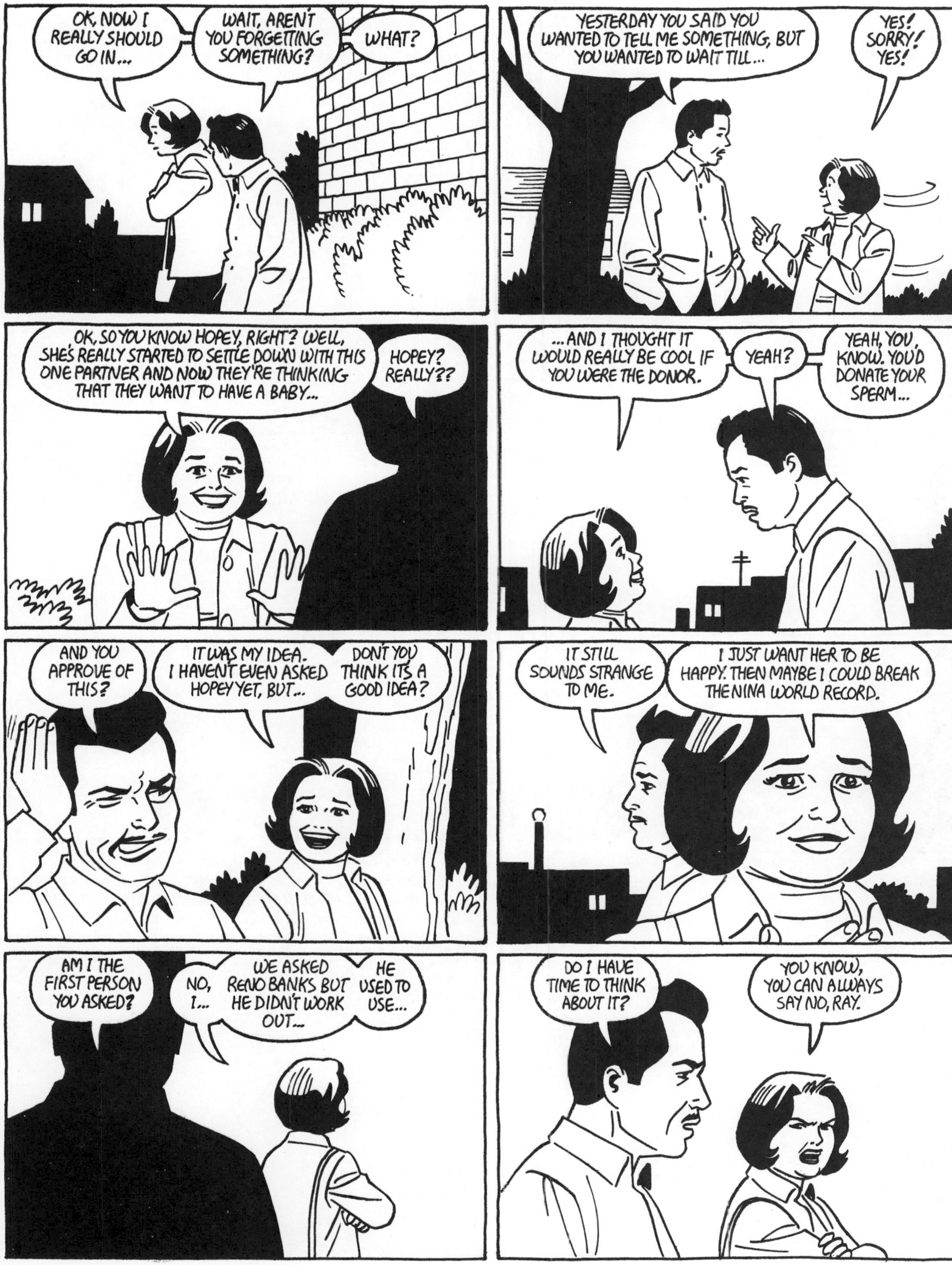
OK, NOW I REALLY SHOULD GO IN...
WAIT, AREN'T YOU FORGETTING SOMETHING?
WHAT?
YESTERDAY YOU SAID YOU WANTED TO TELL ME SOMETHING, BUT YOU WANTED TO WAIT TILL...
YES! SORRY! YES!
OK, SO YOU KNOW HOPEY, RIGHT? WELL, SHE'S REALLY STARTED TO SETTLE DOWN WITH THIS ONE PARTNER AND NOW THEY'RE THINKING THAT THEY WANT TO HAVE A BABY...
HOPEY? REALLY??
...AND I THOUGHT IT WOULD REALLY BE COOL IF YOU WERE THE DONOR.
YEAH?
YEAH, YOU, KNOW. YOU'D DONATE YOUR SPERM...
AND YOU APPROVE OF THIS?
IT WAS MY IDEA. I HAVEN'T EVEN ASKED HOPEY YET, BUT...
DON'T YOU THINK IT'S A GOOD IDEA?
IT STILL SOUNDS STRANGE TO ME.
I JUST WANT HER TO BE HAPPY. THEN MAYBE I COULD BREAK THE NINA WORLD RECORD.
AM I THE FIRST PERSON YOU ASKED?
NO, I...
WE ASKED RENO BANKS BUT HE DIDN'T WORK OUT...
HE USED TO USE...
DO I HAVE TIME TO THINK ABOUT IT?
YOU KNOW, YOU CAN ALWAYS SAY NO, RAY.

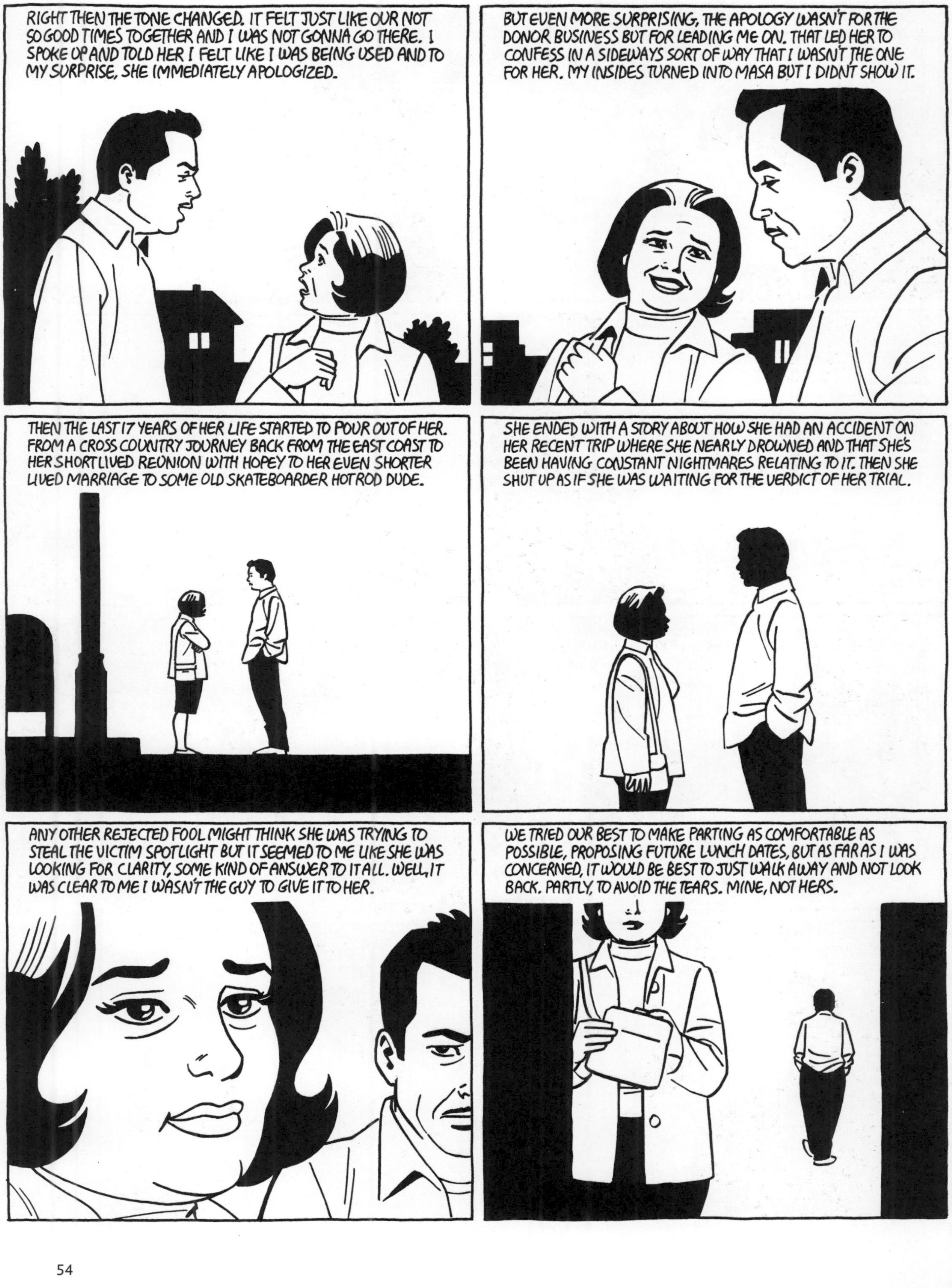
RIGHT THEN THE TONE CHANGED. IT FELT JUST LIKE OUR NOT SO GOOD TIMES TOGETHER AND I WAS NOT GONNA GO THERE. I SPOKE UP AND TOLD HER I FELT LIKE I WAS BEING USED AND TO MY SURPRISE, SHE IMMEDIATELY APOLOGIZED.
BUT EVEN MORE SURPRISING, THE APOLOGY WASN'T FOR THE DONOR BUSINESS BUT FOR LEADING ME ON. THAT LED HER TO CONFESS IN A SIDEWAYS SORT OF WAY THAT I WASN'T THE ONE FOR HER. MY INSIDES TURNED INTO MASA BUT I DIDN'T SHOW IT.
THEN THE LAST 17 YEARS OF HER LIFE STARTED TO POUR OUT OF HER. FROM A CROSS COUNTRY JOURNEY BACK FROM THE EAST COAST TO HER SHORTLIVED REUNION WITH HOPEY TO HER EVEN SHORTER LIVED MARRIAGE TO SOME OLD SKATEBOARDER HOT ROD DUDE.
SHE ENDED WITH A STORY ABOUT HOW SHE HAD AN ACCIDENT ON HER RECENT TRIP WHERE SHE NEARLY DROWNED AND THAT SHE'S BEEN HAVING CONSTANT NIGHTMARES RELATING TO IT. THEN SHE SHUT UP AS IF SHE WAS WAITING FOR THE VERDICT OF HER TRIAL.
ANY OTHER REJECTED FOOL MIGHT THINK SHE WAS TRYING TO STEAL THE VICTIM SPOTLIGHT BUT IT SEEMED TO ME LIKE SHE WAS LOOKING FOR CLARITY, SOME KIND OF ANSWER TO IT ALL. WELL, IT WAS CLEAR TO ME I WASN'T THE GUY TO GIVE IT TO HER.
WE TRIED OUR BEST TO MAKE PARTING AS COMFORTABLE AS POSSIBLE, PROPOSING FUTURE LUNCH DATES, BUT AS FAR AS I WAS CONCERNED, IT WOULD BE BEST TO JUST WALK AWAY AND NOT LOOK BACK. PARTLY, TO AVOID THE TEARS. MINE, NOT HERS.

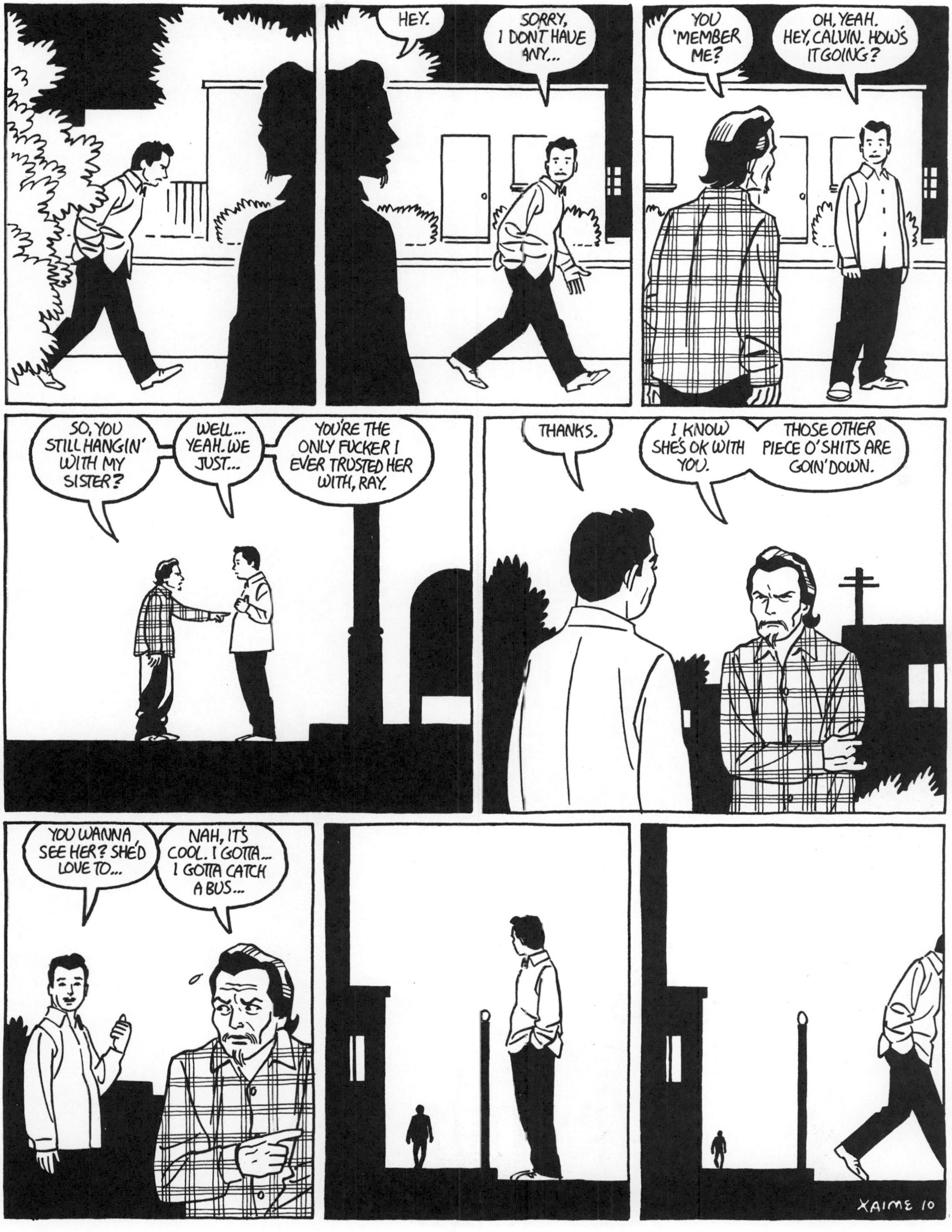
HEY.
SORRY, I DON'T HAVE ANY...
YOU 'MEMBER ME?
OH, YEAH. HEY, CALVIN. HOW'S IT GOING?
SO, YOU STILL HANGIN' WITH MY SISTER?
WELL... YEAH. WE JUST...
YOU'RE THE ONLY FUCKER I EVER TRUSTED HER WITH, RAY.
THANKS.
I KNOW SHE'S OK WITH YOU.
THOSE OTHER PIECE O' SHITS ARE GOIN' DOWN.
YOU WANNA SEE HER? SHE'D LOVE TO...
NAH, IT'S COOL. I GOTTA... I GOTTA CATCH A BUS...
XAIME 10

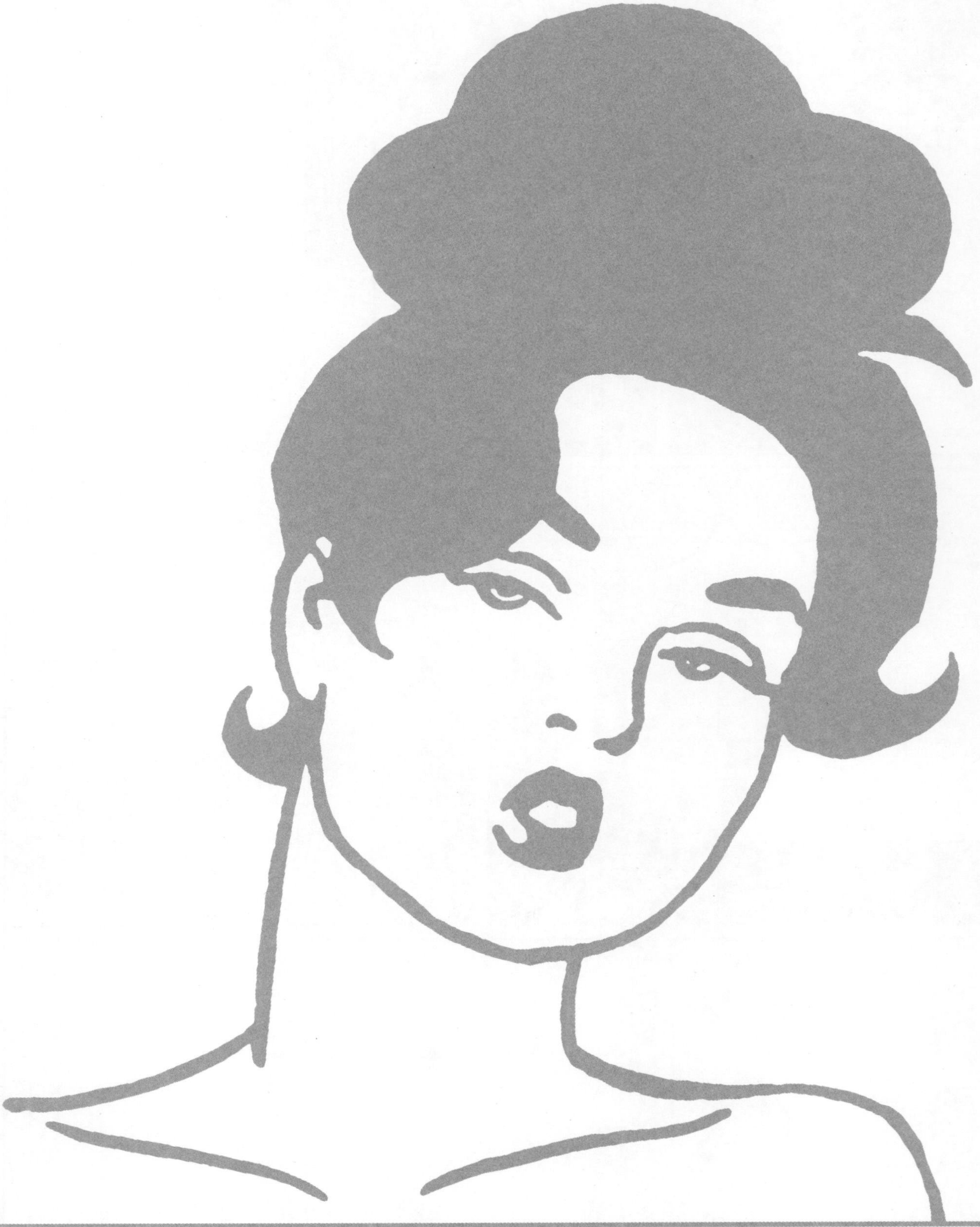

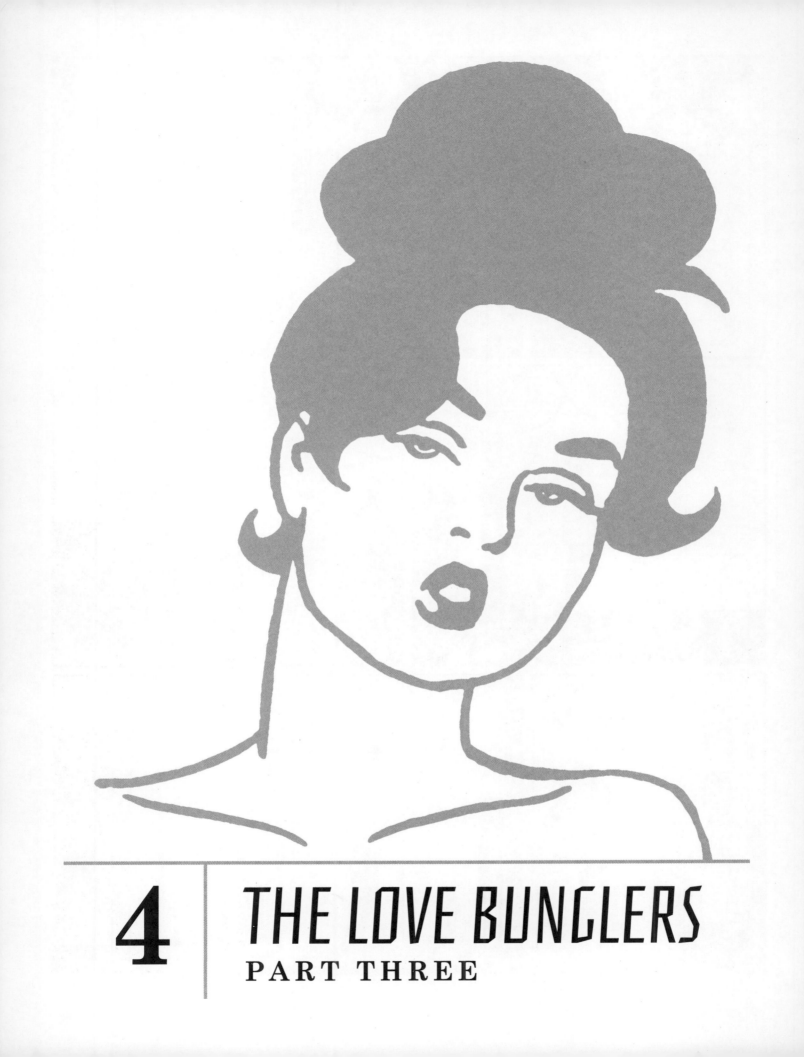

4 THE LOVE BUNGLERS

PART THREE

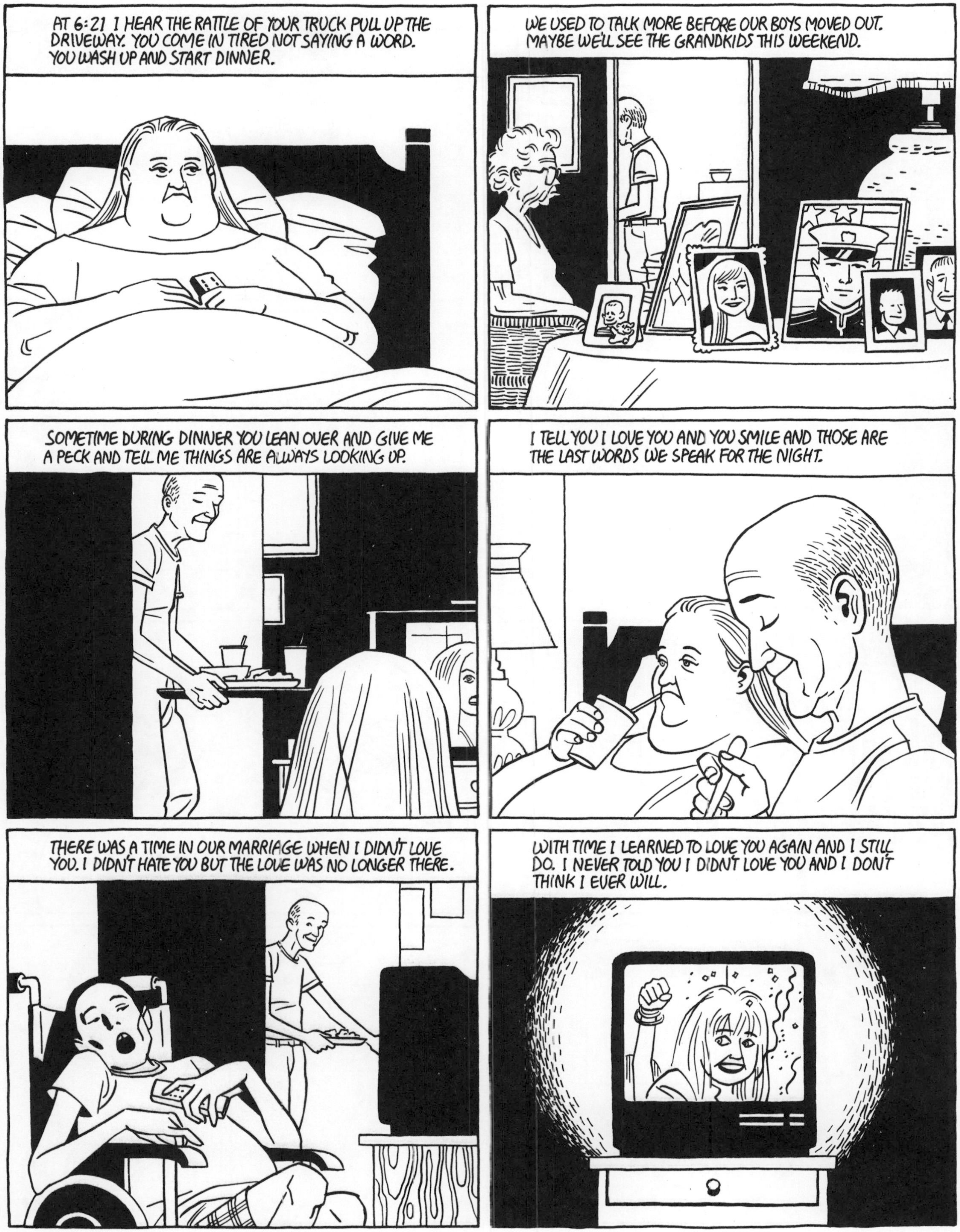
AT 6:21 I HEAR THE RATTLE OF YOUR TRUCK PULL UP THE DRIVEWAY. YOU COME IN TIRED NOT SAYING A WORD. YOU WASH UP AND START DINNER.
WE USED TO TALK MORE BEFORE OUR BOYS MOVED OUT. MAYBE WE'LL SEE THE GRANDKIDS THIS WEEKEND.
SOMETIME DURING DINNER YOU LEAN OVER AND GIVE ME A PECK AND TELL ME THINGS ARE ALWAYS LOOKING UP.
I TELL YOU I LOVE YOU AND YOU SMILE AND THOSE ARE THE LAST WORDS WE SPEAK FOR THE NIGHT.
THERE WAS A TIME IN OUR MARRIAGE WHEN I DIDN'T LOVE YOU. I DIDN'T HATE YOU BUT THE LOVE WAS NO LONGER THERE.
WITH TIME I LEARNED TO LOVE YOU AGAIN AND I STILL DO. I NEVER TOLD YOU I DIDN'T LOVE YOU AND I DON'T THINK I EVER WILL.

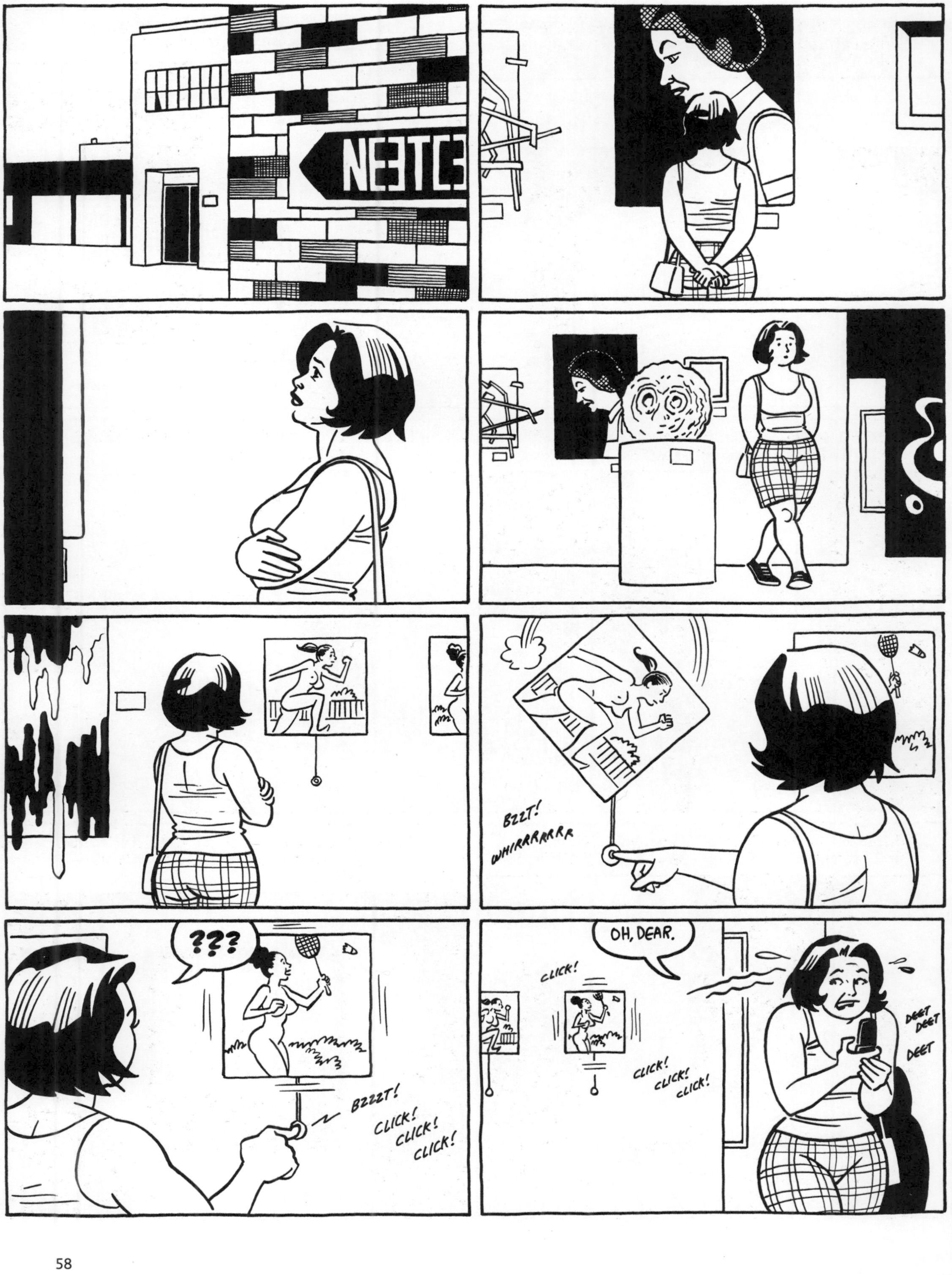
NE3TC3
BZZT!
WHIRRRRRRR
???
BZZZT!
CLICK!
CLICK!
CLICK!
OH, DEAR.
CLICK!
CLICK!
CLICK!
CLICK!
DEET
DEET
DEET

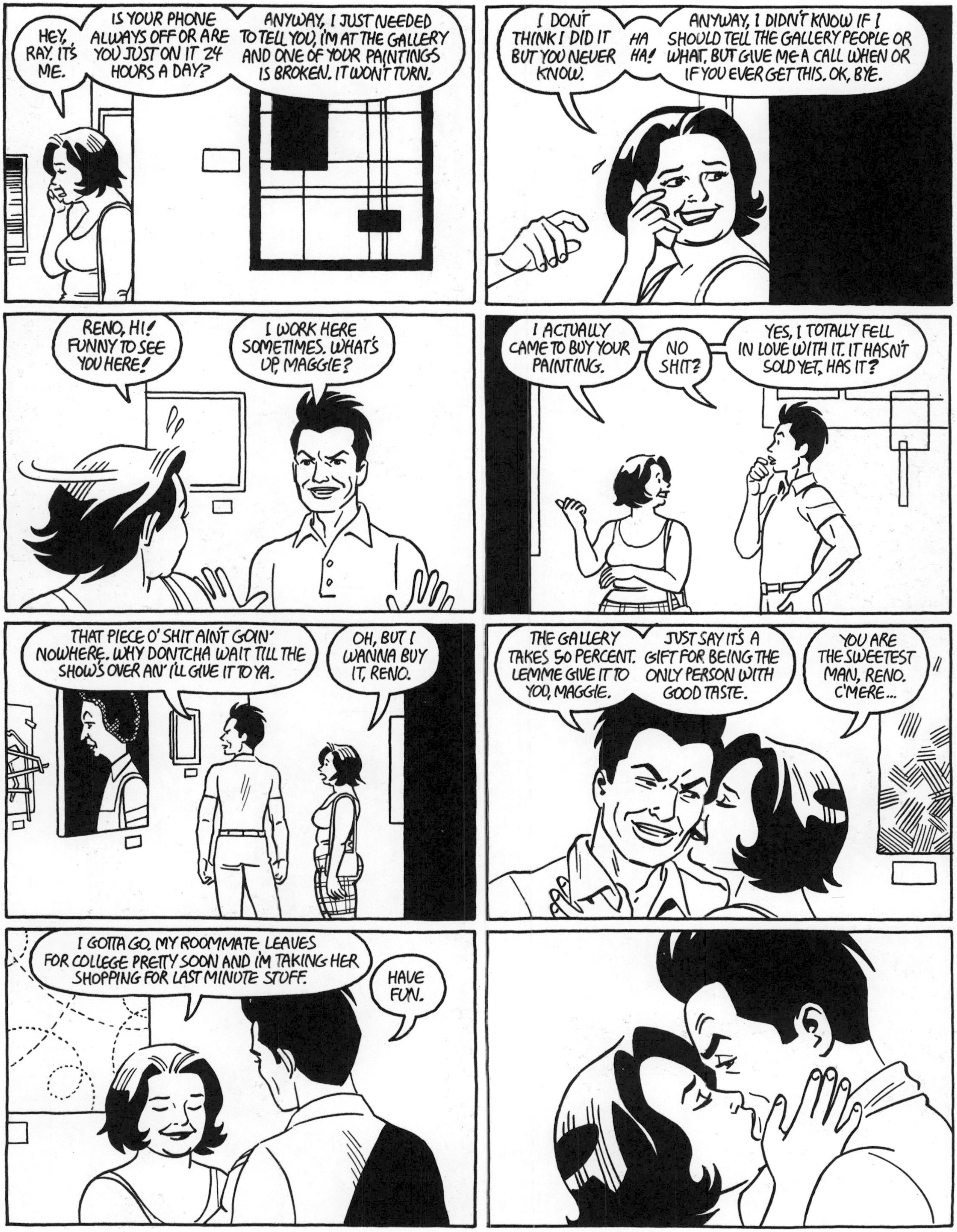
HEY, RAY. IT'S ME.
IS YOUR PHONE ALWAYS OFF OR ARE YOU JUST ON IT 24 HOURS A DAY?
ANYWAY, I JUST NEEDED TO TELL YOU, I'M AT THE GALLERY AND ONE OF YOUR PAINTINGS IS BROKEN. IT WON'T TURN.
I DON'T THINK I DID IT BUT YOU NEVER KNOW.
HA HA!
ANYWAY, I DIDN'T KNOW IF I SHOULD TELL THE GALLERY PEOPLE OR WHAT, BUT GIVE ME A CALL WHEN OR IF YOU EVER GET THIS. OK, BYE.
RENO, HI! FUNNY TO SEE YOU HERE!
I WORK HERE SOMETIMES. WHAT'S UP, MAGGIE?
I ACTUALLY CAME TO BUY YOUR PAINTING.
NO SHIT?
YES, I TOTALLY FELL IN LOVE WITH IT. IT HASN'T SOLD YET, HAS IT?
THAT PIECE O' SHIT AIN'T GOIN' NOWHERE. WHY DONTCHA WAIT TILL THE SHOW'S OVER AN' I'LL GIVE IT TO YA.
OH, BUT I WANNA BUY IT, RENO.
THE GALLERY TAKES 50 PERCENT. LEMME GIVE IT TO YOU, MAGGIE.
JUST SAY IT'S A GIFT FOR BEING THE ONLY PERSON WITH GOOD TASTE.
YOU ARE THE SWEETEST MAN, RENO. C'MERE...
I GOTTA GO. MY ROOMMATE LEAVES FOR COLLEGE PRETTY SOON AND I'M TAKING HER SHOPPING FOR LAST MINUTE STUFF.
HAVE FUN.

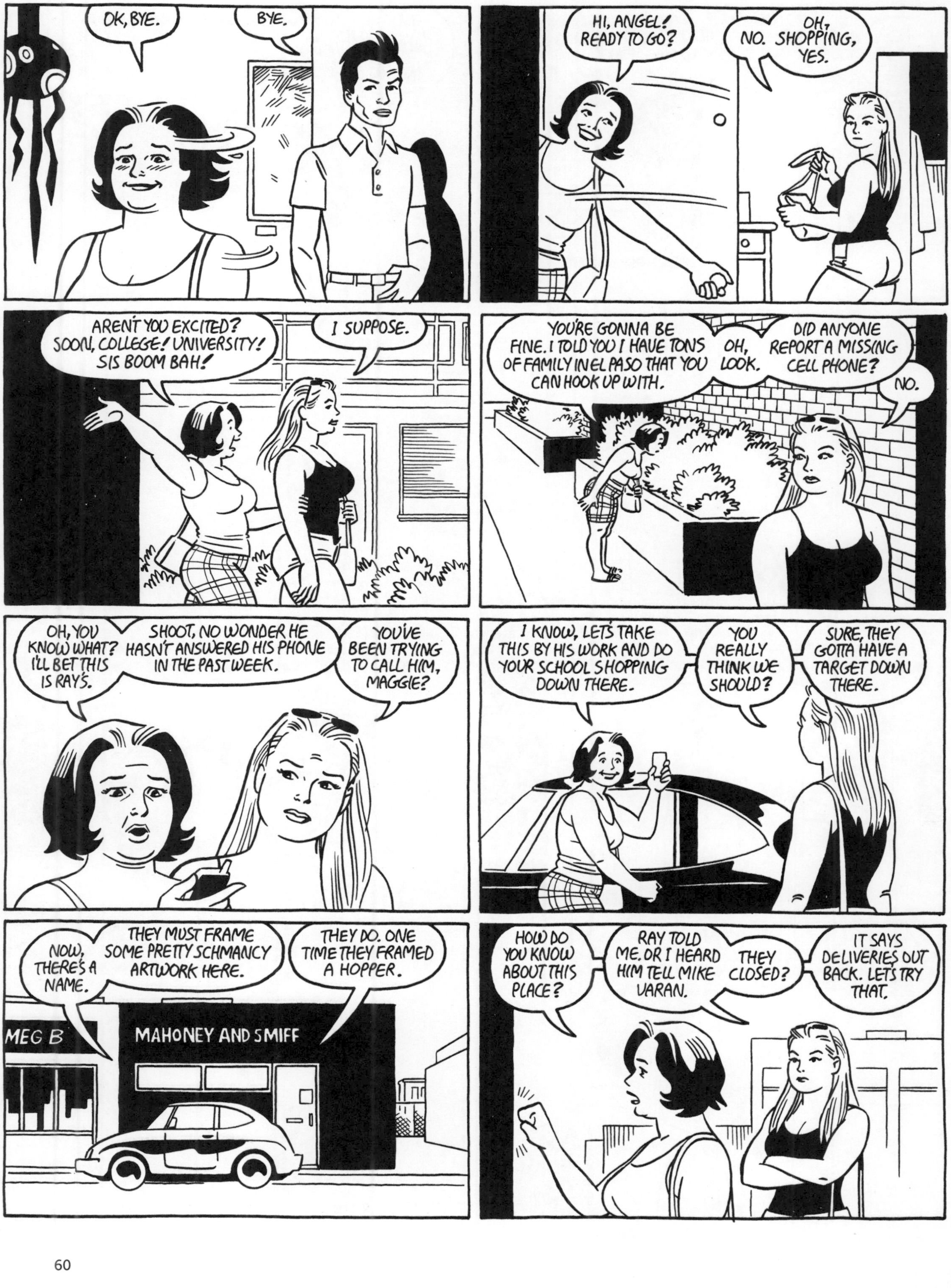
OK, BYE.
BYE.
HI, ANGEL! READY TO GO?
OH, NO. SHOPPING, YES.
AREN'T YOU EXCITED? SOON, COLLEGE! UNIVERSITY! SIS BOOM BAH!
I SUPPOSE.
YOU'RE GONNA BE FINE. I TOLD YOU I HAVE TONS OF FAMILY IN EL PASO THAT YOU CAN HOOK UP WITH.
OH, LOOK.
DID ANYONE REPORT A MISSING CELL PHONE?
NO.
OH, YOU KNOW WHAT? I'LL BET THIS IS RAY'S.
SHOOT, NO WONDER HE HASN'T ANSWERED HIS PHONE IN THE PAST WEEK.
YOU'VE BEEN TRYING TO CALL HIM, MAGGIE?
I KNOW, LET'S TAKE THIS BY HIS WORK AND DO YOUR SCHOOL SHOPPING DOWN THERE.
YOU REALLY THINK WE SHOULD?
SURE, THEY GOTTA HAVE A TARGET DOWN THERE.
NOW, THERE'S A NAME.
THEY MUST FRAME SOME PRETTY SCHMANCY ARTWORK HERE.
THEY DO. ONE TIME THEY FRAMED A HOPPER.
MEG B
MAHONEY AND SMIFF
HOW DO YOU KNOW ABOUT THIS PLACE?
RAY TOLD ME. OR I HEARD HIM TELL MIKE VARAN.
THEY CLOSED?
IT SAYS DELIVERIES OUT BACK. LET'S TRY THAT.

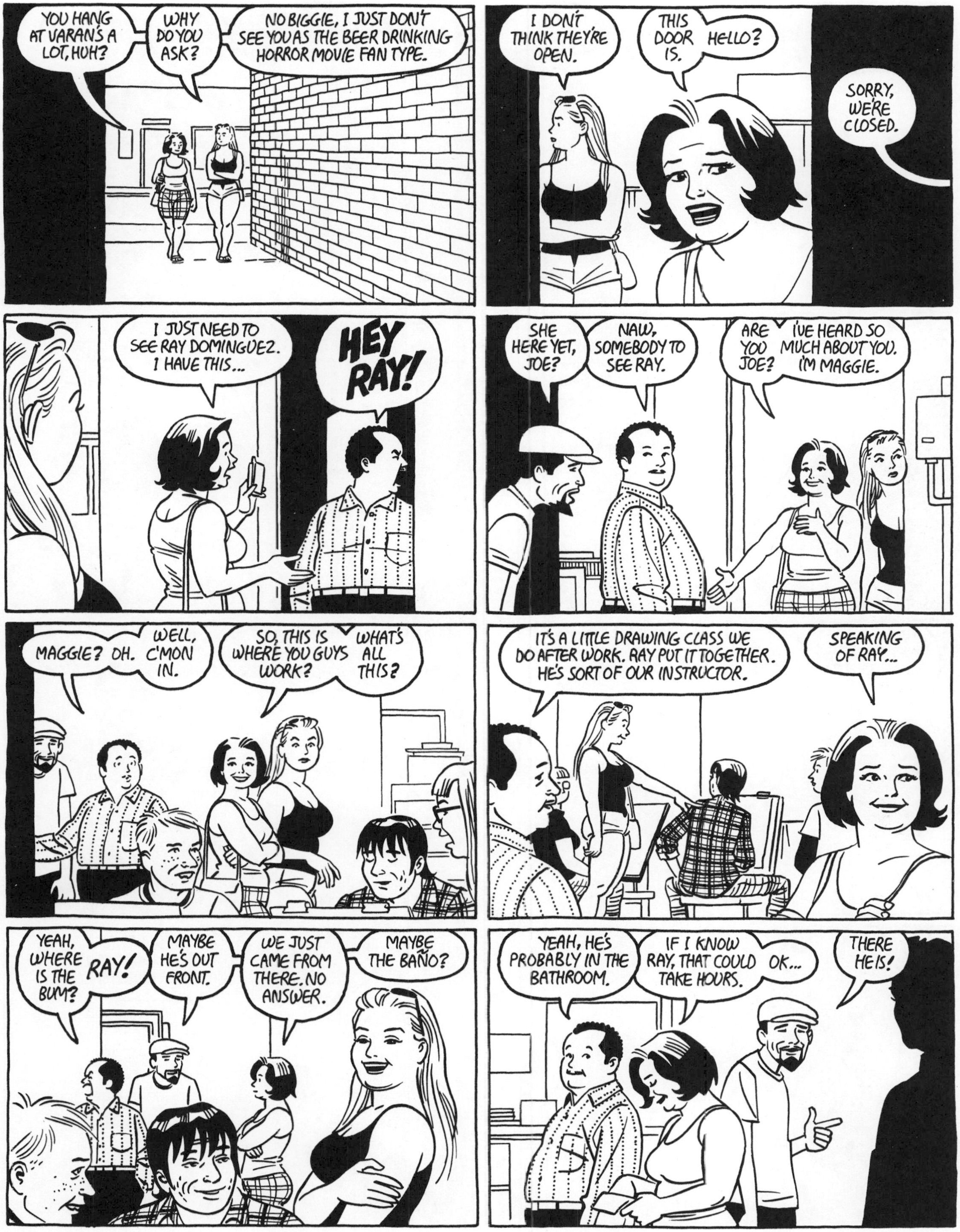

YOU HANG AT VARAN'S A LOT, HUH?
WHY DO YOU ASK?
NO BIGGIE, I JUST DON'T SEE YOU AS THE BEER DRINKING HORROR MOVIE FAN TYPE.
I DON'T THINK THEY'RE OPEN.
THIS DOOR IS.
HELLO?
SORRY, WE'RE CLOSED.
I JUST NEED TO SEE RAY DOMINGUEZ. I HAVE THIS...
HEY RAY!
SHE HERE YET, JOE?
NAW, SOMEBODY TO SEE RAY.
ARE YOU JOE?
I'VE HEARD SO MUCH ABOUT YOU. I'M MAGGIE.
MAGGIE? OH.
WELL, C'MON IN.
SO, THIS IS WHERE YOU GUYS WORK?
WHAT'S ALL THIS?
IT'S A LITTLE DRAWING CLASS WE DO AFTER WORK. RAY PUT IT TOGETHER. HE'S SORT OF OUR INSTRUCTOR.
SPEAKING OF RAY...
YEAH, WHERE IS THE BUM?
RAY!
MAYBE HE'S OUT FRONT.
WE JUST CAME FROM THERE. NO ANSWER.
MAYBE THE BAÑO?
YEAH, HE'S PROBABLY IN THE BATHROOM.
IF I KNOW RAY, THAT COULD TAKE HOURS.
OK...
THERE HE IS!

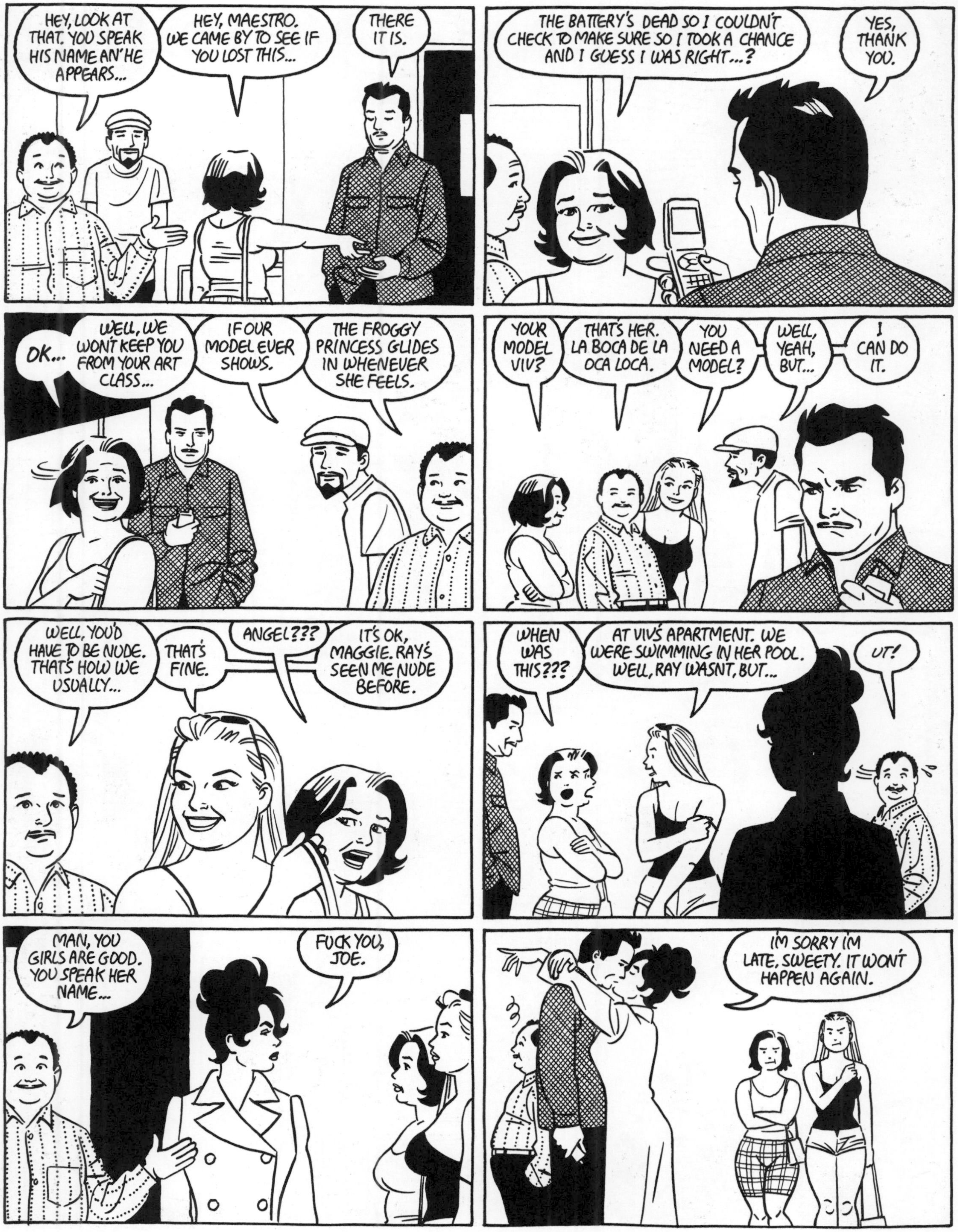
HEY, LOOK AT THAT. YOU SPEAK HIS NAME AN' HE APPEARS...
HEY, MAESTRO. WE CAME BY TO SEE IF YOU LOST THIS...
THERE IT IS.
THE BATTERY'S DEAD SO I COULDN'T CHECK TO MAKE SURE SO I TOOK A CHANCE AND I GUESS I WAS RIGHT...?
YES, THANK YOU.
OK...
WELL, WE WON'T KEEP YOU FROM YOUR ART CLASS...
IF OUR MODEL EVER SHOWS.
THE FROGGY PRINCESS GLIDES IN WHENEVER SHE FEELS.
YOUR MODEL VIV?
THAT'S HER. LA BOCA DE LA OCA LOCA.
YOU NEED A MODEL?
WELL, YEAH, BUT...
I CAN DO IT.
WELL, YOU'D HAVE TO BE NUDE. THAT'S HOW WE USUALLY...
THAT'S FINE.
ANGEL???
IT'S OK, MAGGIE. RAY'S SEEN ME NUDE BEFORE.
WHEN WAS THIS???
AT VIV'S APARTMENT. WE WERE SWIMMING IN HER POOL. WELL, RAY WASN'T, BUT...
UT!
MAN, YOU GIRLS ARE GOOD. YOU SPEAK HER NAME...
FUCK YOU, JOE.
I'M SORRY I'M LATE, SWEETY. IT WON'T HAPPEN AGAIN.

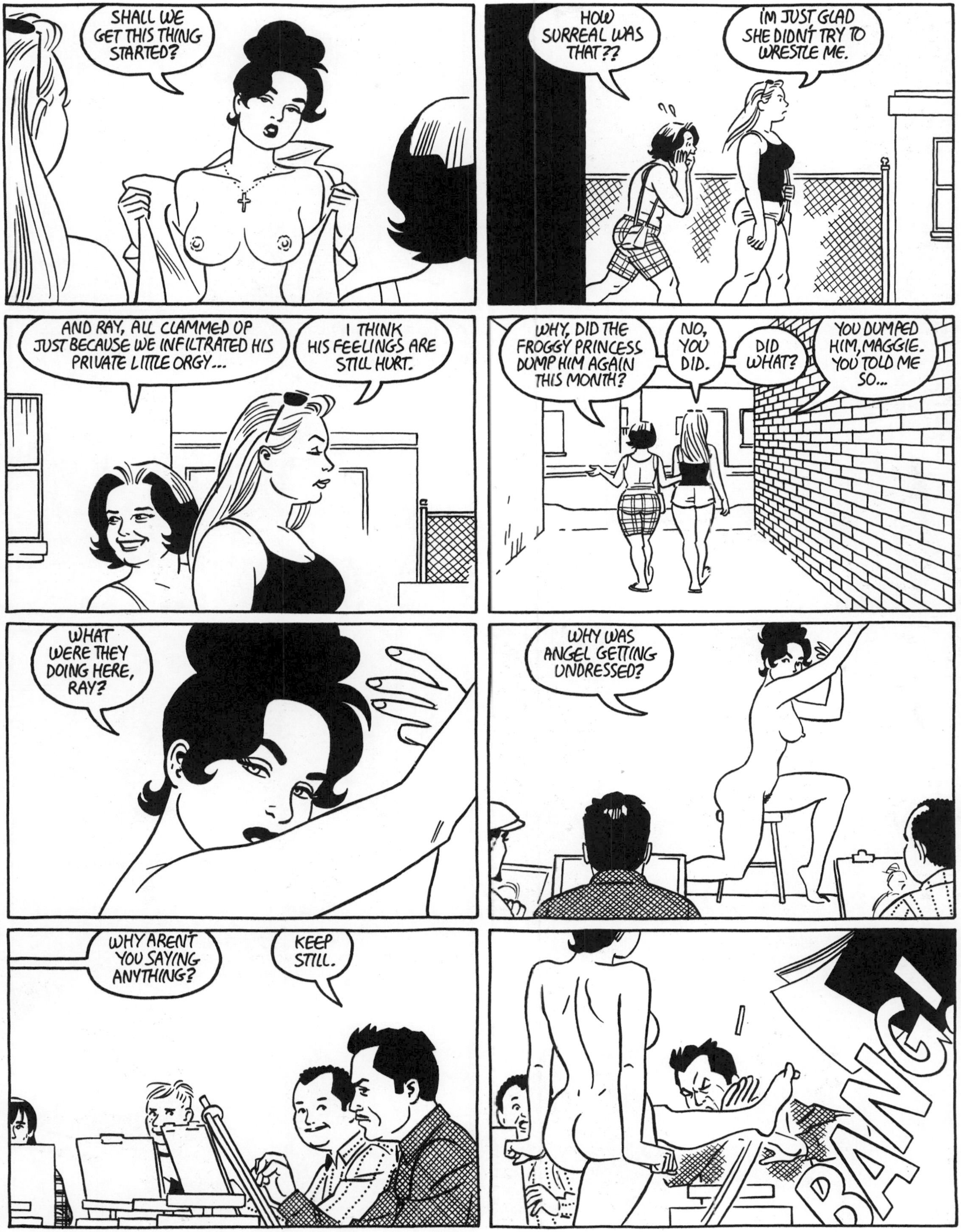
SHALL WE GET THIS THING STARTED?
HOW SURREAL WAS THAT??
I'M JUST GLAD SHE DIDN'T TRY TO WRESTLE ME.
AND RAY, ALL CLAMMED UP JUST BECAUSE WE INFILTRATED HIS PRIVATE LITTLE ORGY...
I THINK HIS FEELINGS ARE STILL HURT.
WHY, DID THE FROGGY PRINCESS DUMP HIM AGAIN THIS MONTH?
NO, YOU DID.
DID WHAT?
YOU DUMPED HIM, MAGGIE. YOU TOLD ME SO...
WHAT WERE THEY DOING HERE, RAY?
WHY WAS ANGEL GETTING UNDRESSED?
WHY AREN'T YOU SAYING ANYTHING?
KEEP STILL.
BANG!

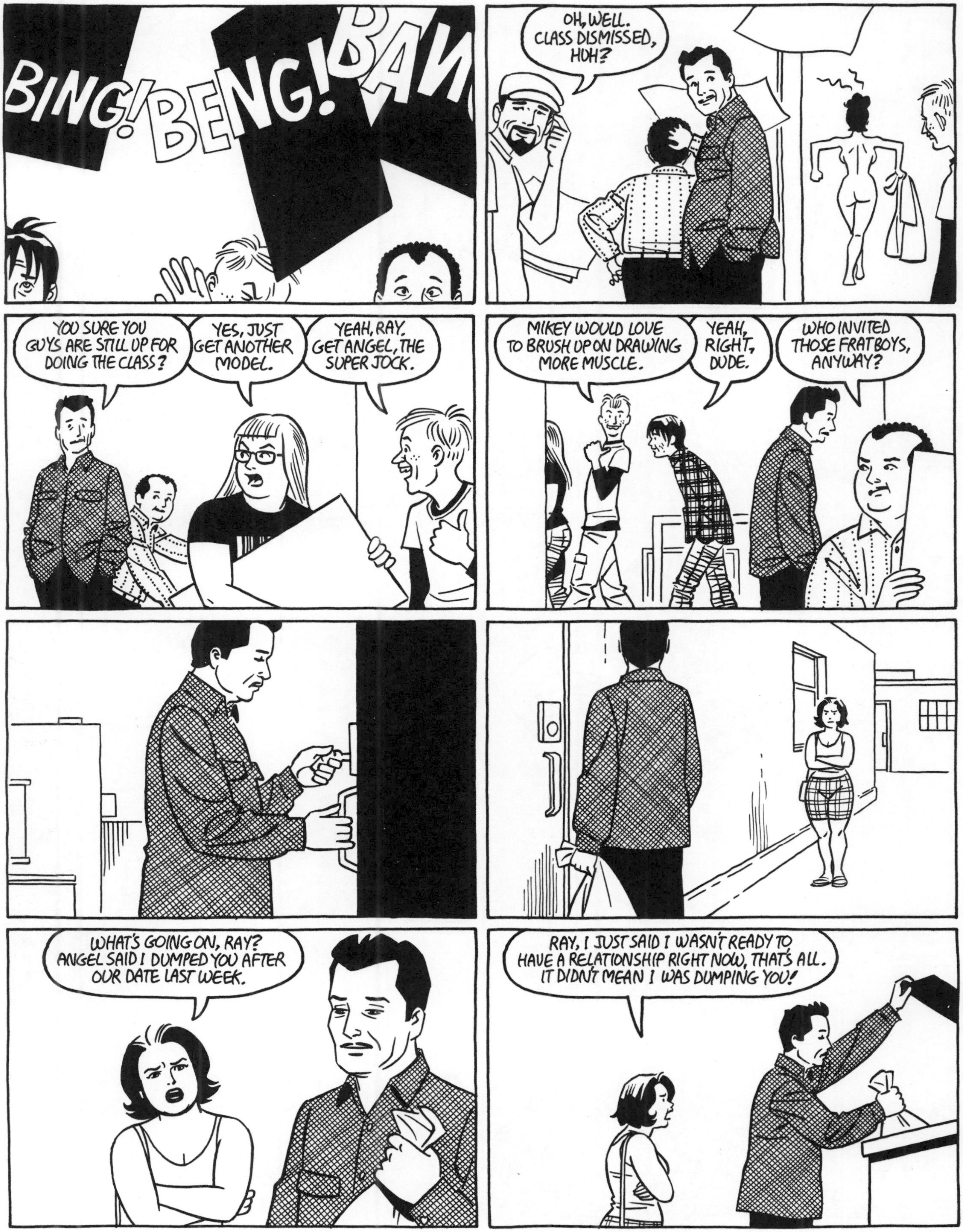
BING! BENG! BAN
OH, WELL. CLASS DISMISSED, HUH?
YOU SURE YOU GUYS ARE STILL UP FOR DOING THE CLASS?
YES, JUST GET ANOTHER MODEL.
YEAH, RAY. GET ANGEL, THE SUPER JOCK.
MIKEY WOULD LOVE TO BRUSH UP ON DRAWING MORE MUSCLE.
YEAH, RIGHT, DUDE.
WHO INVITED THOSE FRATBOYS, ANYWAY?
WHAT'S GOING ON, RAY? ANGEL SAID I DUMPED YOU AFTER OUR DATE LAST WEEK.
RAY, I JUST SAID I WASN'T READY TO HAVE A RELATIONSHIP RIGHT NOW, THAT'S ALL. IT DIDN'T MEAN I WAS DUMPING YOU!

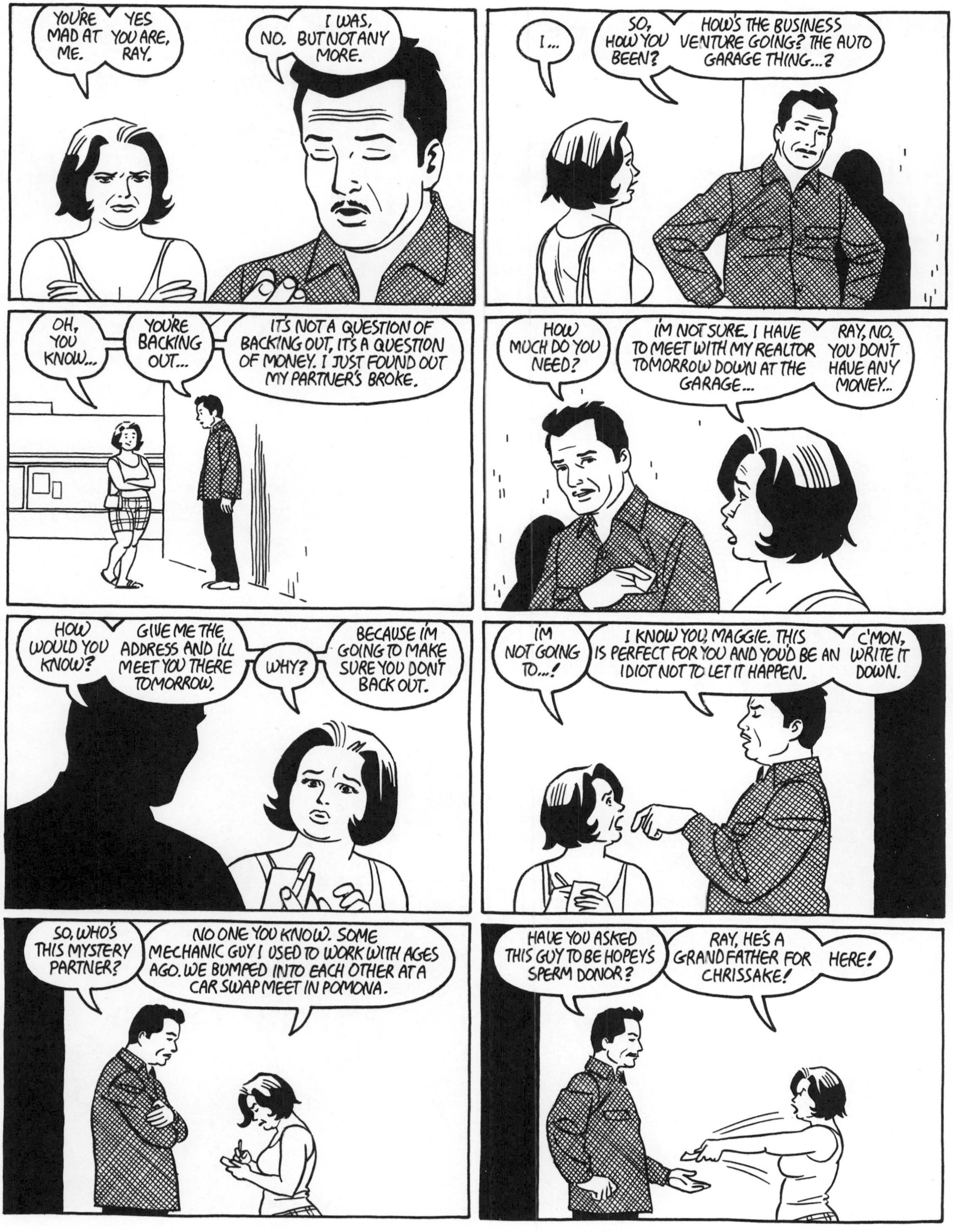
YOU'RE MAD AT ME.
YES YOU ARE, RAY.
NO.
I WAS, BUT NOT ANY MORE.
I...
SO, HOW YOU BEEN?
HOW'S THE BUSINESS VENTURE GOING? THE AUTO GARAGE THING...?
OH, YOU KNOW...
YOU'RE BACKING OUT...
IT'S NOT A QUESTION OF BACKING OUT, IT'S A QUESTION OF MONEY. I JUST FOUND OUT MY PARTNER'S BROKE.
HOW MUCH DO YOU NEED?
I'M NOT SURE. I HAVE TO MEET WITH MY REALTOR TOMORROW DOWN AT THE GARAGE...
RAY, NO. YOU DON'T HAVE ANY MONEY...
HOW WOULD YOU KNOW?
GIVE ME THE ADDRESS AND I'LL MEET YOU THERE TOMORROW.
WHY?
BECAUSE I'M GOING TO MAKE SURE YOU DON'T BACK OUT.
I'M NOT GOING TO...!
I KNOW YOU, MAGGIE. THIS IS PERFECT FOR YOU AND YOU'D BE AN IDIOT NOT TO LET IT HAPPEN.
C'MON, WRITE IT DOWN.
SO, WHO'S THIS MYSTERY PARTNER?
NO ONE YOU KNOW. SOME MECHANIC GUY I USED TO WORK WITH AGES AGO. WE BUMPED INTO EACH OTHER AT A CAR SWAP MEET IN POMONA.
HAVE YOU ASKED THIS GUY TO BE HOPEY'S SPERM DONOR?
RAY, HE'S A GRANDFATHER FOR CHRISSAKE!
HERE!

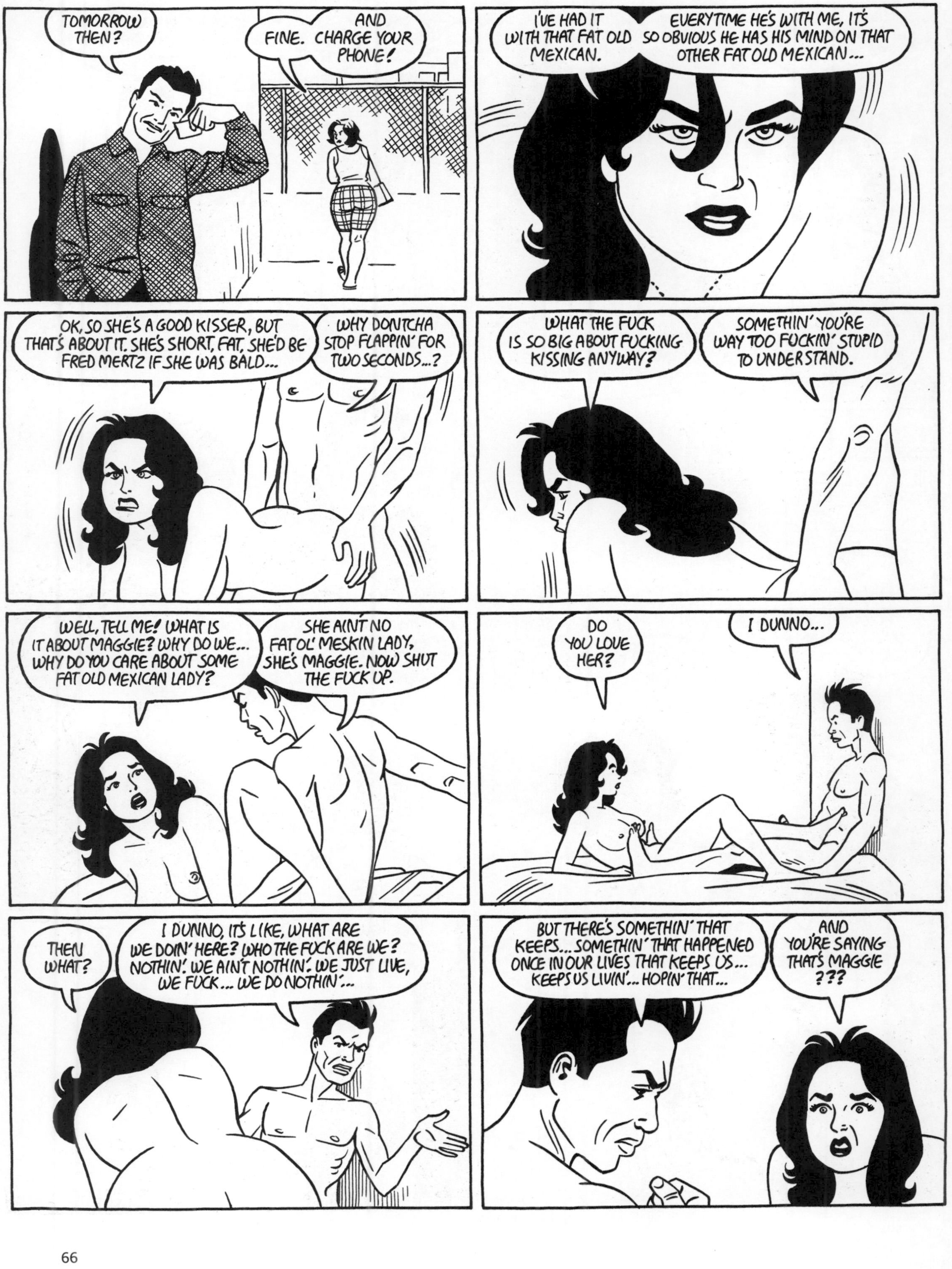
TOMORROW THEN?
FINE.
AND CHARGE YOUR PHONE!
I'VE HAD IT WITH THAT FAT OLD MEXICAN.
EVERYTIME HE'S WITH ME, IT'S SO OBVIOUS HE HAS HIS MIND ON THAT OTHER FAT OLD MEXICAN...
OK, SO SHE'S A GOOD KISSER, BUT THAT'S ABOUT IT. SHE'S SHORT, FAT, SHE'D BE FRED MERTZ IF SHE WAS BALD...
WHY DONTCHA STOP FLAPPIN' FOR TWO SECONDS...?
WHAT THE FUCK IS SO BIG ABOUT FUCKING KISSING ANYWAY?
SOMETHIN' YOU'RE WAY TOO FUCKIN' STUPID TO UNDERSTAND.
WELL, TELL ME! WHAT IS IT ABOUT MAGGIE? WHY DO WE... WHY DO YOU CARE ABOUT SOME FAT OLD MEXICAN LADY?
SHE AIN'T NO FAT OL' MESKIN LADY, SHE'S MAGGIE. NOW SHUT THE FUCK UP.
DO YOU LOVE HER?
I DUNNO...
THEN WHAT?
I DUNNO, IT'S LIKE, WHAT ARE WE DOIN' HERE? WHO THE FUCK ARE WE? NOTHIN'. WE AIN'T NOTHIN'. WE JUST LIVE, WE FUCK... WE DO NOTHIN'...
BUT THERE'S SOMETHIN' THAT KEEPS... SOMETHIN' THAT HAPPENED ONCE IN OUR LIVES THAT KEEPS US... KEEPS US LIVIN'... HOPIN' THAT...
AND YOU'RE SAYING THAT'S MAGGIE ???

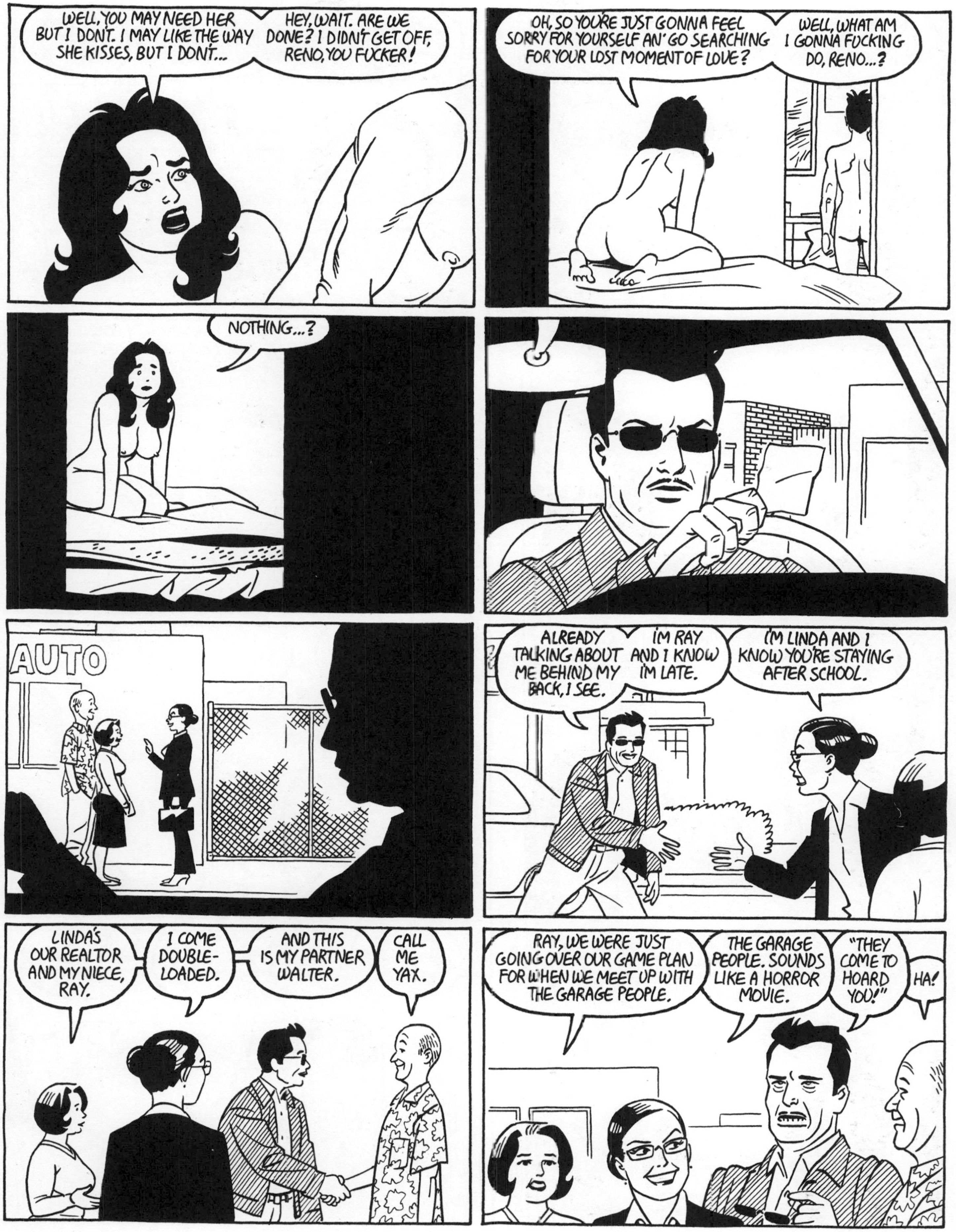
WELL, YOU MAY NEED HER BUT I DON'T. I MAY LIKE THE WAY SHE KISSES, BUT I DON'T...
HEY, WAIT. ARE WE DONE? I DIDN'T GET OFF, RENO, YOU FUCKER!
OH, SO YOU'RE JUST GONNA FEEL SORRY FOR YOURSELF AN' GO SEARCHING FOR YOUR LOST MOMENT OF LOVE?
WELL, WHAT AM I GONNA FUCKING DO, RENO...?
NOTHING...?
AUTO
ALREADY TALKING ABOUT ME BEHIND MY BACK, I SEE.
I'M RAY AND I KNOW I'M LATE.
I'M LINDA AND I KNOW YOU'RE STAYING AFTER SCHOOL.
LINDA'S OUR REALTOR AND MY NIECE, RAY.
I COME DOUBLE-LOADED.
AND THIS IS MY PARTNER WALTER.
CALL ME YAX.
RAY, WE WERE JUST GOING OVER OUR GAME PLAN FOR WHEN WE MEET UP WITH THE GARAGE PEOPLE.
THE GARAGE PEOPLE. SOUNDS LIKE A HORROR MOVIE.
"THEY COME TO HOARD YOU!"
HA!

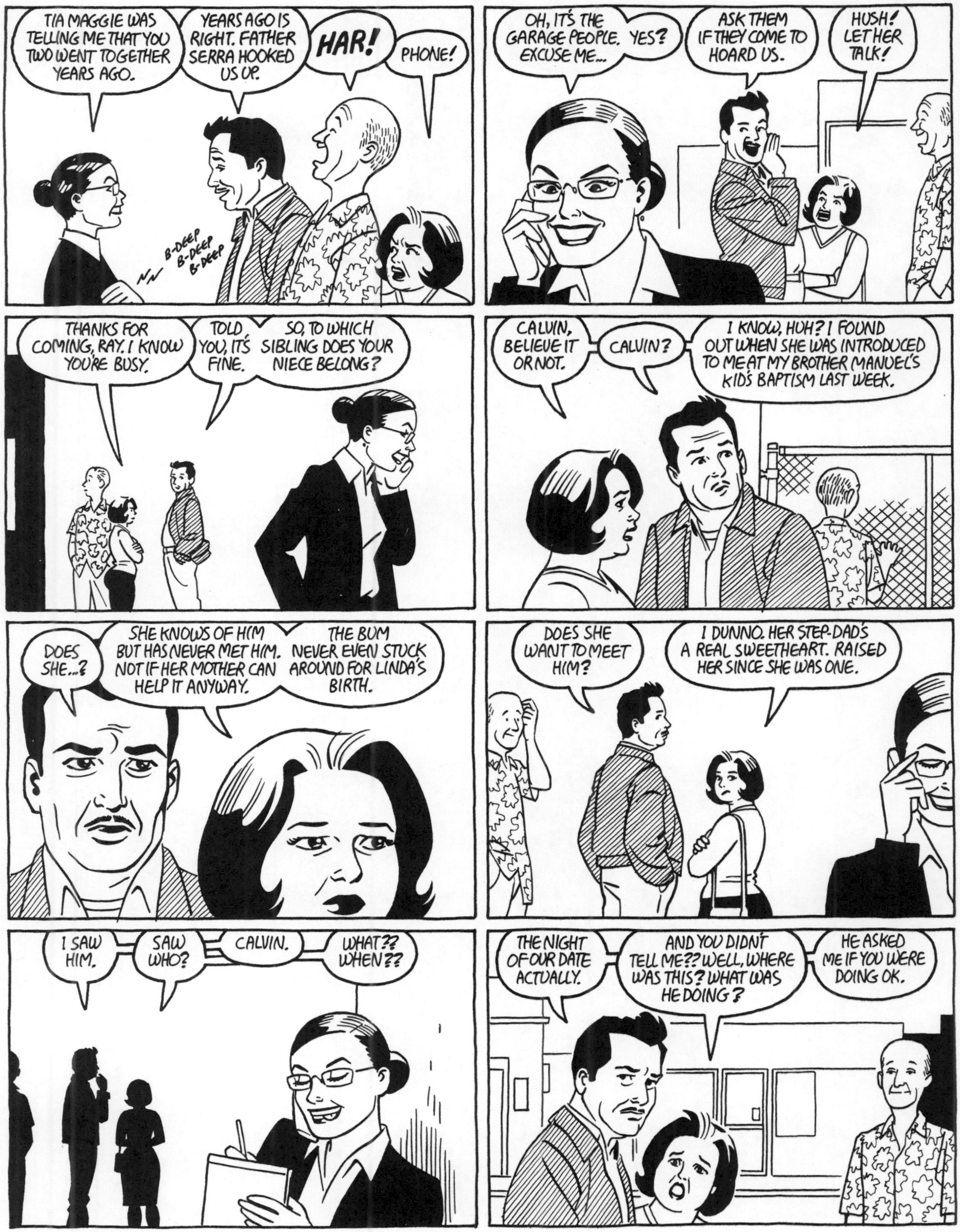
TIA MAGGIE WAS TELLING ME THAT YOU TWO WENT TOGETHER YEARS AGO.
YEARS AGO IS RIGHT. FATHER SERRA HOOKED US UP.
HAR!
PHONE!
B-DEEP B-DEEP B-DEEP
OH, IT'S THE GARAGE PEOPLE. EXCUSE ME...
YES?
ASK THEM IF THEY COME TO HOARD US.
HUSH! LET HER TALK!
THANKS FOR COMING, RAY. I KNOW YOU'RE BUSY.
TOLD YOU, IT'S FINE.
SO, TO WHICH SIBLING DOES YOUR NIECE BELONG?
CALVIN, BELIEVE IT OR NOT.
CALVIN?
I KNOW, HUH? I FOUND OUT WHEN SHE WAS INTRODUCED TO ME AT MY BROTHER MANUEL'S KID'S BAPTISM LAST WEEK.
DOES SHE...?
SHE KNOWS OF HIM BUT HAS NEVER MET HIM. NOT IF HER MOTHER CAN HELP IT ANYWAY.
THE BUM NEVER EVEN STUCK AROUND FOR LINDA'S BIRTH.
DOES SHE WANT TO MEET HIM?
I DUNNO. HER STEP-DAD'S A REAL SWEETHEART. RAISED HER SINCE SHE WAS ONE.
I SAW HIM.
SAW WHO?
CALVIN.
WHAT?? WHEN??
THE NIGHT OF OUR DATE ACTUALLY.
AND YOU DIDN'T TELL ME?? WELL, WHERE WAS THIS? WHAT WAS HE DOING?
HE ASKED ME IF YOU WERE DOING OK.

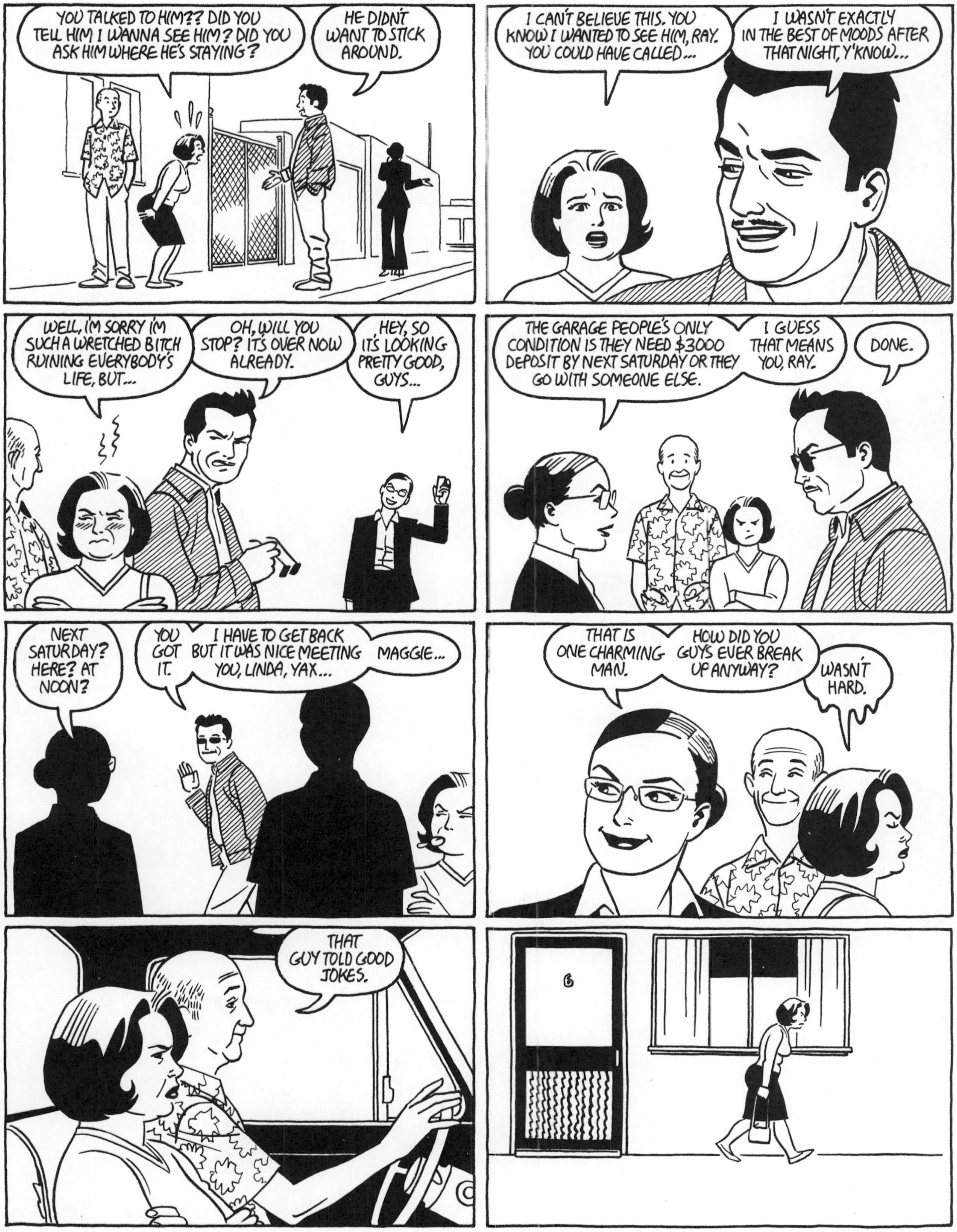
YOU TALKED TO HIM?? DID YOU TELL HIM I WANNA SEE HIM? DID YOU ASK HIM WHERE HE'S STAYING?
HE DIDN'T WANT TO STICK AROUND.
I CAN'T BELIEVE THIS. YOU KNOW I WANTED TO SEE HIM, RAY. YOU COULD HAVE CALLED...
I WASN'T EXACTLY IN THE BEST OF MOODS AFTER THAT NIGHT, Y'KNOW...
WELL, I'M SORRY I'M SUCH A WRETCHED BITCH RUINING EVERYBODY'S LIFE, BUT...
OH, WILL YOU STOP? IT'S OVER NOW ALREADY.
HEY, SO IT'S LOOKING PRETTY GOOD, GUYS...
THE GARAGE PEOPLE'S ONLY CONDITION IS THEY NEED $3000 DEPOSIT BY NEXT SATURDAY OR THEY GO WITH SOMEONE ELSE.
I GUESS THAT MEANS YOU, RAY.
DONE.
NEXT SATURDAY? HERE? AT NOON?
YOU GOT IT.
I HAVE TO GET BACK BUT IT WAS NICE MEETING YOU, LINDA, YAX...
MAGGIE...
THAT IS ONE CHARMING MAN.
HOW DID YOU GUYS EVER BREAK UP ANYWAY?
WASN'T HARD.
THAT GUY TOLD GOOD JOKES.
6

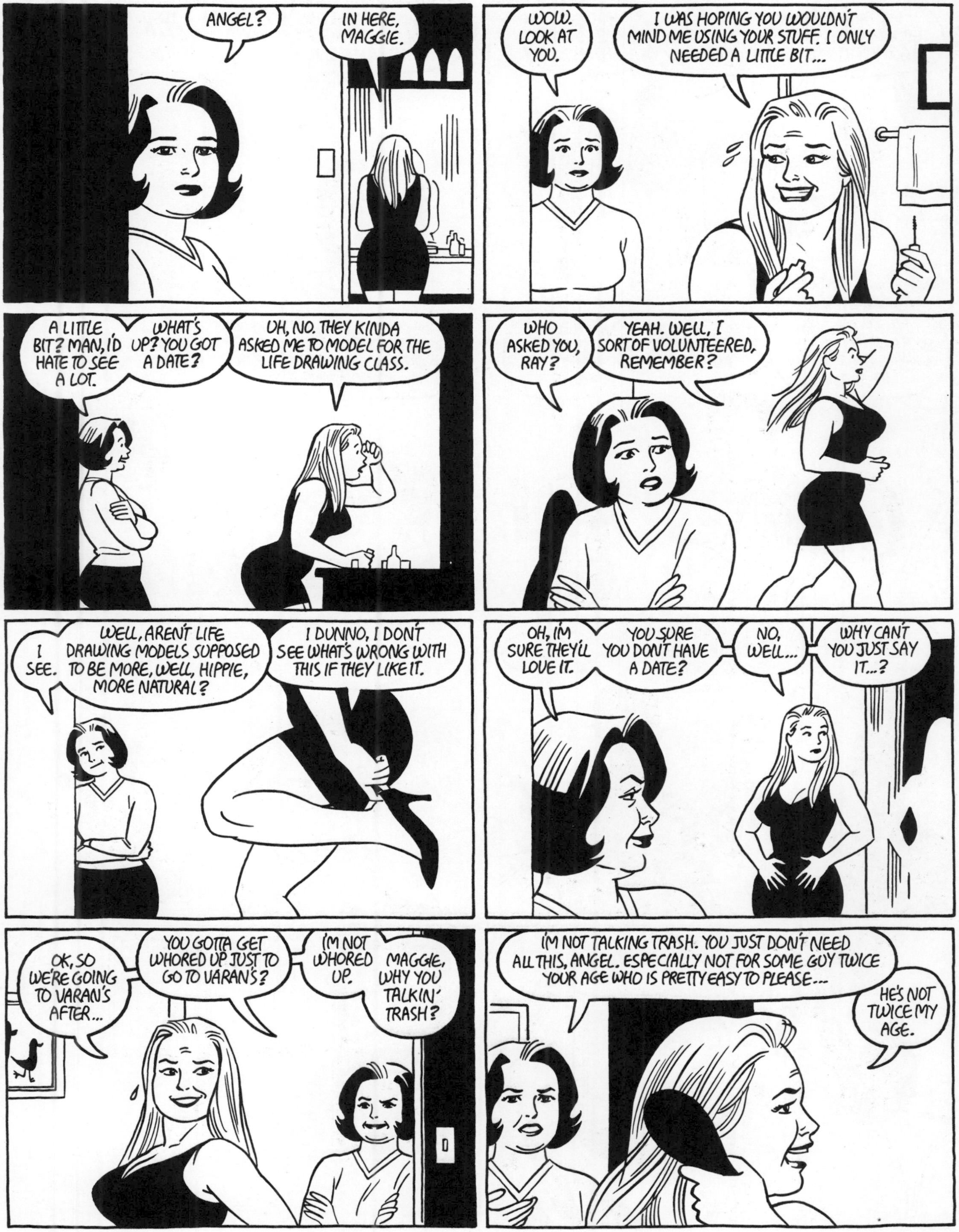
ANGEL?
IN HERE, MAGGIE.
WOW. LOOK AT YOU.
I WAS HOPING YOU WOULDN'T MIND ME USING YOUR STUFF. I ONLY NEEDED A LITTLE BIT...
A LITTLE BIT? MAN, I'D HATE TO SEE A LOT.
WHAT'S UP? YOU GOT A DATE?
UH, NO. THEY KINDA ASKED ME TO MODEL FOR THE LIFE DRAWING CLASS.
WHO ASKED YOU, RAY?
YEAH. WELL, I SORT OF VOLUNTEERED, REMEMBER?
I SEE.
WELL, AREN'T LIFE DRAWING MODELS SUPPOSED TO BE MORE, WELL, HIPPIE, MORE NATURAL?
I DUNNO, I DON'T SEE WHAT'S WRONG WITH THIS IF THEY LIKE IT.
OH, I'M SURE THEY'LL LOVE IT.
YOU SURE YOU DON'T HAVE A DATE?
NO, WELL...
WHY CAN'T YOU JUST SAY IT...?
OK, SO WE'RE GOING TO VARAN'S AFTER...
YOU GOTTA GET WHORED UP JUST TO GO TO VARAN'S?
I'M NOT WHORED UP.
MAGGIE, WHY YOU TALKIN' TRASH?
I'M NOT TALKING TRASH. YOU JUST DON'T NEED ALL THIS, ANGEL. ESPECIALLY NOT FOR SOME GUY TWICE YOUR AGE WHO IS PRETTY EASY TO PLEASE...
HE'S NOT TWICE MY AGE.

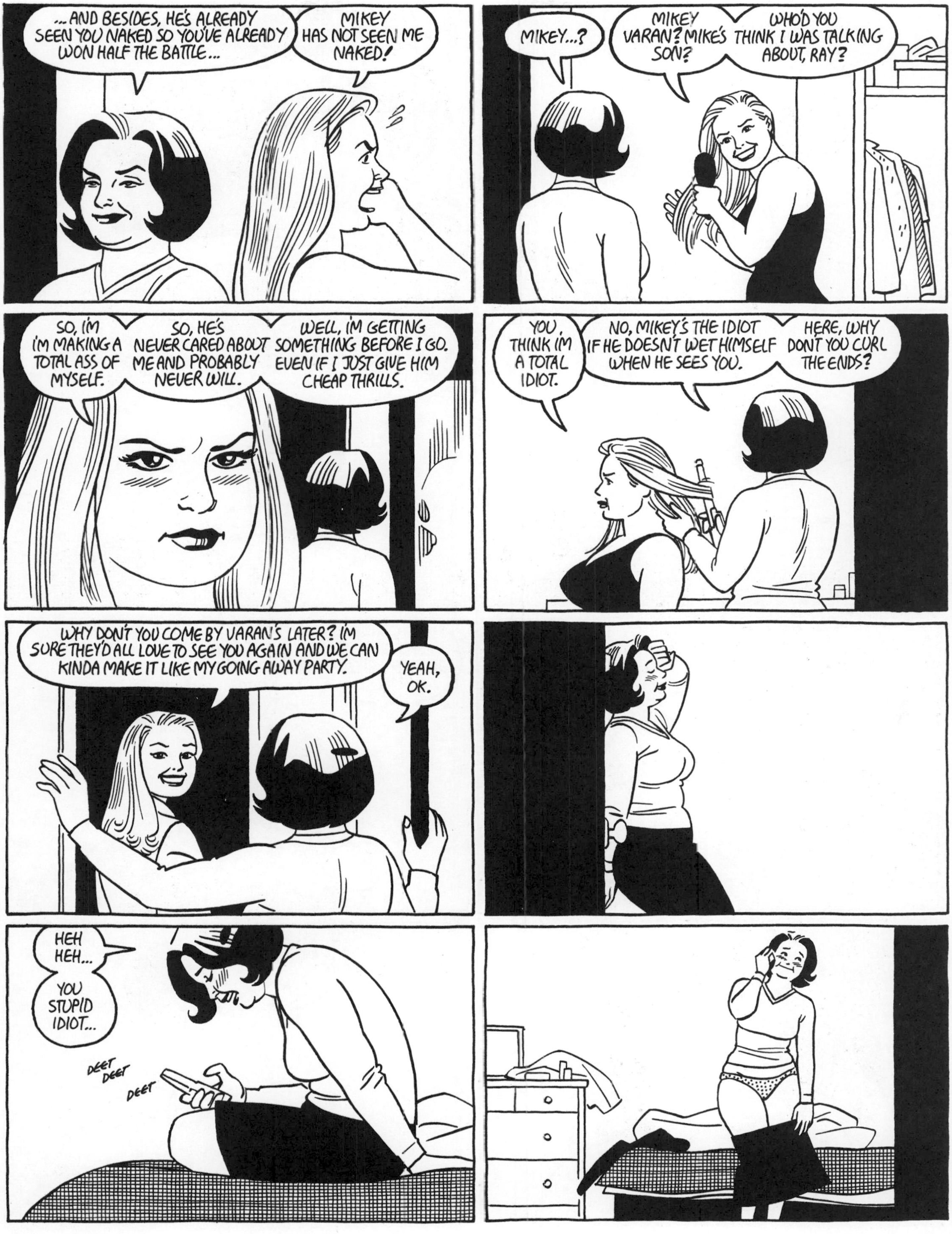
...AND BESIDES, HE'S ALREADY SEEN YOU NAKED SO YOU'VE ALREADY WON HALF THE BATTLE...
MIKEY HAS NOT SEEN ME NAKED!
MIKEY...?
MIKEY VARAN? MIKE'S SON?
WHO'D YOU THINK I WAS TALKING ABOUT, RAY?
SO, I'M I'M MAKING A TOTAL ASS OF MYSELF.
SO, HE'S NEVER CARED ABOUT ME AND PROBABLY NEVER WILL.
WELL, I'M GETTING SOMETHING BEFORE I GO. EVEN IF I JUST GIVE HIM CHEAP THRILLS.
YOU, THINK I'M A TOTAL IDIOT.
NO, MIKEY'S THE IDIOT IF HE DOESN'T WET HIMSELF WHEN HE SEES YOU.
HERE, WHY DON'T YOU CURL THE ENDS?
WHY DON'T YOU COME BY VARAN'S LATER? I'M SURE THEY'D ALL LOVE TO SEE YOU AGAIN AND WE CAN KINDA MAKE IT LIKE MY GOING AWAY PARTY.
YEAH, OK.
HEH HEH...
YOU STUPID IDIOT...
DEET DEET DEET

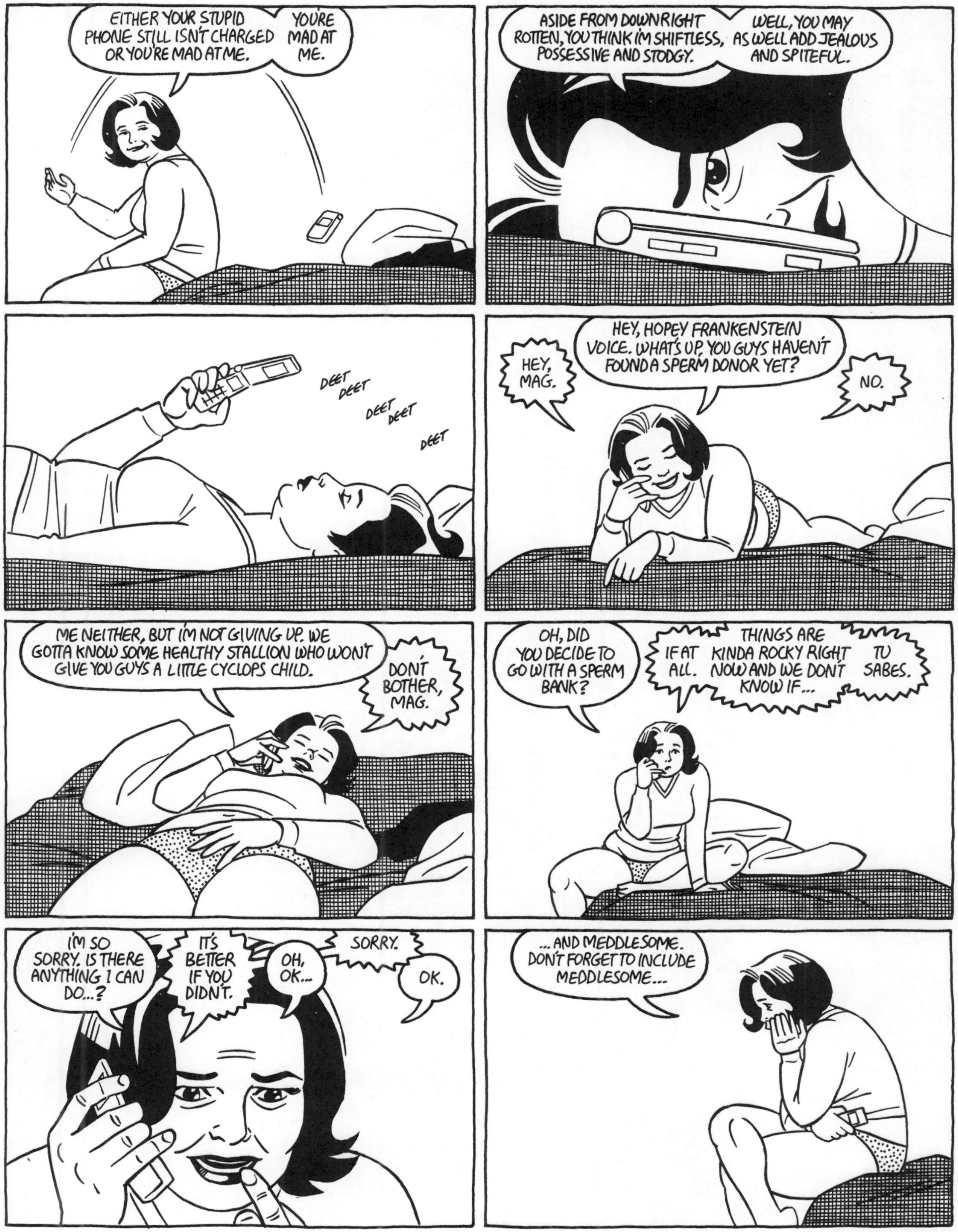
EITHER YOUR STUPID PHONE STILL ISN'T CHARGED OR YOU'RE MAD AT ME.
YOU'RE MAD AT ME.
ASIDE FROM DOWNRIGHT ROTTEN, YOU THINK I'M SHIFTLESS, POSSESSIVE AND STODGY.
WELL, YOU MAY AS WELL ADD JEALOUS AND SPITEFUL.
DEET DEET DEET DEET DEET
HEY, MAG.
HEY, HOPEY FRANKENSTEIN VOICE. WHAT'S UP, YOU GUYS HAVEN'T FOUND A SPERM DONOR YET?
NO.
ME NEITHER, BUT I'M NOT GIVING UP. WE GOTTA KNOW SOME HEALTHY STALLION WHO WON'T GIVE YOU GUYS A LITTLE CYCLOPS CHILD.
DON'T BOTHER, MAG.
OH, DID YOU DECIDE TO GO WITH A SPERM BANK?
IF AT ALL.
THINGS ARE KINDA ROCKY RIGHT NOW AND WE DON'T KNOW IF...
TU SABES.
I'M SO SORRY. IS THERE ANYTHING I CAN DO...?
IT'S BETTER IF YOU DIDN'T.
OH, OK...
SORRY.
OK.
...AND MEDDLESOME. DON'T FORGET TO INCLUDE MEDDLESOME...

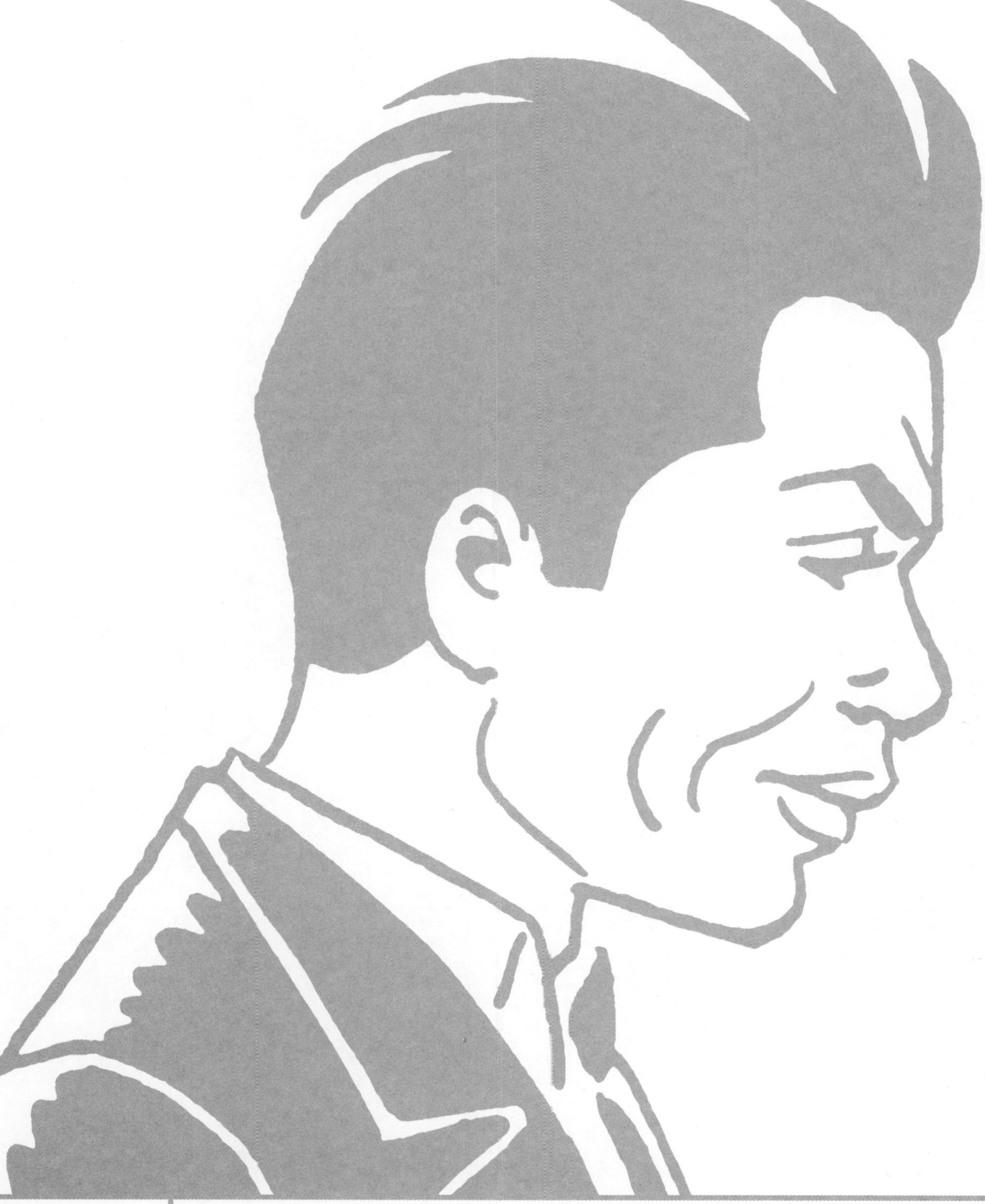

5 THE LOVE BUNGLERS
PART FOUR

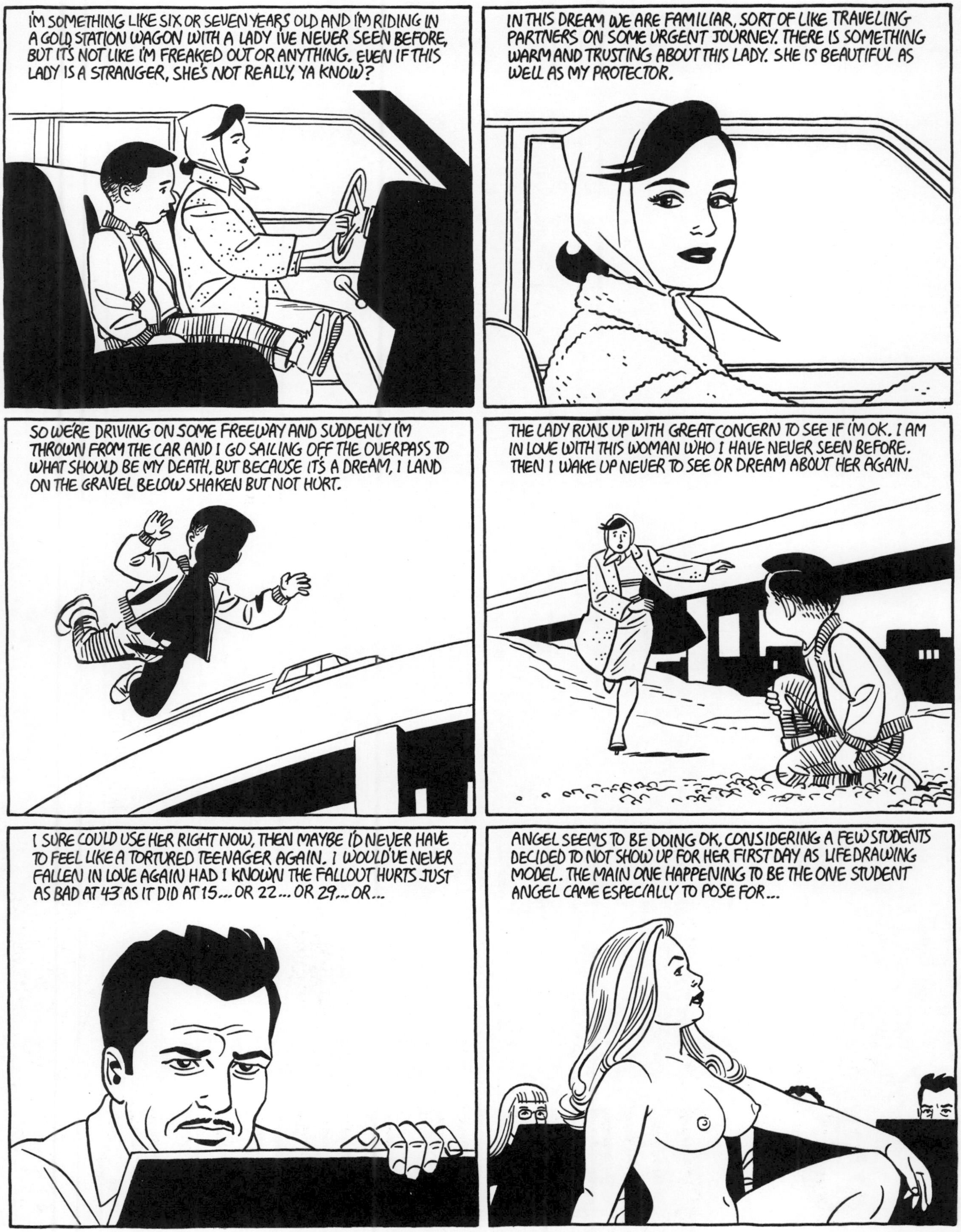
I'M SOMETHING LIKE SIX OR SEVEN YEARS OLD AND I'M RIDING IN A GOLD STATION WAGON WITH A LADY I'VE NEVER SEEN BEFORE, BUT IT'S NOT LIKE I'M FREAKED OUT OR ANYTHING. EVEN IF THIS LADY IS A STRANGER, SHE'S NOT REALLY, YA KNOW?
IN THIS DREAM WE ARE FAMILIAR, SORT OF LIKE TRAVELING PARTNERS ON SOME URGENT JOURNEY. THERE IS SOMETHING WARM AND TRUSTING ABOUT THIS LADY. SHE IS BEAUTIFUL AS WELL AS MY PROTECTOR.
SO WE'RE DRIVING ON SOME FREEWAY AND SUDDENLY I'M THROWN FROM THE CAR AND I GO SAILING OFF THE OVERPASS TO WHAT SHOULD BE MY DEATH, BUT BECAUSE IT'S A DREAM, I LAND ON THE GRAVEL BELOW SHAKEN BUT NOT HURT.
THE LADY RUNS UP WITH GREAT CONCERN TO SEE IF I'M OK. I AM IN LOVE WITH THIS WOMAN WHO I HAVE NEVER SEEN BEFORE. THEN I WAKE UP NEVER TO SEE OR DREAM ABOUT HER AGAIN.
I SURE COULD USE HER RIGHT NOW, THEN MAYBE I'D NEVER HAVE TO FEEL LIKE A TORTURED TEENAGER AGAIN. I WOULD'VE NEVER FALLEN IN LOVE AGAIN HAD I KNOWN THE FALLOUT HURTS JUST AS BAD AT 43 AS IT DID AT 15... OR 22... OR 29... OR...
ANGEL SEEMS TO BE DOING OK, CONSIDERING A FEW STUDENTS DECIDED TO NOT SHOW UP FOR HER FIRST DAY AS LIFEDRAWING MODEL. THE MAIN ONE HAPPENING TO BE THE ONE STUDENT ANGEL CAME ESPECIALLY TO POSE FOR...

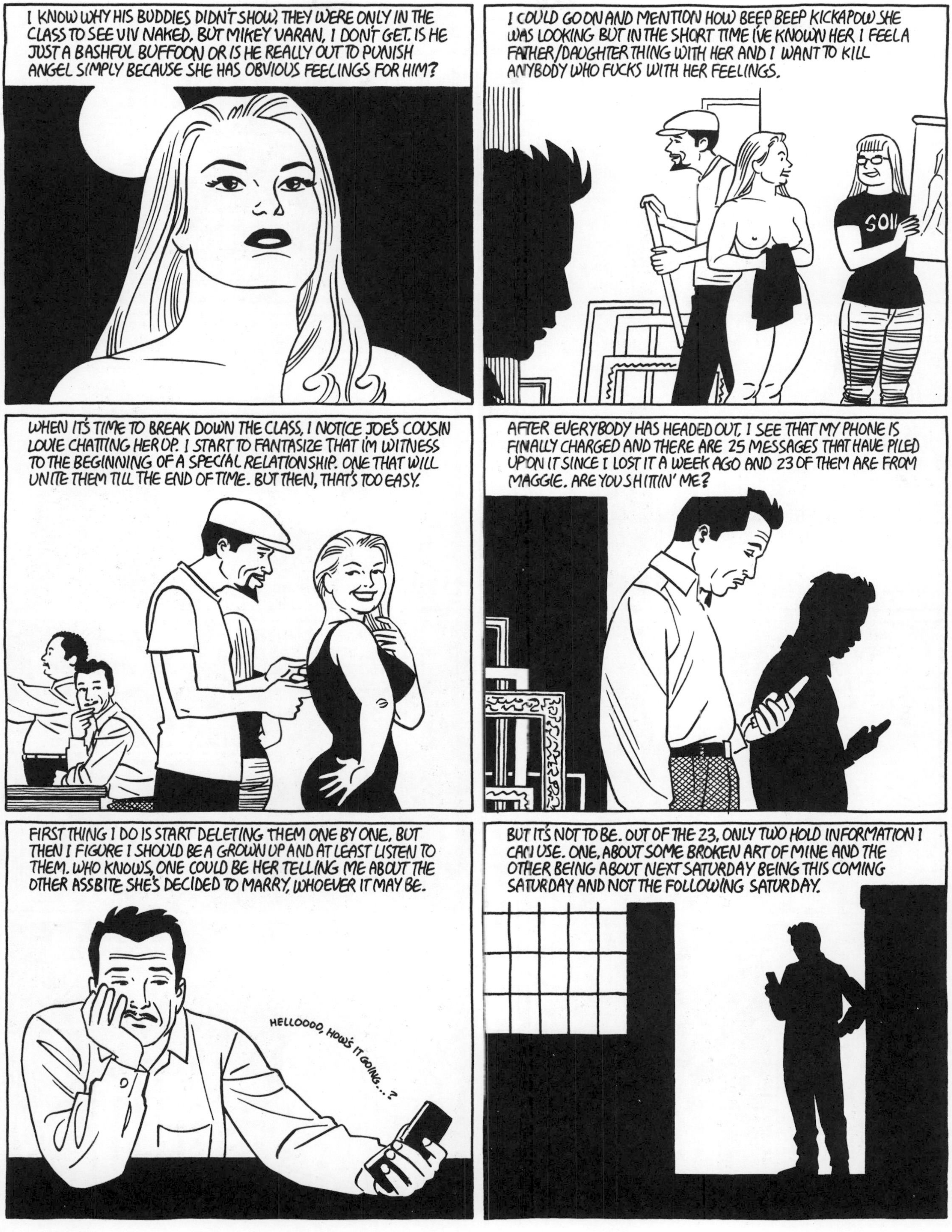
I KNOW WHY HIS BUDDIES DIDN'T SHOW, THEY WERE ONLY IN THE CLASS TO SEE VIV NAKED, BUT MIKEY VARAN, I DON'T GET. IS HE JUST A BASHFUL BUFFOON OR IS HE REALLY OUT TO PUNISH ANGEL SIMPLY BECAUSE SHE HAS OBVIOUS FEELINGS FOR HIM?
I COULD GO ON AND MENTION HOW BEEP BEEP KICKAPOW SHE WAS LOOKING BUT IN THE SHORT TIME I'VE KNOWN HER I FEEL A FATHER/DAUGHTER THING WITH HER AND I WANT TO KILL ANYBODY WHO FUCKS WITH HER FEELINGS.
SOU
WHEN IT'S TIME TO BREAK DOWN THE CLASS, I NOTICE JOE'S COUSIN LOUIE CHATTING HER UP. I START TO FANTASIZE THAT I'M WITNESS TO THE BEGINNING OF A SPECIAL RELATIONSHIP. ONE THAT WILL UNITE THEM TILL THE END OF TIME. BUT THEN, THAT'S TOO EASY.
AFTER EVERYBODY HAS HEADED OUT, I SEE THAT MY PHONE IS FINALLY CHARGED AND THERE ARE 25 MESSAGES THAT HAVE PILED UP ON IT SINCE I LOST IT A WEEK AGO AND 23 OF THEM ARE FROM MAGGIE. ARE YOU SHITTIN' ME?
FIRST THING I DO IS START DELETING THEM ONE BY ONE, BUT THEN I FIGURE I SHOULD BE A GROWN UP AND AT LEAST LISTEN TO THEM. WHO KNOWS, ONE COULD BE HER TELLING ME ABOUT THE OTHER ASSBITE SHE'S DECIDED TO MARRY, WHOEVER IT MAY BE.
HELLOOOO, HOW'S IT GOING...?
BUT IT'S NOT TO BE. OUT OF THE 23, ONLY TWO HOLD INFORMATION I CAN USE. ONE, ABOUT SOME BROKEN ART OF MINE AND THE OTHER BEING ABOUT NEXT SATURDAY BEING THIS COMING SATURDAY AND NOT THE FOLLOWING SATURDAY.

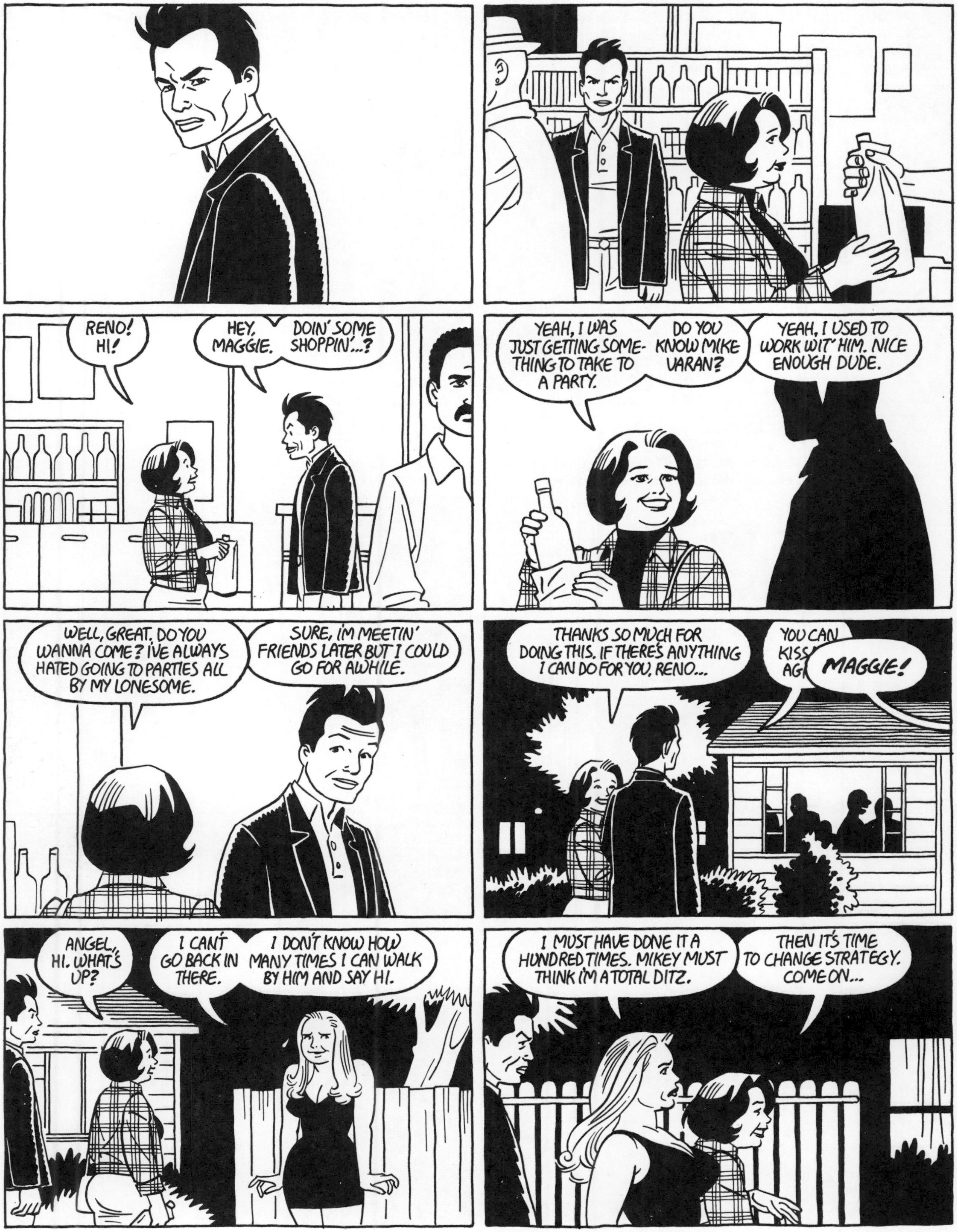
RENO! HI!
HEY, MAGGIE.
DOIN' SOME SHOPPIN'...?
YEAH, I WAS JUST GETTING SOMETHING TO TAKE TO A PARTY.
DO YOU KNOW MIKE VARAN?
YEAH, I USED TO WORK WIT' HIM. NICE ENOUGH DUDE.
WELL, GREAT. DO YOU WANNA COME? I'VE ALWAYS HATED GOING TO PARTIES ALL BY MY LONESOME.
SURE, I'M MEETIN' FRIENDS LATER BUT I COULD GO FOR AWHILE.
THANKS SO MUCH FOR DOING THIS. IF THERE'S ANYTHING I CAN DO FOR YOU, RENO...
YOU CAN
KISS
AG
MAGGIE!
ANGEL, HI. WHAT'S UP?
I CAN'T GO BACK IN THERE.
I DON'T KNOW HOW MANY TIMES I CAN WALK BY HIM AND SAY HI.
I MUST HAVE DONE IT A HUNDRED TIMES. MIKEY MUST THINK I'M A TOTAL DITZ.
THEN IT'S TIME TO CHANGE STRATEGY. COME ON...

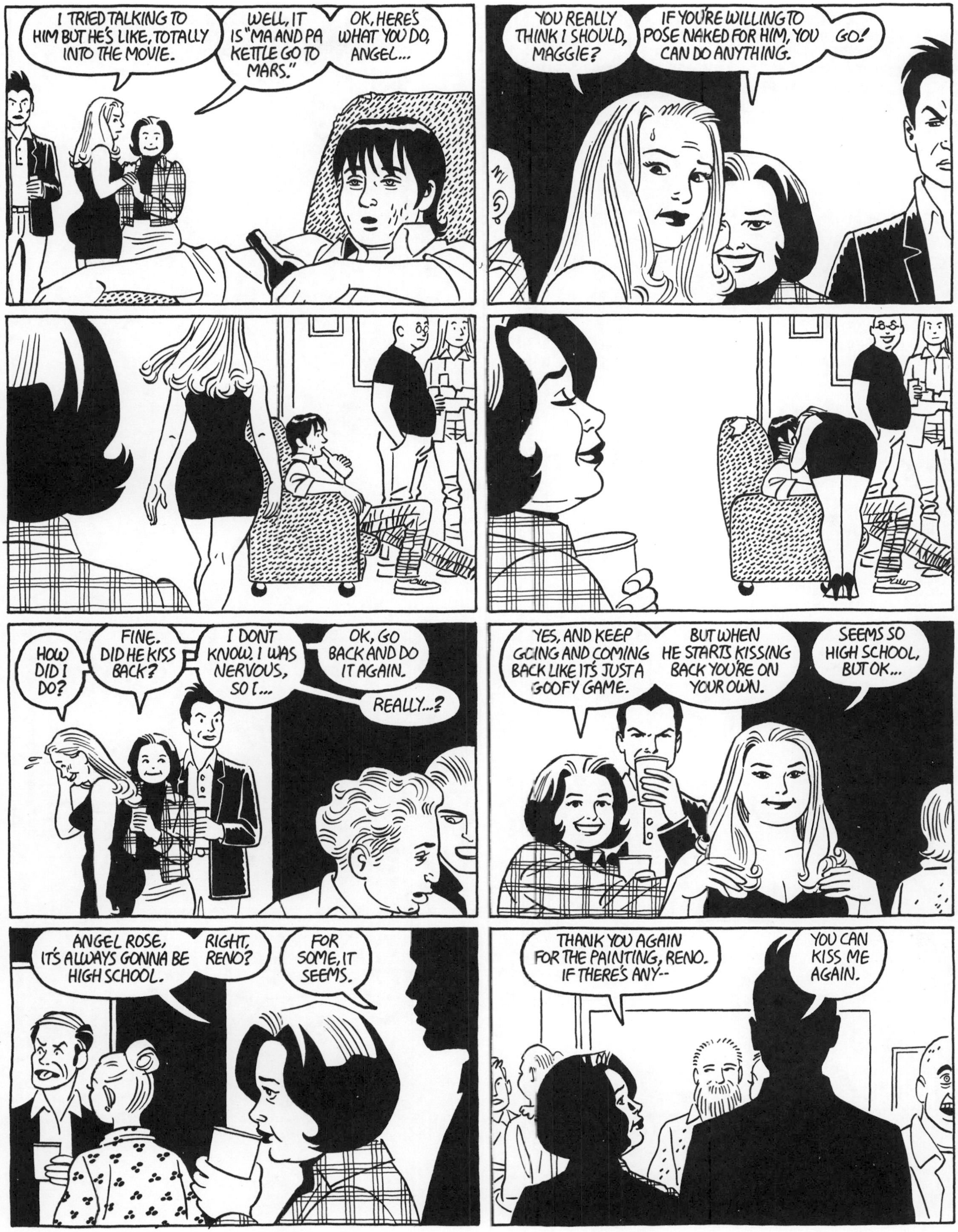
I TRIED TALKING TO HIM BUT HE'S LIKE, TOTALLY INTO THE MOVIE.
WELL, IT IS "MA AND PA KETTLE GO TO MARS."
OK, HERE'S WHAT YOU DO, ANGEL...
YOU REALLY THINK I SHOULD, MAGGIE?
IF YOU'RE WILLING TO POSE NAKED FOR HIM, YOU CAN DO ANYTHING.
GO!
HOW DID I DO?
FINE. DID HE KISS BACK?
I DON'T KNOW. I WAS NERVOUS, SO I...
OK, GO BACK AND DO IT AGAIN.
REALLY...?
YES, AND KEEP GOING AND COMING BACK LIKE IT'S JUST A GOOFY GAME.
BUT WHEN HE STARTS KISSING BACK YOU'RE ON YOUR OWN.
SEEMS SO HIGH SCHOOL, BUT OK...
ANGEL ROSE, IT'S ALWAYS GONNA BE HIGH SCHOOL.
RIGHT, RENO?
FOR SOME, IT SEEMS.
THANK YOU AGAIN FOR THE PAINTING, RENO. IF THERE'S ANY--
YOU CAN KISS ME AGAIN.

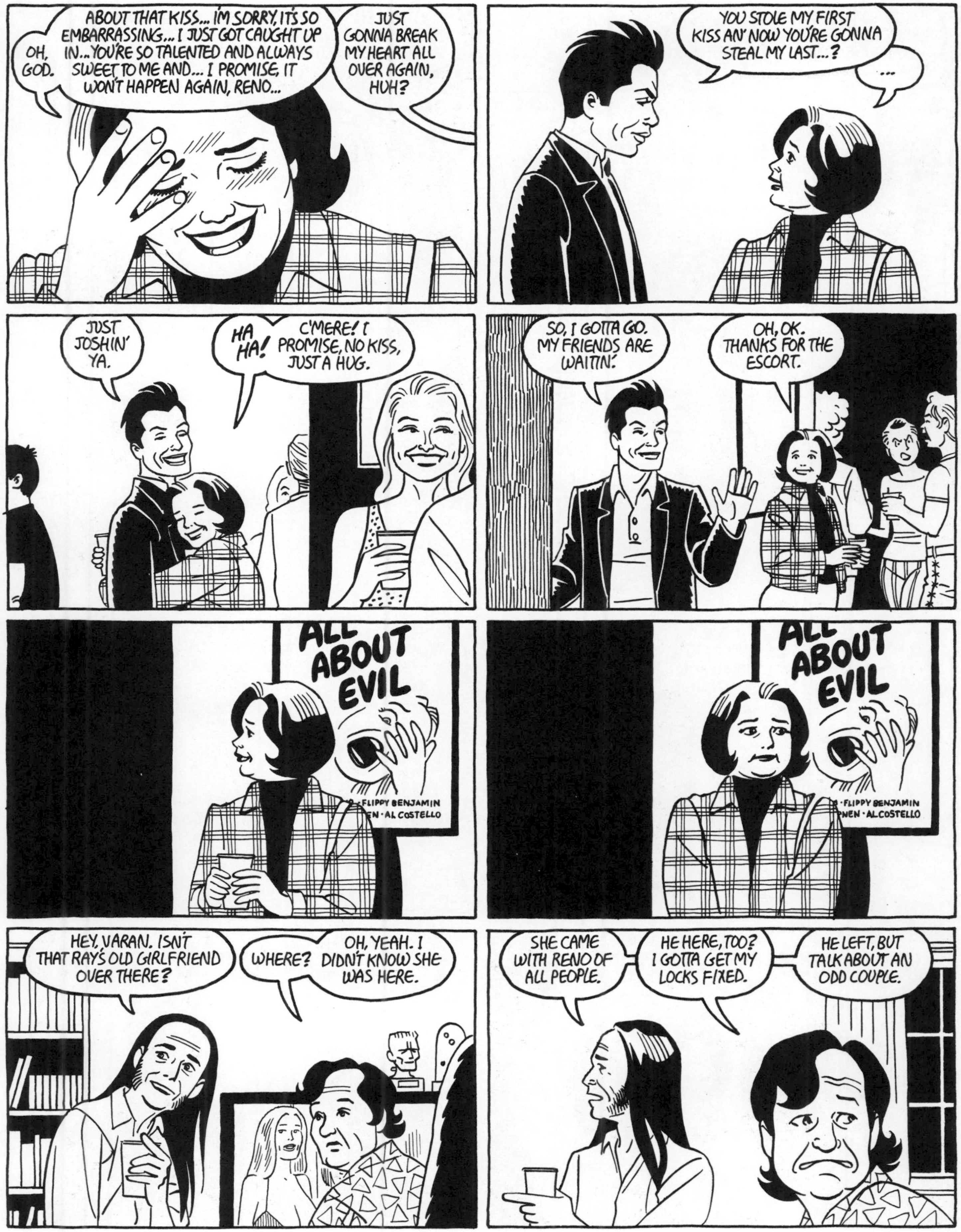
OH, GOD.
ABOUT THAT KISS... I'M SORRY, IT'S SO EMBARRASSING... I JUST GOT CAUGHT UP IN... YOU'RE SO TALENTED AND ALWAYS SWEET TO ME AND... I PROMISE, IT WON'T HAPPEN AGAIN, RENO...
JUST GONNA BREAK MY HEART ALL OVER AGAIN, HUH?
YOU STOLE MY FIRST KISS AN' NOW YOU'RE GONNA STEAL MY LAST...?
...
JUST JOSHIN' YA.
HA HA!
C'MERE! I PROMISE, NO KISS, JUST A HUG.
SO, I GOTTA GO. MY FRIENDS ARE WAITIN'.
OH, OK. THANKS FOR THE ESCORT.
ALL ABOUT EVIL
FLIPPY BENJAMIN
AL COSTELLO
ALL ABOUT EVIL
FLIPPY BENJAMIN
AL COSTELLO
HEY, VARAN. ISN'T THAT RAY'S OLD GIRLFRIEND OVER THERE?
WHERE?
OH, YEAH. I DIDN'T KNOW SHE WAS HERE.
SHE CAME WITH RENO OF ALL PEOPLE.
HE HERE, TOO? I GOTTA GET MY LOCKS FIXED.
HE LEFT, BUT TALK ABOUT AN ODD COUPLE.

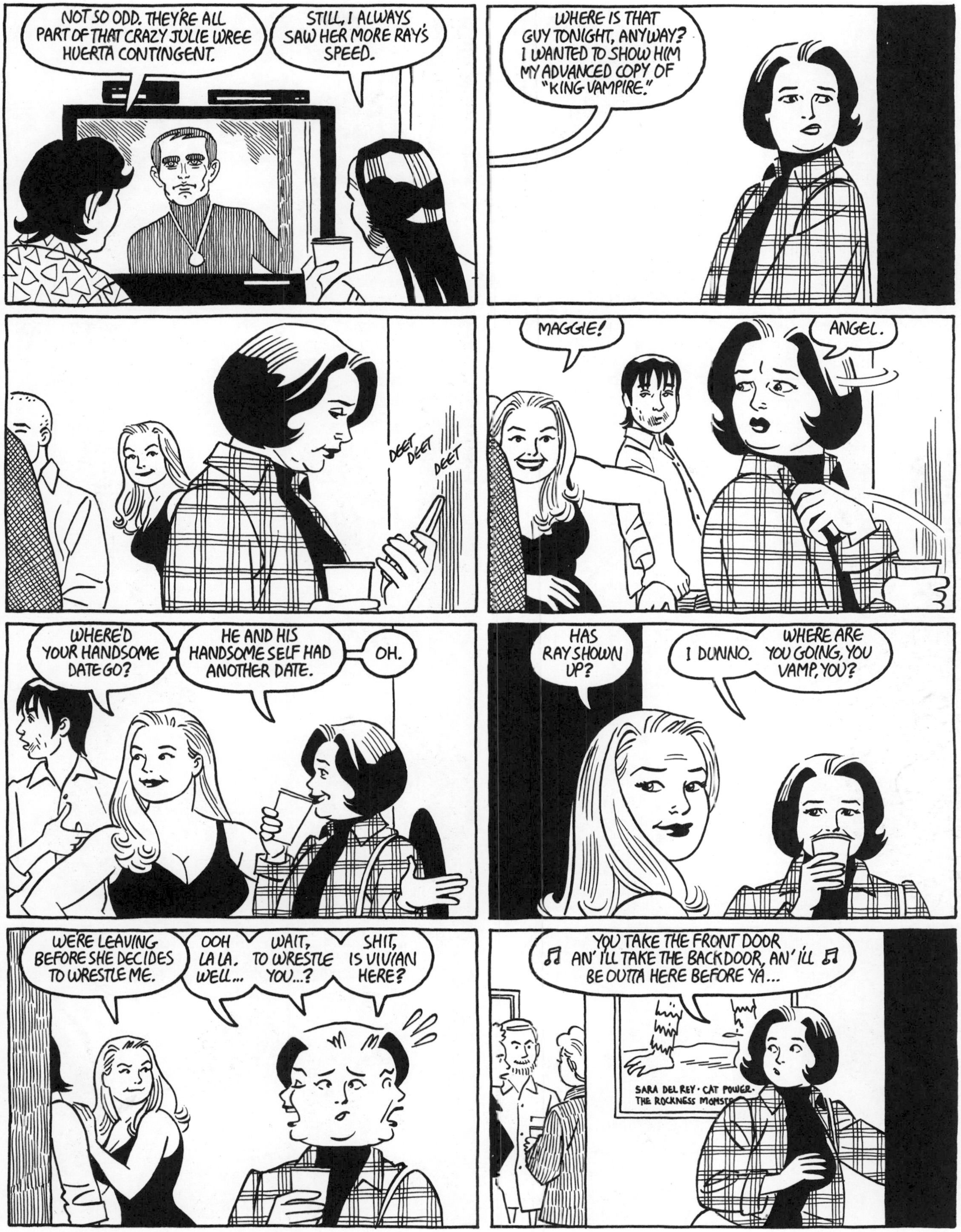
NOT SO ODD. THEY'RE ALL PART OF THAT CRAZY JULIE WREE HUERTA CONTINGENT.
STILL, I ALWAYS SAW HER MORE RAY'S SPEED.
WHERE IS THAT GUY TONIGHT, ANYWAY? I WANTED TO SHOW HIM MY ADVANCED COPY OF "KING VAMPIRE."
DEET DEET DEET
MAGGIE!
ANGEL.
WHERE'D YOUR HANDSOME DATE GO?
HE AND HIS HANDSOME SELF HAD ANOTHER DATE.
OH.
HAS RAY SHOWN UP?
I DUNNO.
WHERE ARE YOU GOING, YOU VAMP, YOU?
WE'RE LEAVING BEFORE SHE DECIDES TO WRESTLE ME.
OOH LA LA. WELL...
WAIT, TO WRESTLE YOU...?
SHIT, IS VIVIAN HERE?
YOU TAKE THE FRONT DOOR AN' I'LL TAKE THE BACKDOOR, AN' I'LL BE OUTTA HERE BEFORE YA...
SARA DEL REY · CAT POWER · THE ROCKNESS MONSTE

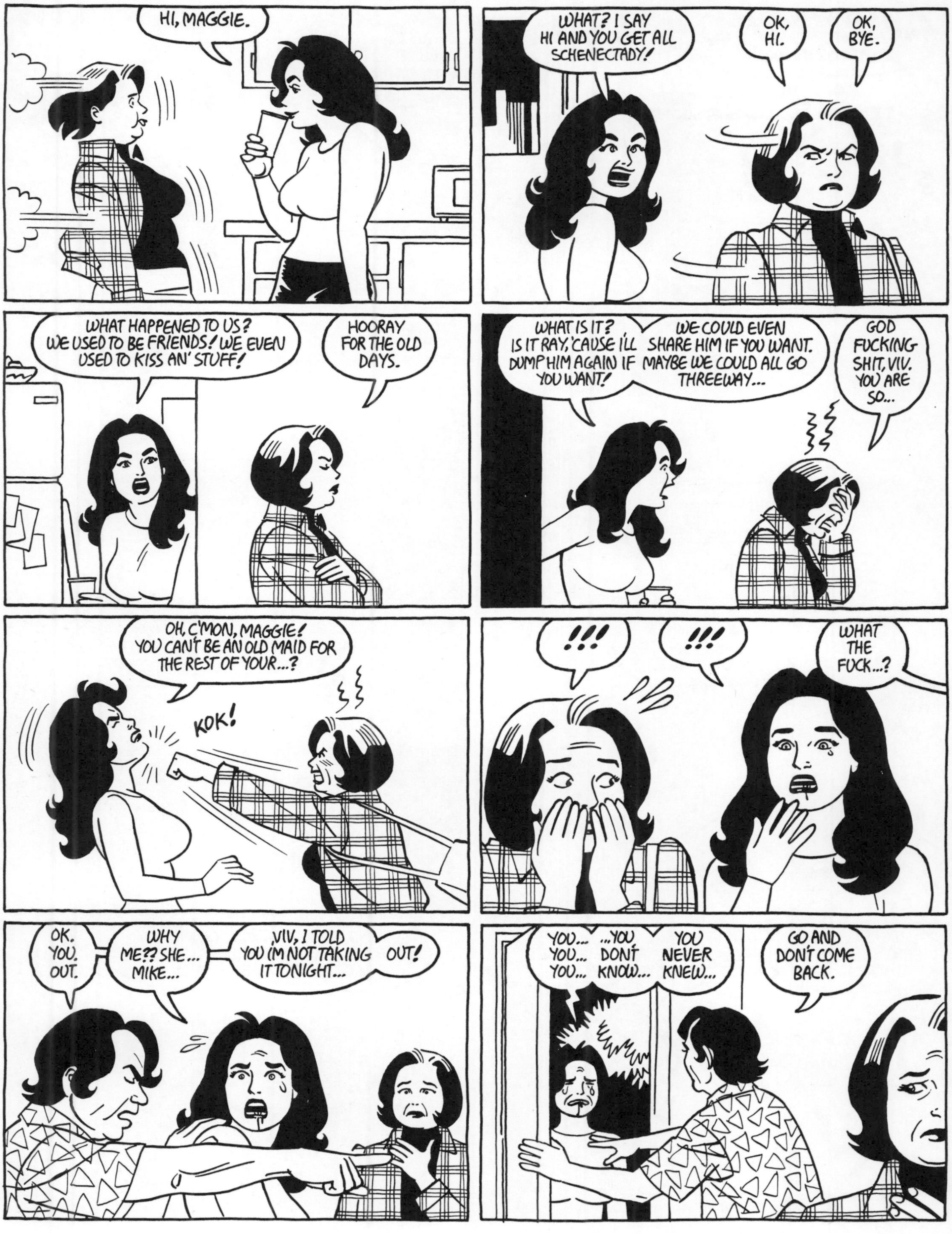
HI, MAGGIE.
WHAT? I SAY HI AND YOU GET ALL SCHENECTADY!
OK, HI.
OK, BYE.
WHAT HAPPENED TO US? WE USED TO BE FRIENDS! WE EVEN USED TO KISS AN' STUFF!
HOORAY FOR THE OLD DAYS.
WHAT IS IT? IS IT RAY, 'CAUSE I'LL DUMP HIM AGAIN IF YOU WANT!
WE COULD EVEN SHARE HIM IF YOU WANT. MAYBE WE COULD ALL GO THREEWAY...
GOD FUCKING SHIT, VIV. YOU ARE SO...
OH, C'MON, MAGGIE! YOU CAN'T BE AN OLD MAID FOR THE REST OF YOUR...?
KOK!
!!!
!!!
WHAT THE FUCK...?
OK. YOU. OUT.
WHY ME?? SHE... MIKE...
VIV, I TOLD YOU I'M NOT TAKING IT TONIGHT...
OUT!
YOU... YOU... YOU...
...YOU DON'T KNOW...
YOU NEVER KNEW...
GO AND DON'T COME BACK.

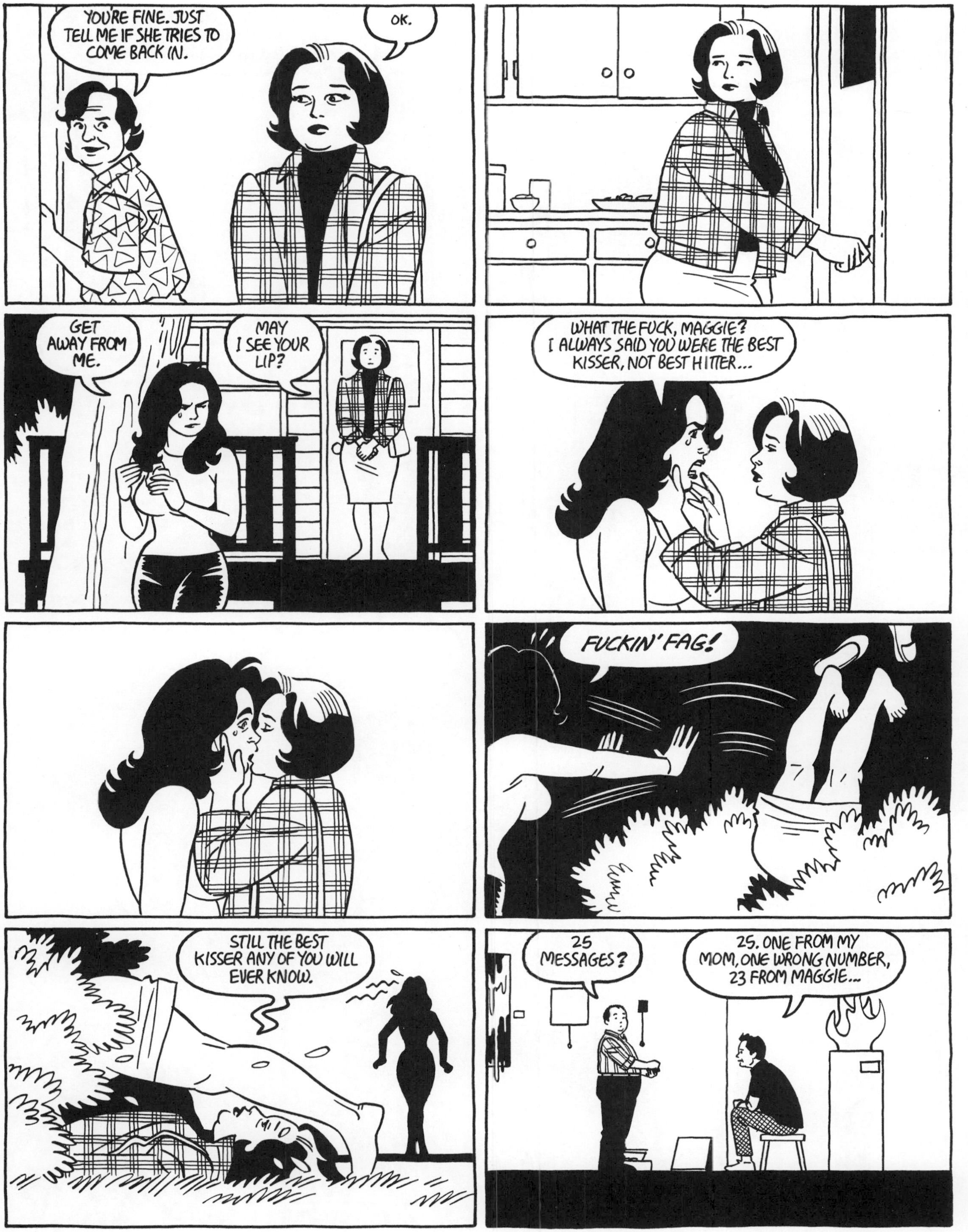
YOU'RE FINE. JUST TELL ME IF SHE TRIES TO COME BACK IN.
OK.
GET AWAY FROM ME.
MAY I SEE YOUR LIP?
WHAT THE FUCK, MAGGIE? I ALWAYS SAID YOU WERE THE BEST KISSER, NOT BEST HITTER...
FUCKIN' FAG!
STILL THE BEST KISSER ANY OF YOU WILL EVER KNOW.
25 MESSAGES?
25. ONE FROM MY MOM, ONE WRONG NUMBER, 23 FROM MAGGIE...

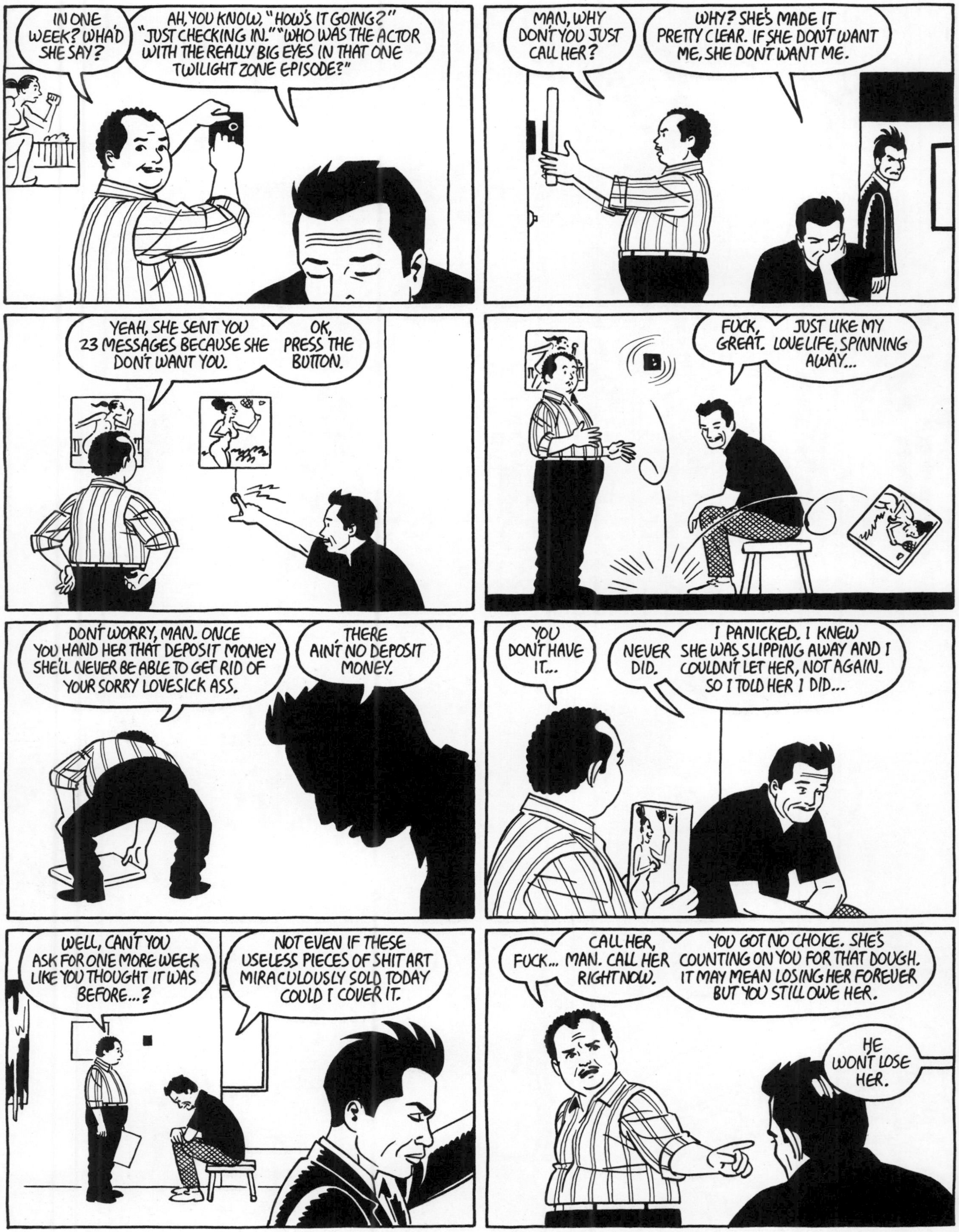
IN ONE WEEK? WHA'D SHE SAY?
AH, YOU KNOW, "HOW'S IT GOING?" "JUST CHECKING IN." "WHO WAS THE ACTOR WITH THE REALLY BIG EYES IN THAT ONE TWILIGHT ZONE EPISODE?"
MAN, WHY DON'T YOU JUST CALL HER?
WHY? SHE'S MADE IT PRETTY CLEAR. IF SHE DON'T WANT ME, SHE DON'T WANT ME.
YEAH, SHE SENT YOU 23 MESSAGES BECAUSE SHE DON'T WANT YOU.
OK, PRESS THE BUTTON.
FUCK, GREAT.
JUST LIKE MY LOVE LIFE, SPINNING AWAY...
DON'T WORRY, MAN. ONCE YOU HAND HER THAT DEPOSIT MONEY SHE'LL NEVER BE ABLE TO GET RID OF YOUR SORRY LOVESICK ASS.
THERE AIN'T NO DEPOSIT MONEY.
YOU DON'T HAVE IT...
NEVER DID.
I PANICKED. I KNEW SHE WAS SLIPPING AWAY AND I COULDN'T LET HER, NOT AGAIN. SO I TOLD HER I DID...
WELL, CAN'T YOU ASK FOR ONE MORE WEEK LIKE YOU THOUGHT IT WAS BEFORE...?
NOT EVEN IF THESE USELESS PIECES OF SHIT ART MIRACULOUSLY SOLD TODAY COULD I COVER IT.
FUCK...
CALL HER, MAN. CALL HER RIGHT NOW.
YOU GOT NO CHOICE. SHE'S COUNTING ON YOU FOR THAT DOUGH. IT MAY MEAN LOSING HER FOREVER BUT YOU STILL OWE HER.
HE WON'T LOSE HER.

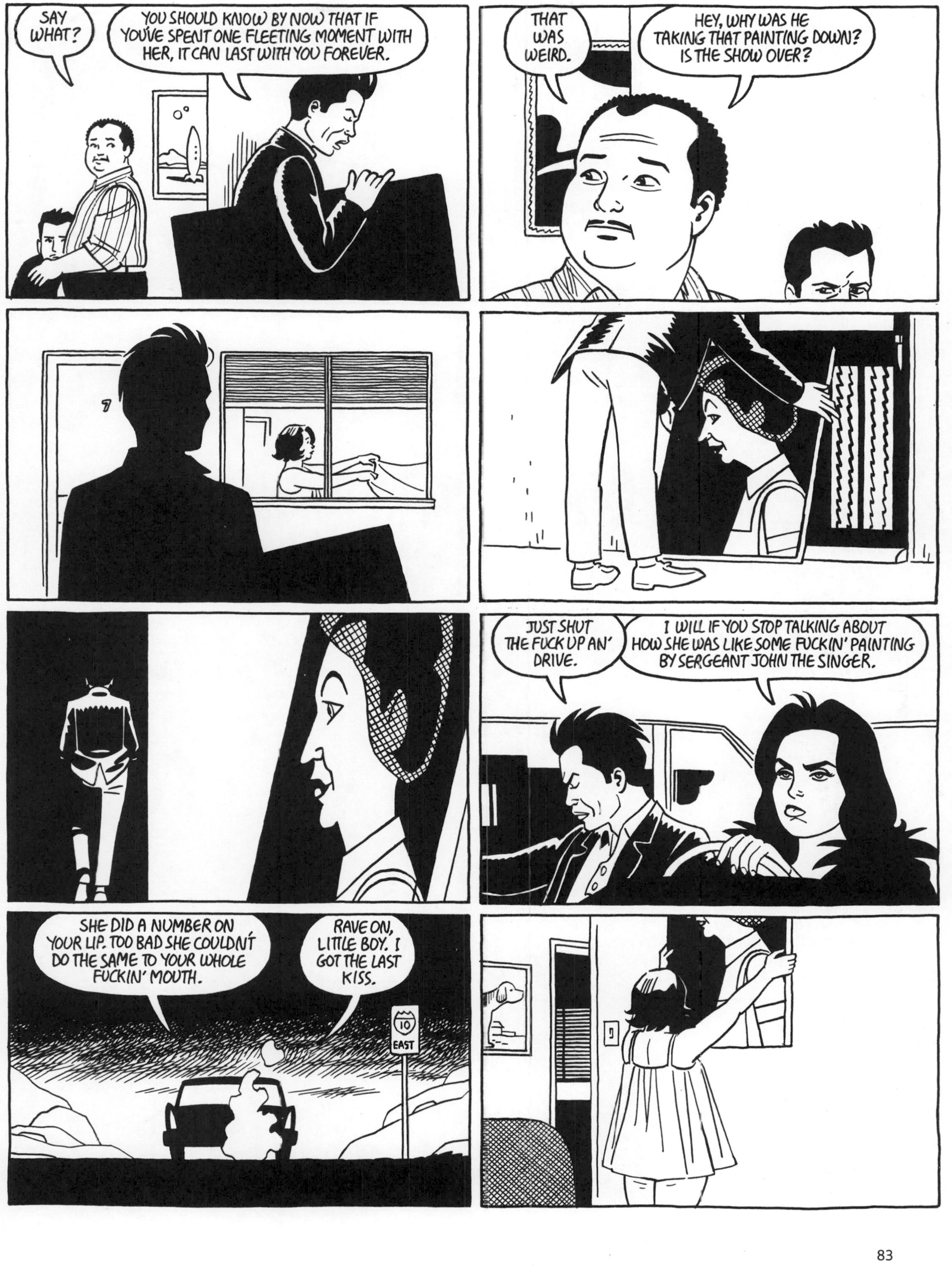
SAY WHAT?
YOU SHOULD KNOW BY NOW THAT IF YOU'VE SPENT ONE FLEETING MOMENT WITH HER, IT CAN LAST WITH YOU FOREVER.
THAT WAS WEIRD.
HEY, WHY WAS HE TAKING THAT PAINTING DOWN? IS THE SHOW OVER?
JUST SHUT THE FUCK UP AN' DRIVE.
I WILL IF YOU STOP TALKING ABOUT HOW SHE WAS LIKE SOME FUCKIN' PAINTING BY SERGEANT JOHN THE SINGER.
SHE DID A NUMBER ON YOUR LIP. TOO BAD SHE COULDN'T DO THE SAME TO YOUR WHOLE FUCKIN' MOUTH.
RAVE ON, LITTLE BOY. I GOT THE LAST KISS.
10
EAST

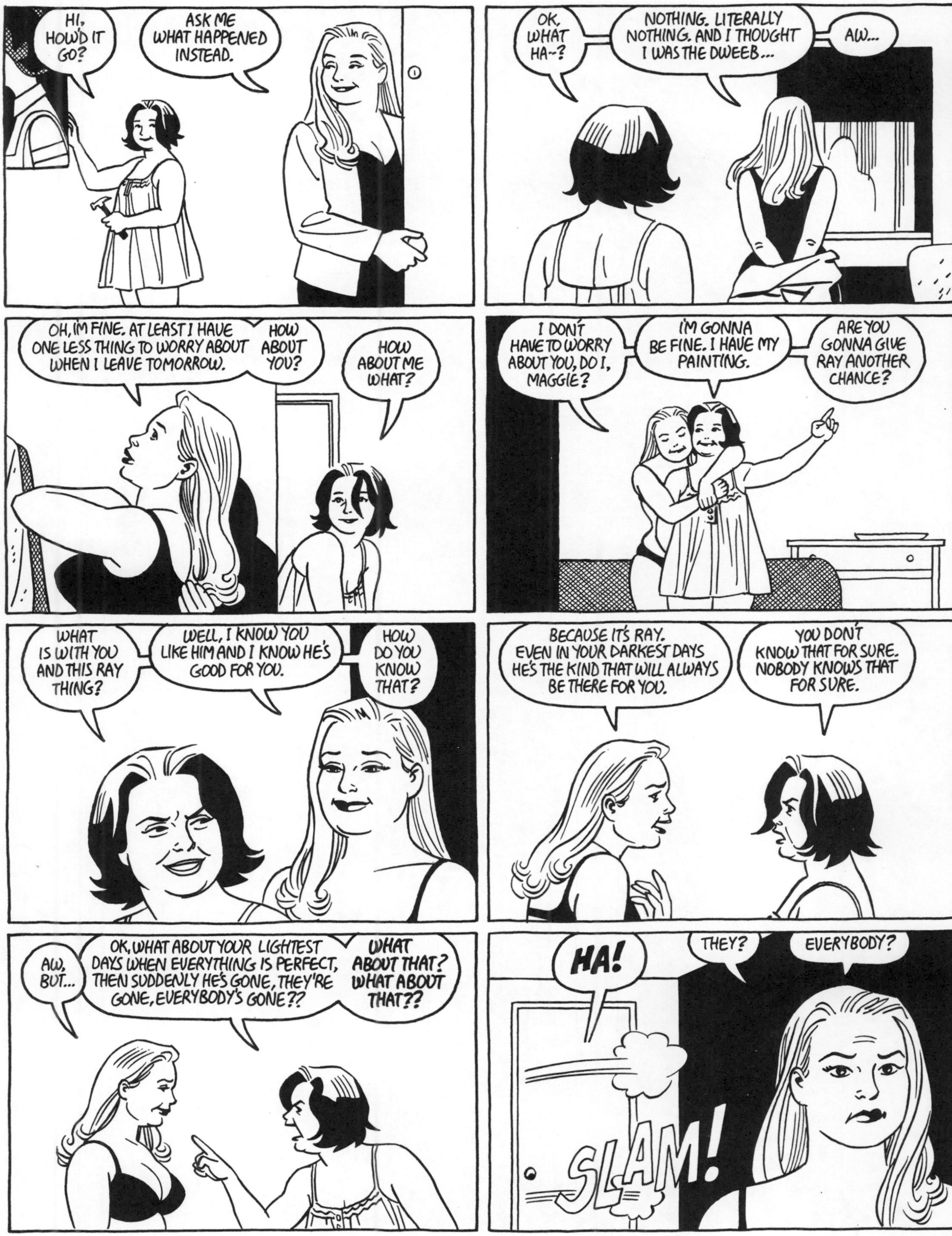
HI, HOW'D IT GO?
ASK ME WHAT HAPPENED INSTEAD.
OK, WHAT HA--?
NOTHING. LITERALLY NOTHING. AND I THOUGHT I WAS THE DWEEB...
AW...
OH, I'M FINE. AT LEAST I HAVE ONE LESS THING TO WORRY ABOUT WHEN I LEAVE TOMORROW.
HOW ABOUT YOU?
HOW ABOUT ME WHAT?
I DON'T HAVE TO WORRY ABOUT YOU, DO I, MAGGIE?
I'M GONNA BE FINE. I HAVE MY PAINTING.
ARE YOU GONNA GIVE RAY ANOTHER CHANCE?
WHAT IS WITH YOU AND THIS RAY THING?
WELL, I KNOW YOU LIKE HIM AND I KNOW HE'S GOOD FOR YOU.
HOW DO YOU KNOW THAT?
BECAUSE IT'S RAY. EVEN IN YOUR DARKEST DAYS HE'S THE KIND THAT WILL ALWAYS BE THERE FOR YOU.
YOU DON'T KNOW THAT FOR SURE. NOBODY KNOWS THAT FOR SURE.
AW, BUT...
OK, WHAT ABOUT YOUR LIGHTEST DAYS WHEN EVERYTHING IS PERFECT, THEN SUDDENLY HE'S GONE, THEY'RE GONE, EVERYBODY'S GONE??
WHAT ABOUT THAT? WHAT ABOUT THAT??
HA!
THEY?
EVERYBODY?
SLAM!

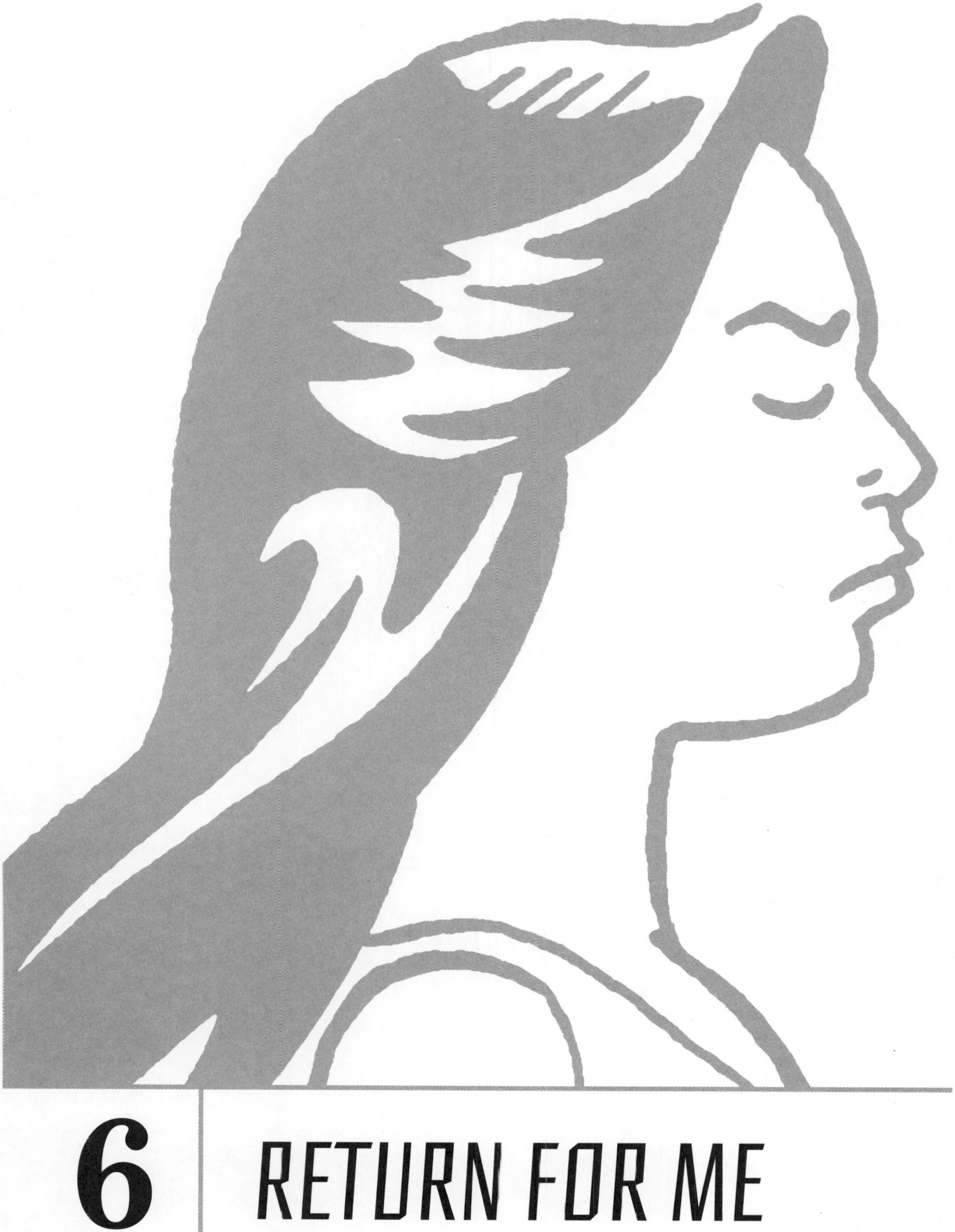

6 RETURN FOR ME

RETURN FOR ME

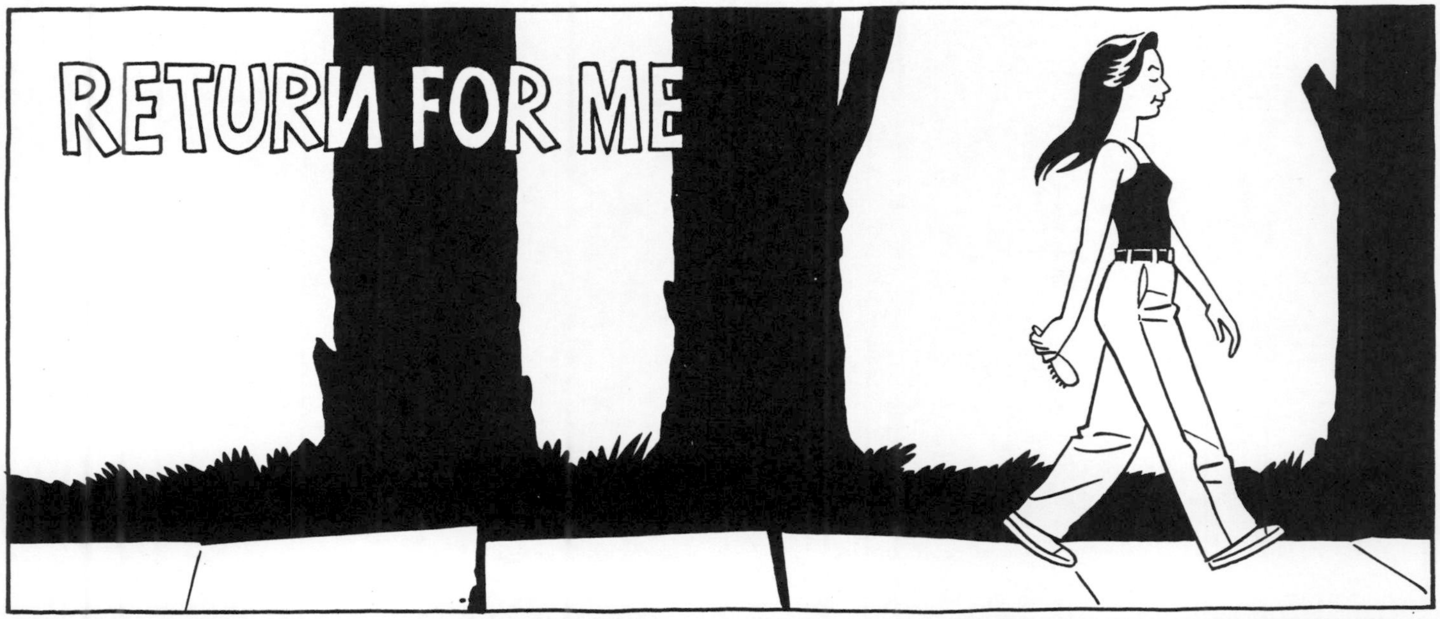

AT FIRST I WAS SO EXCITED THAT MAGGIE WAS MOVING BACK TO OUR OLD NEIGHBORHOOD. SHE WAS GONE FOR THREE WHOLE YEARS AN' SHE ONLY CAME TO VISIT A FEW TIMES EVEN IF WE WROTE A LOTTA LETTERS BACK AN' FORTH.

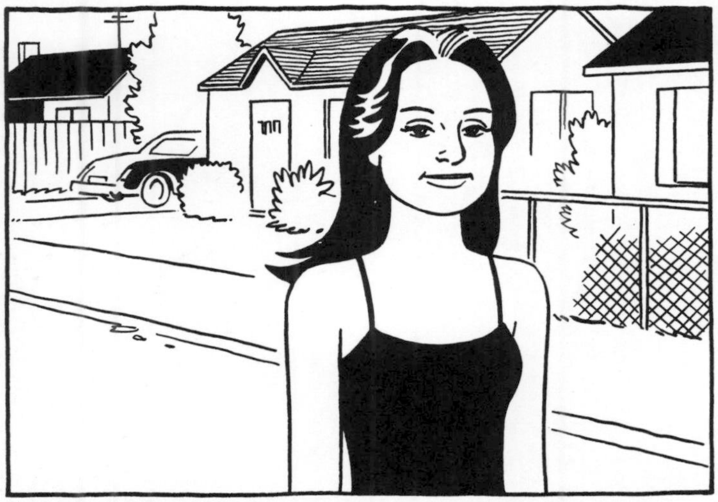

I WAS THINKING OF ALL THE THINGS WE COULD DO TOGETHER BUT THE FIRST TIME I WENT OVER, HER MOM SAID SHE COULDN'T COME OUT, TO TRY LATER. I SAID OK AND WENT HOME.

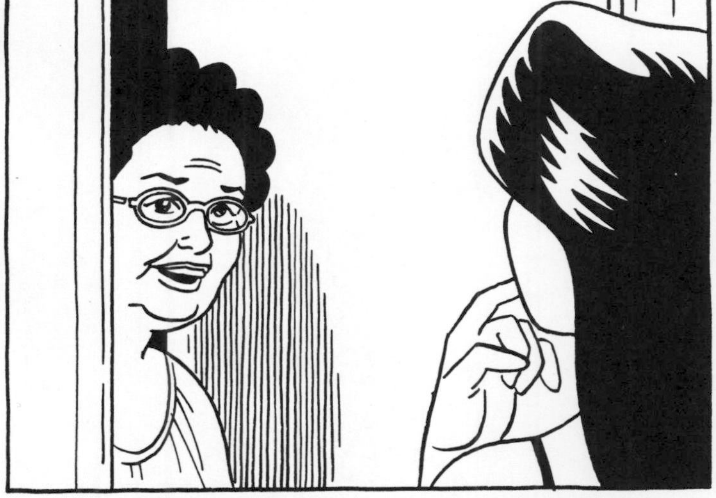

THE NEXT DAY I WENT BACK AND MAGGIE ANSWERED THE DOOR. I THOUGHT, COOL, SHE'LL COME OUT, BUT SHE SAID SHE COULDN'T. SHE HAD TO STAY IN THE HOUSE. I SAID OK AND WENT HOME AGAIN. THE NEXT TIME I WENT OVER SHE SAID IT AGAIN.

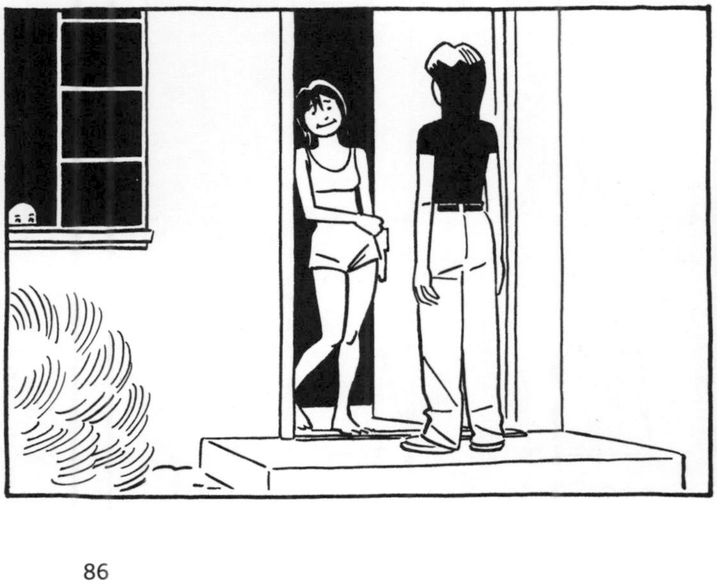

THE TIME AFTER THAT I HEARD HER AN' ESTHER AN' HER BROTHERS PLAYING IN THEIR BACKYARD. I CALLED FOR HER TO COME OUT AN' SHE SAID SHE HAD A LOTTA CHORES TO DO BUT MAYBE SHE COULD COME OUT TOMORROW. THAT'S WHAT SHE ALWAYS SAID, MAYBE TOMORROW.

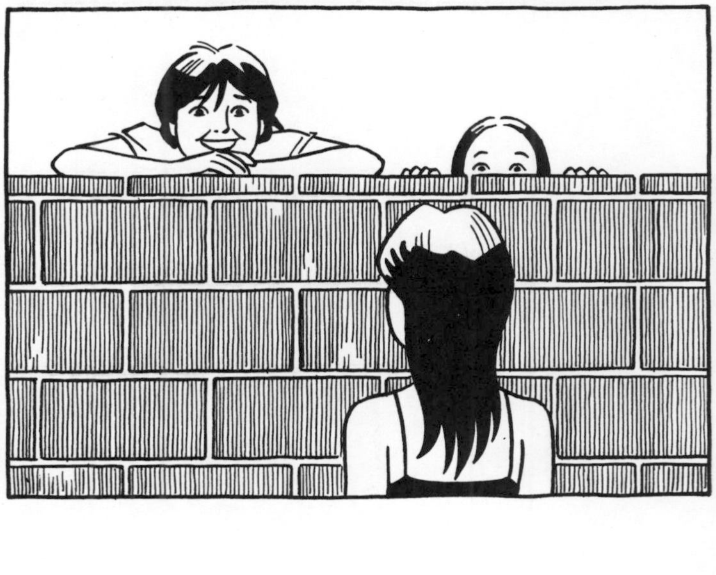

TWO WEEKS LATER AN' SHE STILL COULDN'T COME OUT. I STARTED TO GET SUSPICIOUS. MAYBE SHE DIDN'T WANNA COME OUT. MAYBE SHE DIDN'T WANNA BE MY FRIEND NO MORE. WHAT WAS SO COOL ABOUT THOSE DAYS IN CADEZZA ANYWAY?

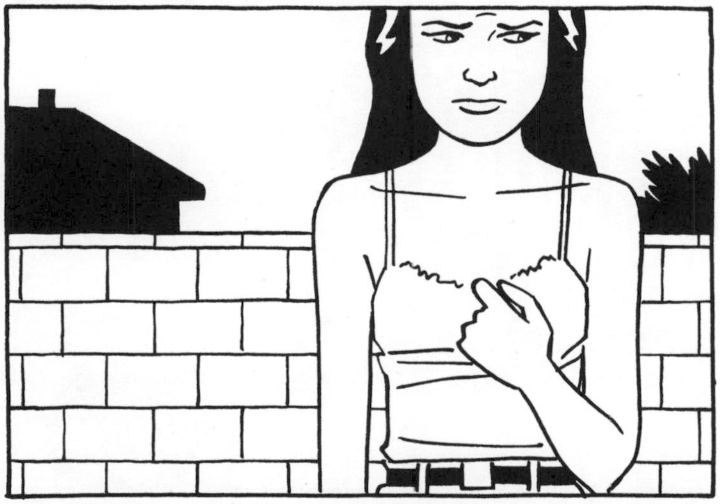

WELL, I HAD ENOUGH SO I STOPPED TRYING. IF SHE DIDN'T WANNA BE MY BEST FRIEND ANY MORE THAT WAS FINE WITH ME. ONE TIME I SAW HER WALKING HOME FROM THE STORE. INSTEAD OF BEING EXCITED THAT SHE WAS OUT, IT WAS MY CHANCE TO SHINE HER ON AN' I DID.

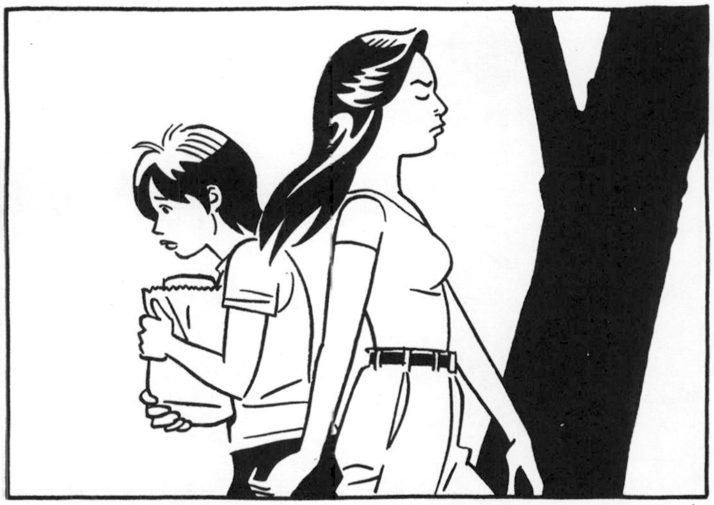

MY OLDER BROTHER TOLD ME I WAS BEING STUPID. HE SAID THAT MAGGIE'S MOM AN' DAD GOT DIVORCED AN' THAT'S WHY MAGGIE AN' HER FAMILY ARE ACTING LIKE HERMITS. LIKE HE THINKS HE KNOWS EVERYTHING. I NEVER EVEN HEARD THAT WORD, DIVORCED, EXCEPT ON TV.

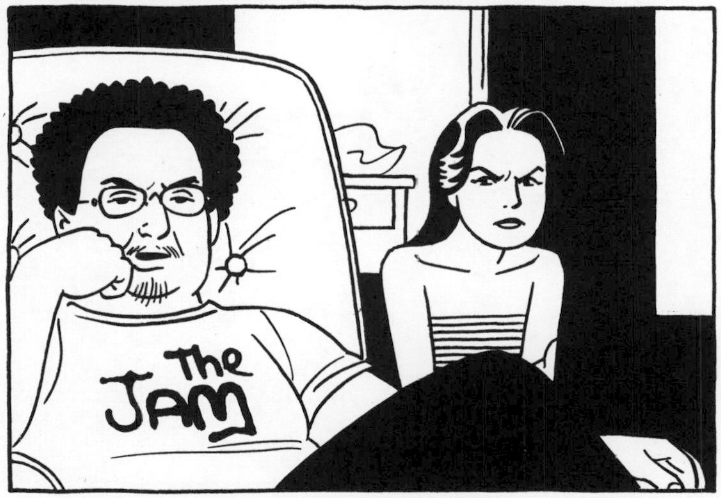
The JAM

BUT I TRIED TO UNDERSTAND SO I TRIED TO STILL BE HER FRIEND, EVEN IF I COULDN'T HANG OUT WITH HER. I HAD TO THINK OF A WAY TO MAKE HER COME OUT SO I STARTED HANGING WITH THE KIDS WHO PLAYED IN THE EMPTY FIELD ACROSS THE ALLEY FROM MAGGIE'S BACKYARD.

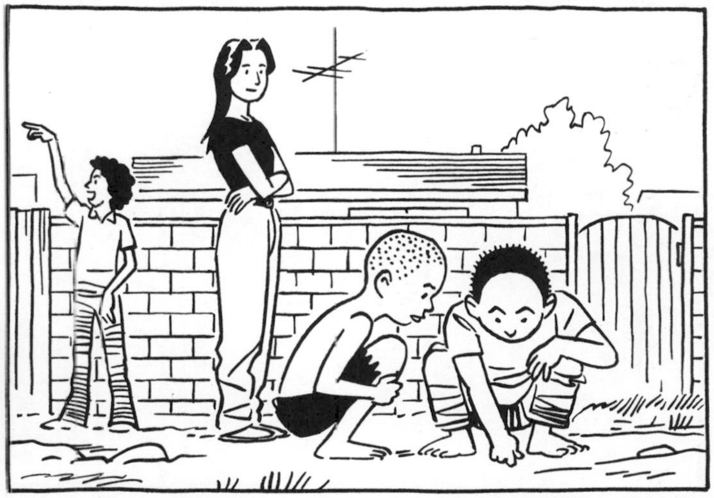

IT STARTED TO WORK A LITTLE. SHE WOULD AT LEAST WATCH FROM THE TOP OF HER FENCE, EVEN IF SHE WOULDN'T REALLY COME OUT. SHE WOULDN'T SAY ANYTHING, SHE'D JUST WATCH. I THOUGHT MAYBE SHE WAS MAD AT ME FOR SHINING HER ON. I WAS TOO SCARED TO ASK HER.

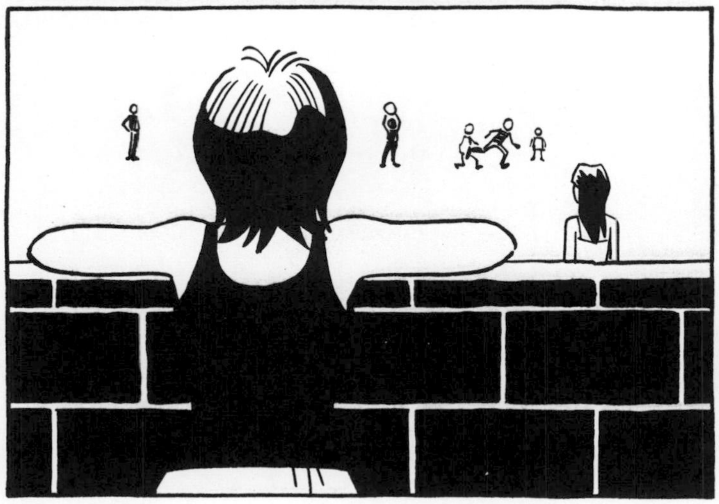

ONE FUNNY DAY, ROBERT AN' SPEEDY AN' THE GUYS STARTED A GAME OF LINE IN THE EMPTY FIELD. IT SEEMED LIKE EVERY KID IN THE NEIGHBORHOOD WAS OUT. EVEN THE CHASCARRILLO KIDS, ALL LINING THE TOP OF THAT FENCE.

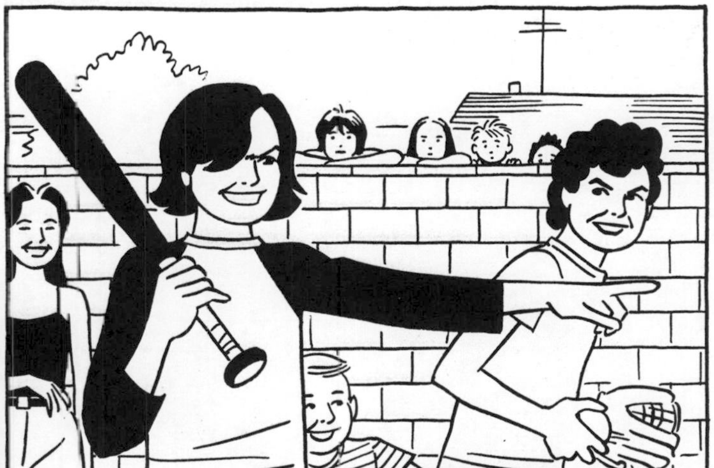

SOMETIME DURING THE GAME, THE GUYS STARTED ARGUING WHERE THE FOUL LINES WERE AN' STARTED MAKING KIDS STAND AS THE FOUL POLES SO NOBODY COULD CHEAT.

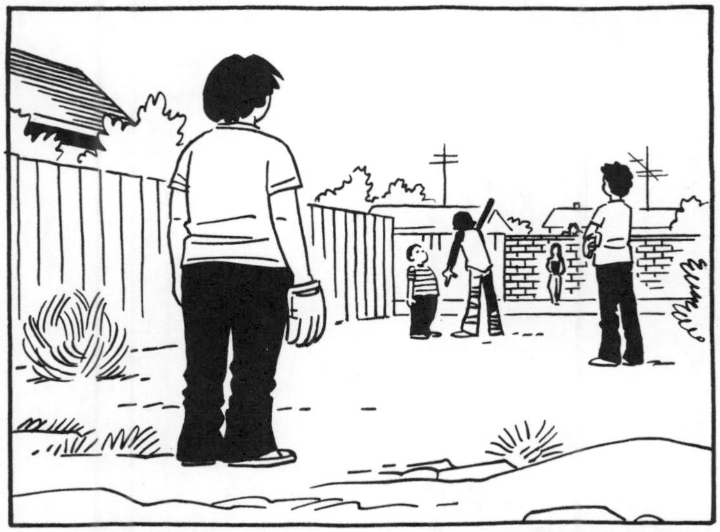

SPEEDY ASKED ME AN' MAGGIE TO DO IT BUT WE BOTH SAID NO AN' WE SAID IT AT THE SAME TIME AN' THAT MADE ME THINK THAT MAYBE MAGGIE WAS COMING BACK TO NORMAL. SO, SPEEDY WAS GOING AWAY ALL MAD AN' THEN BLANCA SAID SHE WOULD DO IT.

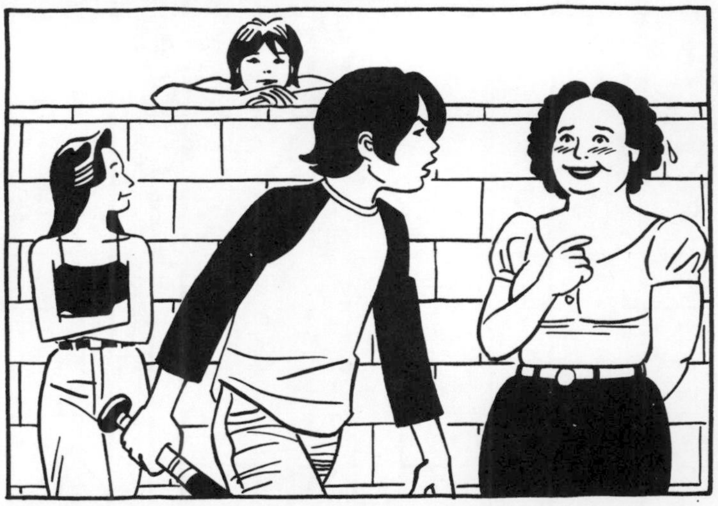

I'M SO SURE. YOU KNOW SHE WAS ONLY DOING IT TO IMPRESS SPEEDY 'CAUSE SHE LIKED HIM. SHE EVEN WORE HER SCHOOL BLOUSE AN' IT WASN'T EVEN SCHOOL YET. SO, BLANCA WAS THE THIRD BASE LINE.

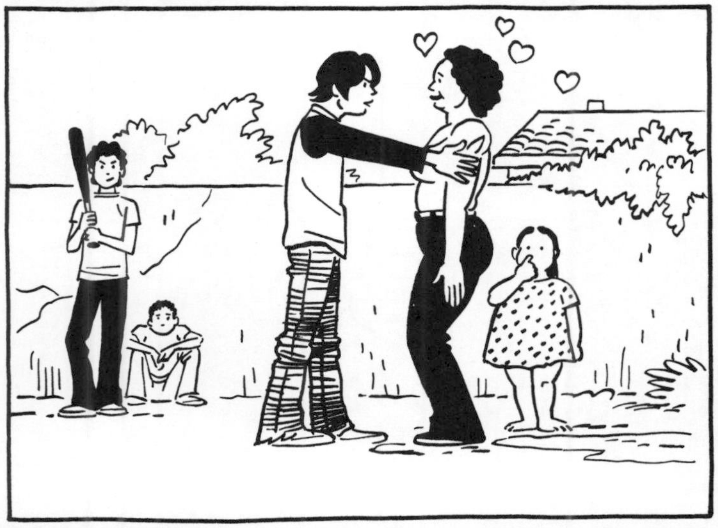

MAGGIE MUMBLED SOMETHING ABOUT HOW BIG BLANCA'S BOOBS GOT AN' THAT REALLY BROKE THE ICE AN' WE WERE BEST FRIENDS AGAIN. MAN, YOU SHOULDA HEARD US WITH THE BOOB JOKES, BUT NOT TO HER FACE OF COURSE. PRETTY SOON WE WERE TALKIN' MESS ABOUT EVERYBODY.

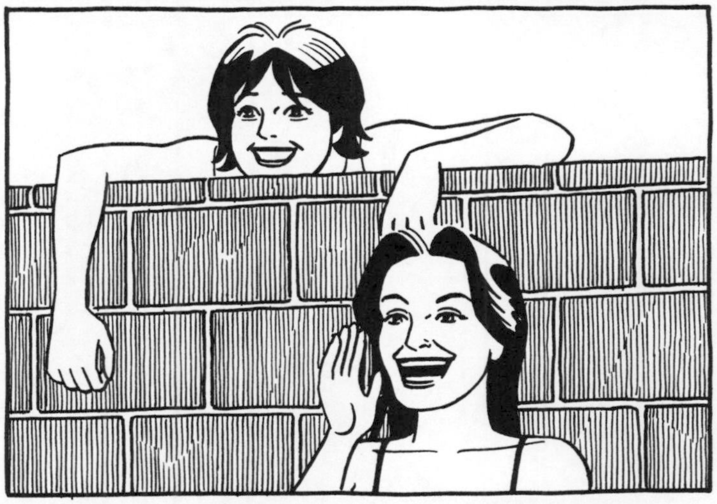

SPEEDY GOT UP TO BAT AN' WE WERE ON HIM LIKE NOTHIN'. HE HIT A FOUL BALL AN' IT NEARLY HIT BLANCA BUT IT SPLASHED MUD ON HER SCHOOL BLOUSE. BOY, WAS SHE EMBARRASSED AN' MAD AS HELL, TOO.

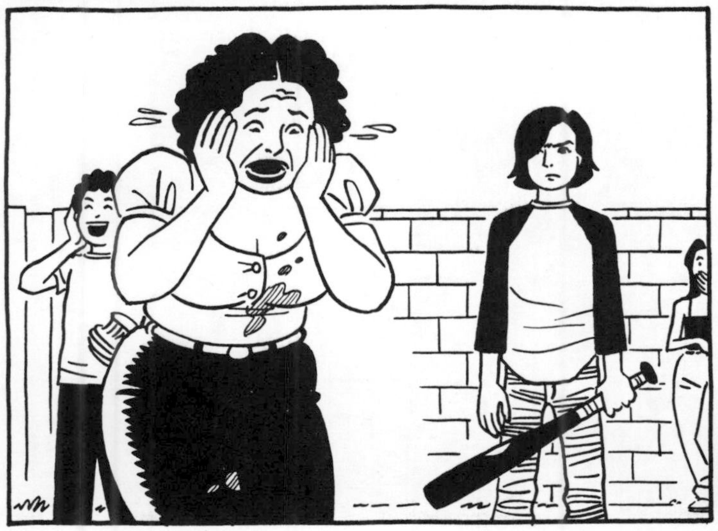

I GUESS ME AN' MAGGIE DIDN'T KEEP OUR GIGGLES TO OURSELF ENOUGH 'CAUSE BLANCA GAVE US THE BIGGEST MADDOGGING BEFORE SHE RAN HOME. THAT'S NERVE, I THOUGHT. WHY MADDOG US? WE WEREN'T THE ONLY ONES LAUGHING. WE DIDN'T SPLASH HER NEITHER.

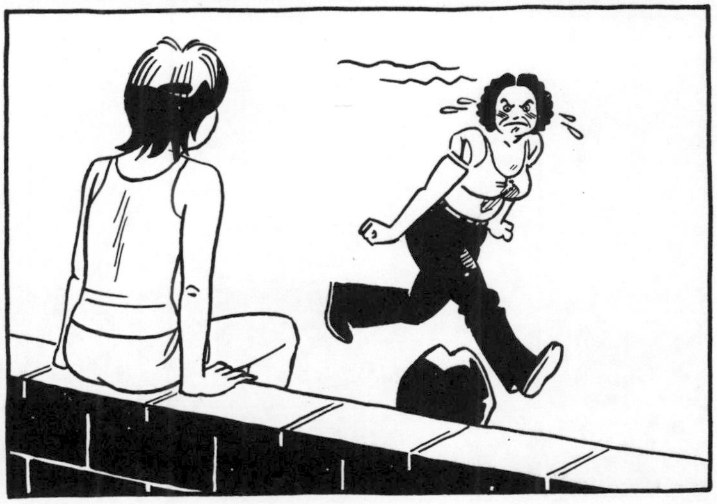

THE NEXT TIME SPEEDY WAS UP HE HIT A LONG ONE INTO SPOOKY THE SMOKEY'S YARD. NOBODY WANTED TO GET IT. WHEN WE WERE LITTLE, PEOPLE USED TO SAY THAT SPOOKY USED TO KIDNAP CHILDREN AN' USE 'EM AS DARTBOARDS. I GUESS SPEEDY WAS STILL SCARED.

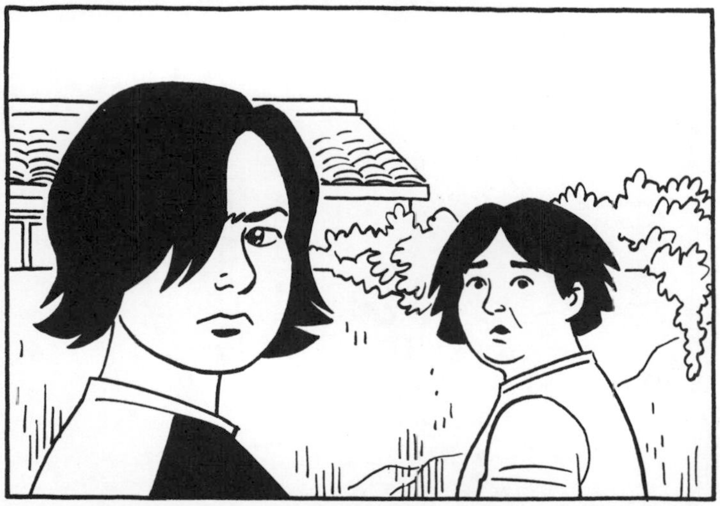

EVERYBODY WAS CALLING HIM A WUSS SO HE SAID HE'D GO GET IT IF SOMEBODY WENT WITH HIM AND GUESS WHO VOLUNTEERED? MAGGIE! DON'T TELL ME SHE LIKED SPEEDY, TOO! HE WAS BARELY GOING INTO JUNIOR HIGH AN' MAGGIE AN' BLANCA WERE GOING INTO HIGH SCHOOL.

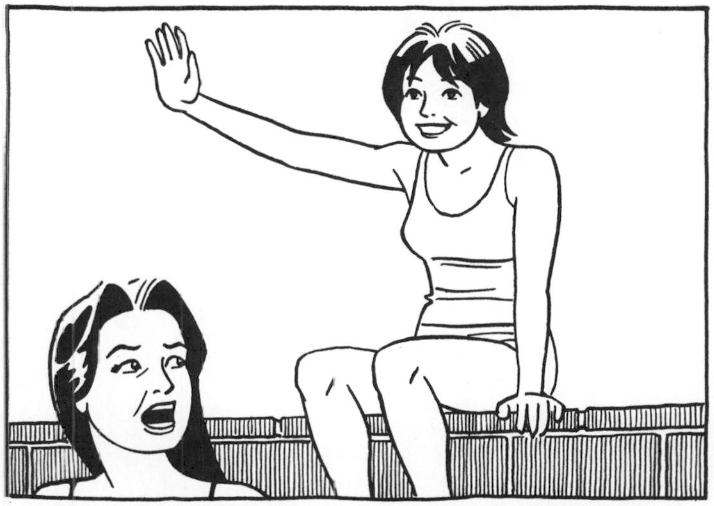

OH, WELL. SO THEY BOTH WENT OVER THE FENCE. WE ALL WAITED DOWN THE ALLEY. I DIDN'T WANNA HEAR NO SCREAMING CHILDREN OR ANYTHING EVEN IF I DIDN'T BELIEVE THOSE STORIES.

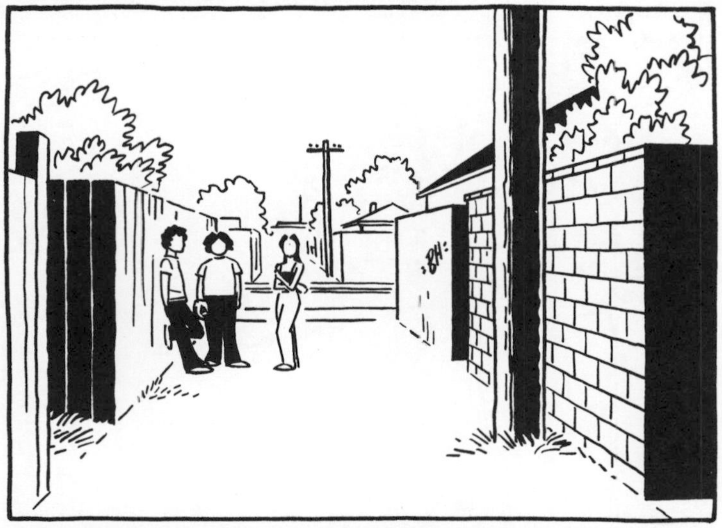

IT SEEMED LIKE FOREVER BEFORE THEY CAME OUT. THEY WEREN'T RUNNING SO WE FIGURED MR. SMOKEY WASN'T HOME. ROBERT WAS MAKING ALL LIKE THEY WERE LOVEBIRDS AN' SHIT AN' ALL SPEEDY DID WAS TALK ABOUT HOW SCARED MAGGIE WAS AN' ALL THAT.

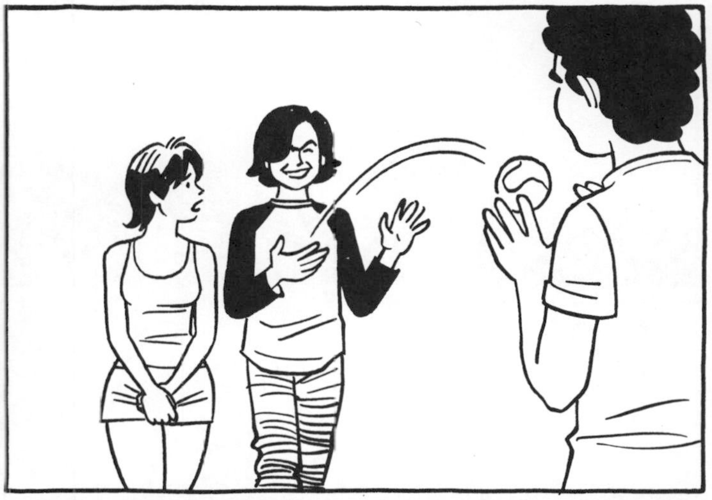

IT WAS FUNNY WHEN MAGGIE PUSHED HIM ALL MAD AN' WALKED AWAY BUT IT WAS KINDA WEIRD BECAUSE SHE HAD THE SAME MAD LOOK ON HER FACE THAT BLANCA HAD. ALMOST SAD AS IT WAS MAD. COULD IT REALLY BE 'CAUSE OF SOME STUPID ELEVEN YEAR OLD?

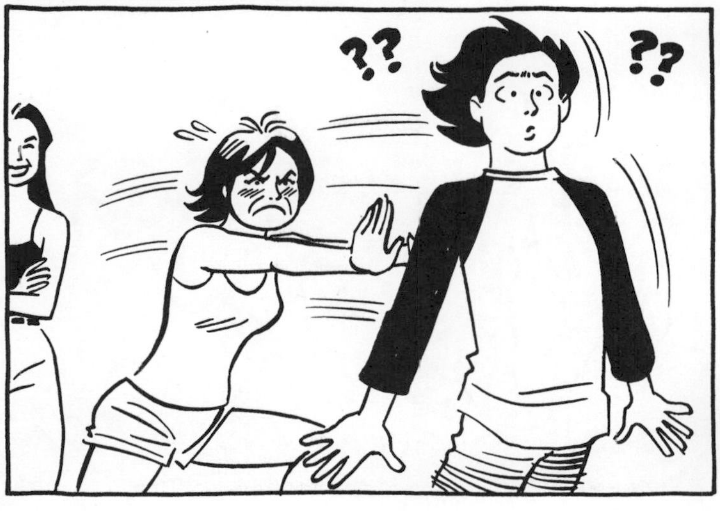
??
??

I HAD TO KNOW WHAT WENT ON AN' ME AN' MAGGIE TOOK OFF DOWN THE ALLEY. SHE WAS TOO MAD TO NOTICE THAT SHE WAS GOING AWAY FROM HER HOUSE BUT I WASN'T GONNA TELL HER. I DIDN'T WANNA MESS UP ONE OF THE BEST DAYS IN A LONG TIME.

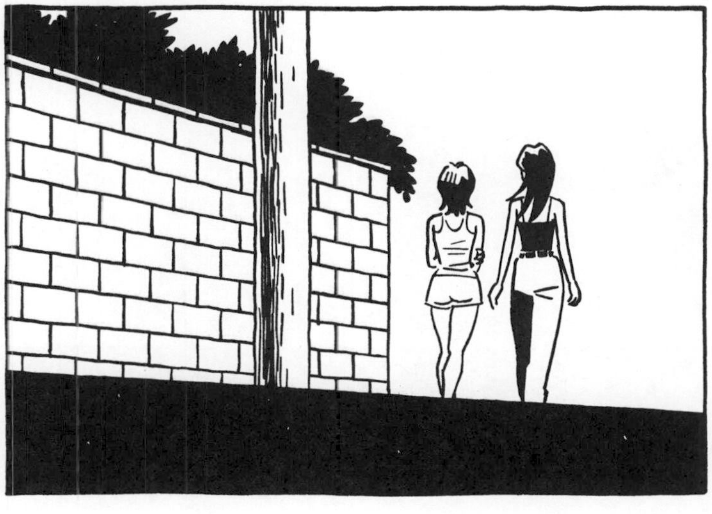

I KEPT ON BUGGING HER ABOUT WHAT HAPPENED IN SPOOKY'S YARD. SHE FINALLY SAID SHE WAS MAD 'CAUSE SPEEDY WAS DIFFERENT WHEN THEY WERE ALONE. SHE SAID THEY WERE SCARED TOGETHER AN' THEY TALKED FOR A LONG TIME, ABOUT STUFF, SHE SAID. WAS THAT ALL, I SAID?

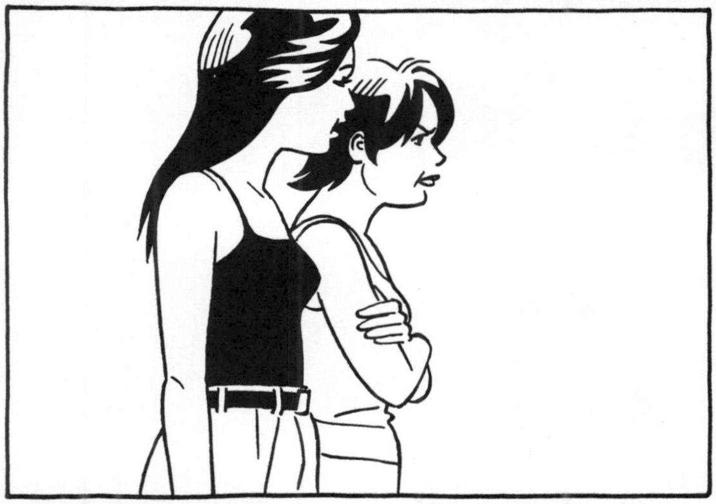

THE ONLY INTERESTING THING SHE SAID WAS SHE KNEW A BOY IN CADEZZA WHO HAD HAIR THAT WENT DOWN OVER ONE EYE LIKE SPEEDY, IF THAT'S INTERESTING AT ALL. MAYBE IT WAS INTERESTING TO ME 'CAUSE SHE NEVER WROTE TO ME ABOUT THAT BOY.

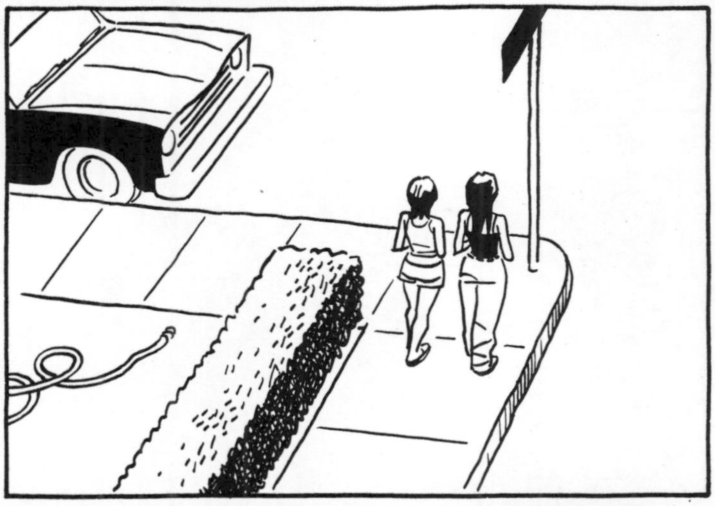

I STOPPED BUGGING HER ABOUT SPEEDY AN' WE JUST KEPT WALKING. WE WALKED BY OLD PLACES KINDA GETTING MAGGIE USED TO THE OLD NEIGHBORHOOD AGAIN, EXCEPT NOW IT WAS HOPPERS AN' WE WERE BADASS CHAVAS CLAIMING OUR TURF. DON'T EVEN MESS WITH US, MAN.

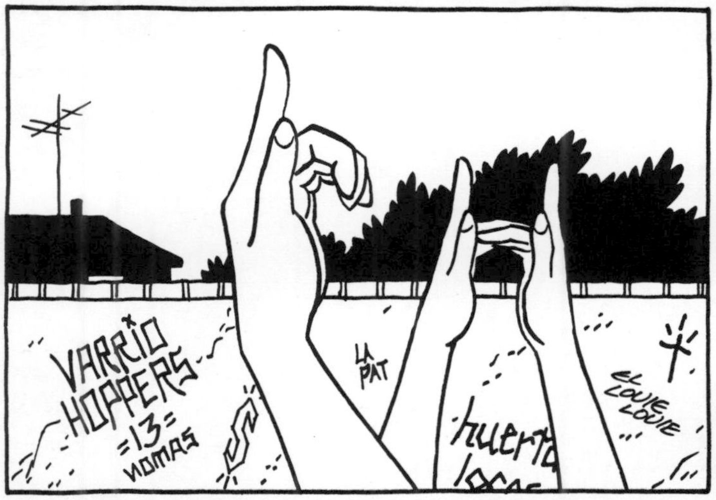
VARRIO
HOPPERS
=13=
NOMAS
LA PAT
EL LOUIE LOUIE

MOSTLY EVERYBODY WE PASSED WELCOMED MAGGIE BACK BUT SHE DIDN'T SEEM TOO HAPPY ABOUT IT. SHE HATED THAT THEY WERE CALLING HER THAT NEW NAME. YOU CAN'T REALLY BLAME 'EM 'CAUSE THAT'S HOW PEOPLE KNEW HER NOW. PERLA LEFT AN' MAGGIE RETURNED.

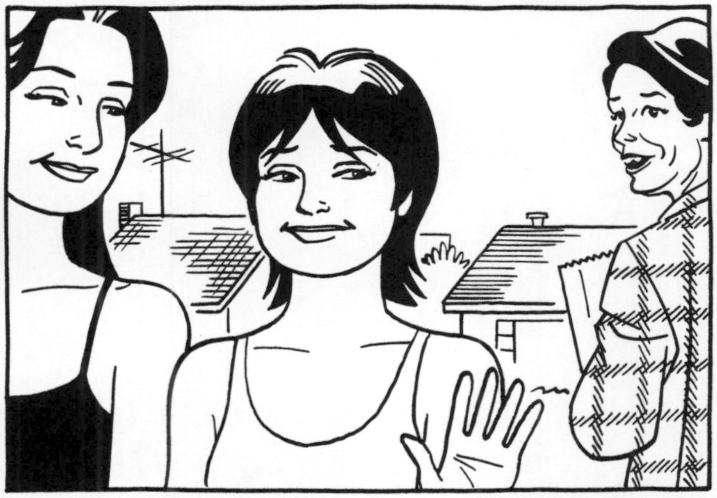

I TOOK HER DOWN A STREET A FEW BLOCKS AWAY WHERE SOME OF THE OLDER HOMEBOYS HUNG OUT. THEY WEREN'T THE BADDEST VATOS LIKE BIG EDDIE AN' LITOS AN' THOSE SAVS BUT I STILL THOUGHT THEY WERE COOL. ESPECIALLY MANDO. OOPS, I GAVE IT AWAY, I GUESS, HUH?

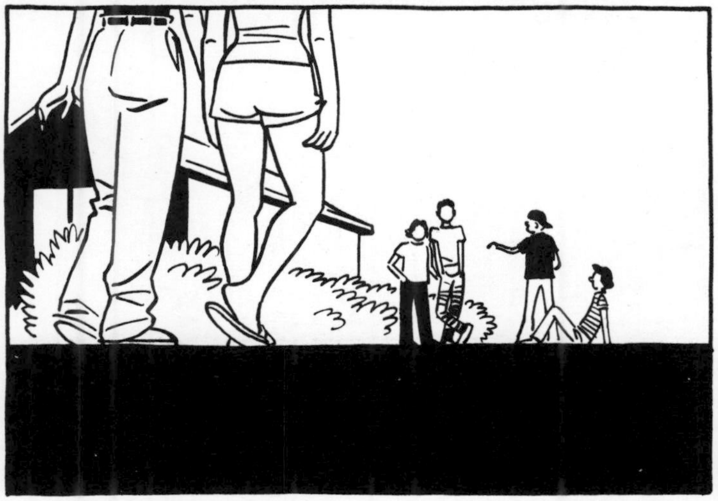

MANDO DID HIS USUAL SLACKTALKING WHEN WE WENT BY. AFTER THAT, I ASKED MAGGIE WHAT SHE THOUGHT OF HIM AN' SHE JUST SAID SHE HATED THE WAY THEY ALL LOOKED AT HER. WELL, ALL EXCEPT THE TALLEST ONE WHO SHE THOUGHT WAS JUST PLAIN STUCK UP.

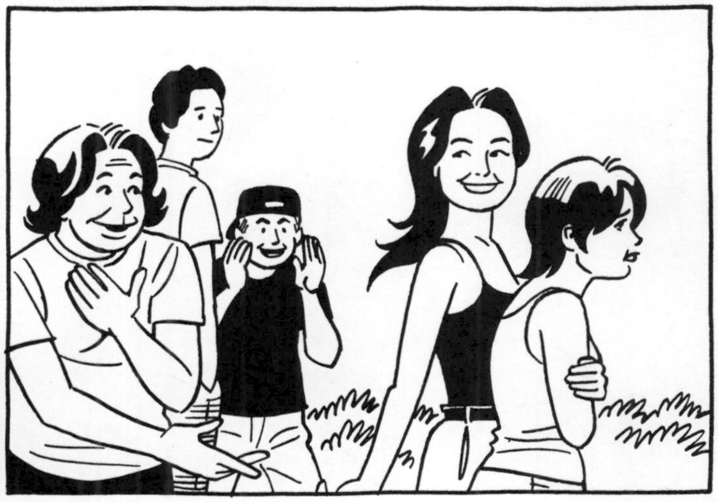

BOY, WAS SHE SHOCKED WHEN I TOLD HER THAT WAS LI'L RAY WHO GREW ALMOST A FOOT SINCE SHE WAS GONE. SHE CHANGED HER MIND ON THE SPOT AN' SAID SHE LIKED HIM, BUT TO NEVER TELL ANYBODY. I SAID OK 'CAUSE SHE ACTED REAL SERIOUS ABOUT IT.

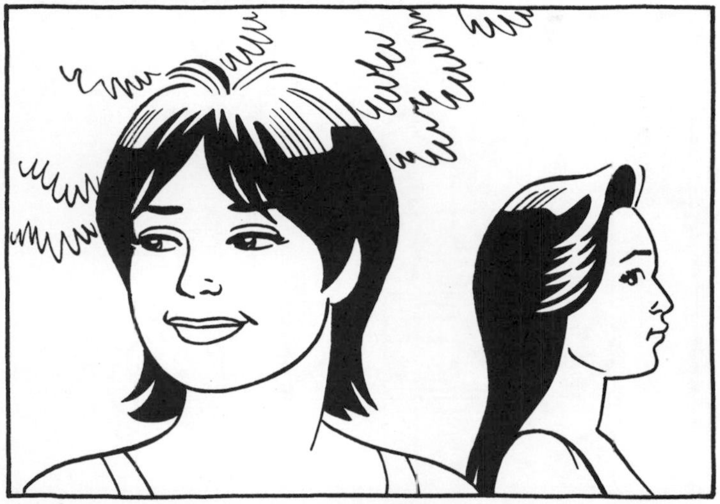

WE CAME UP TO SAL'S GARAGE WHERE HARVEY AN' LOUIS WORKED. HARVEY CAME OUT AN' WAS ALL EXCITED TO SEE MAGGIE LIKE HE WAS HER UNCLE OR SOMETHING. LOUIS JUST KEPT CALLING HER MAGGIE O MAGGIE LIKE HE ALWAYS DID SINCE SHE WAS LIKE, BORN.

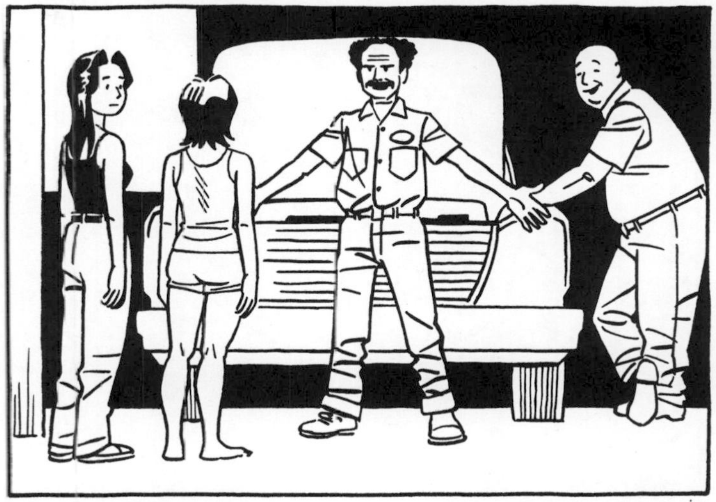

HARVEY KEPT ASKING MAGGIE IF EVERYTHING WAS OK AT HOME LIKE HE KNEW ABOUT HER MOM AN' DAD BUT SHE DIDN'T SEEM TO WANNA TALK ABOUT IT BUT SHE DID TELL HIM SHE KNEW ABOUT FIXING CARS. WELL, EVERYBODY, INCLUDING ME, WAS LIKE, WHERE DID THAT COME FROM??

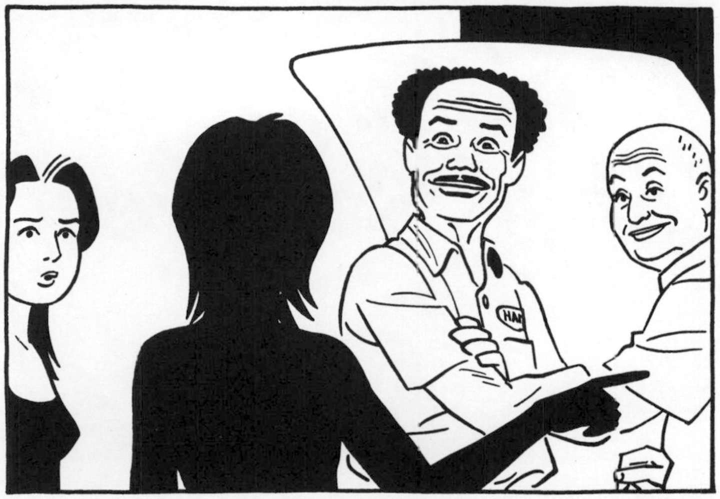

SHE SAID THAT IN CADEZZA WHENEVER SHE GOT IN TROUBLE HER DAD WOULD MAKE HER TAKE SOMETHING OUT OF THE ENGINE OF THEIR CAR AN' CLEAN IT AN' HAVE TO PUT IT BACK IN CORRECTLY OR SHE WOULD HAVE TO DO IT AGAIN.

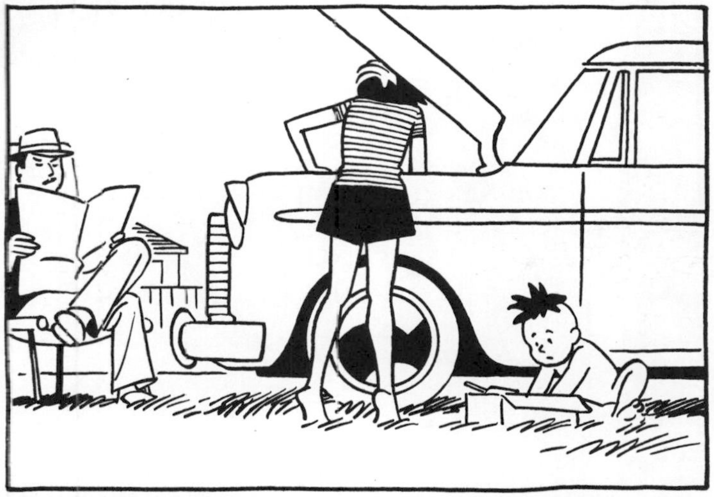

TO TEST HER, HARVEY ASKED HER TO ADJUST THE CARBURETOR IN THE CAR LOUIS WAS WORKING ON BUT MAGGIE SAID THERE WASN'T ONE IN THERE AN' THEY SAID SHE WAS RIGHT SO LOUIS ASKED HER IF SHE WANTED TO HELP HIM PUT IT IN AN' GUESS WHAT, SHE DID!

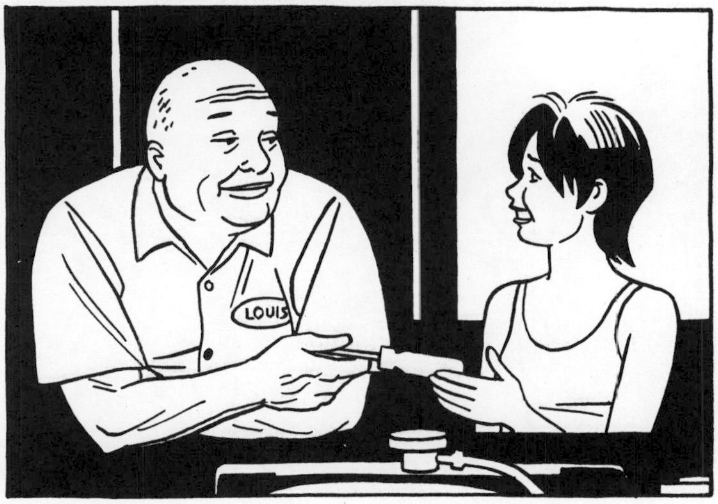
LOUIS

THEY MUSTA BEEN THERE FOREVER WORKING ON THAT THING BUT THE MORE THEY DID IT, THE MORE MAGGIE LIKED IT. I GUESS IT WAS LIKE HER AN' SPEEDY JUST TALKING IN SPOOKY THE SMOKEY'S BACKYARD, BORING THINGS JUST INTEREST HER.

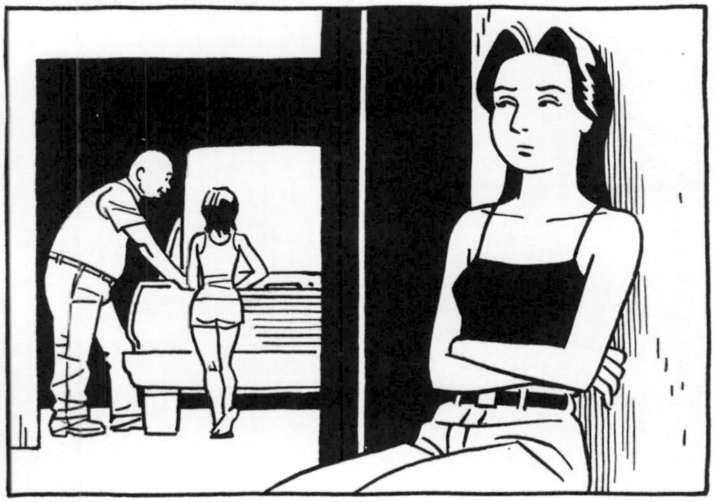

I WAS SO BORED I WAS GONNA LEAVE WHEN MAGGIE'S MOM WALKED UP LOOKING FOR HER AND BOY, DID SHE LOOK MAD. LUCKY FOR MAGGIE HARVEY CALMED HER DOWN AND TOOK THE BLAME.

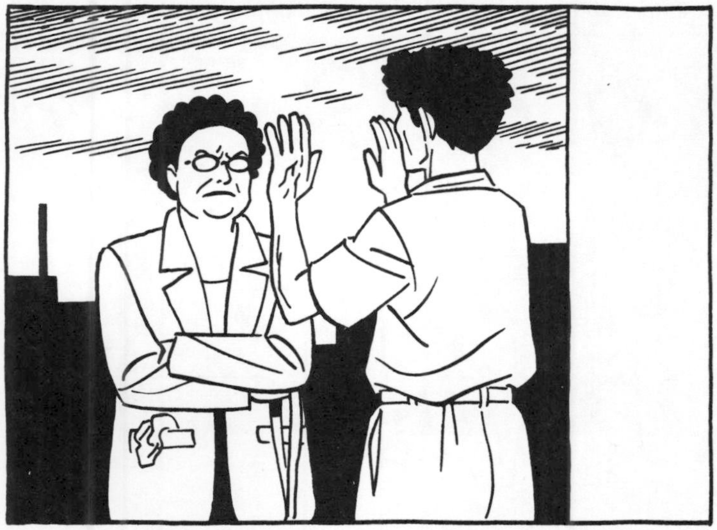

I COULD HEAR HIM ALL BRAGGING TO HER MOM ABOUT MAGGIE FIXING THE CAR. MAGGIE WAS JUST HAPPY SHE WASN'T GONNA GET THE CINTO. IMAGINE, STILL GETTING WHIPPED AT 13. YOU DIDN'T HEAR THIS FROM ME BUT I THINK MAGGIE'S MOM KINDA WENT NUTS IN CADEZZA.

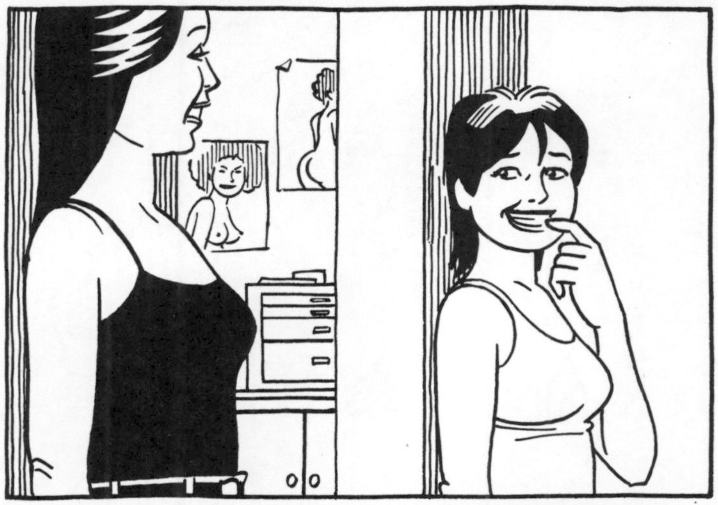

IT MADE ME WONDER WHAT HAPPENS TO PEOPLE WHO GET DIVORCED. I KNOW BLANCA'S PARENTS DIDN'T HAVE TO GET DIVORCED, THEY BOTH JUST SPLIT ON HER. I STARTED TO FEEL GUILTY. THE ONLY PROBLEM I HAD AT HOME WAS A KNOW-IT-ALL BROTHER WHO WAS RIGHT ABOUT MAGGIE.

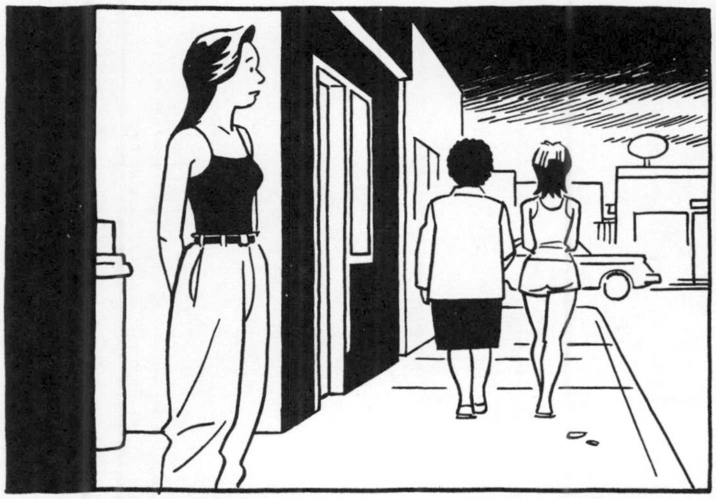

SOON HIGH SCHOOL STARTED AN' I GOT TO SEE MAGGIE MORE. WE SPENT A LOTTA TIME SPYING ON MANDO AN' RAY AN' LISTENING TO PUNK ROCK RECORDS. MAGGIE EVEN GOT AN AFTER SCHOOL JOB AT SAL'S, HELPING FIX CARS. SHE GOT HER PICTURE IN THE PAPER AN' EVERYTHING.

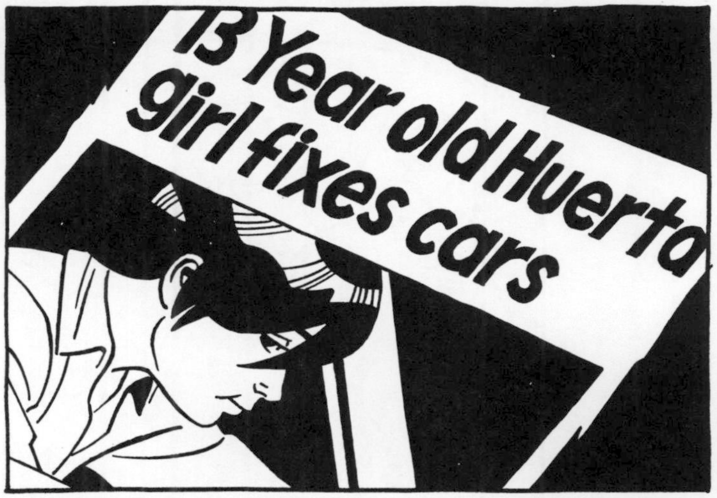
13 Year old Huerta girl fixes cars

THEN CAME THE WEIRD DAY. MAGGIE WAS IN THE ALLEY BY HERSELF CRYING. SHE SAID HER MOM WANTED TO MOVE AGAIN. THIS TIME UP TO DAIRYTOWN TO BE CLOSER TO FAMILY, SINCE SHE HAD A NEW BABY. I COULDN'T BELIEVE IT. MAGGIE JUST CAME BACK TO ME, YOU KNOW?

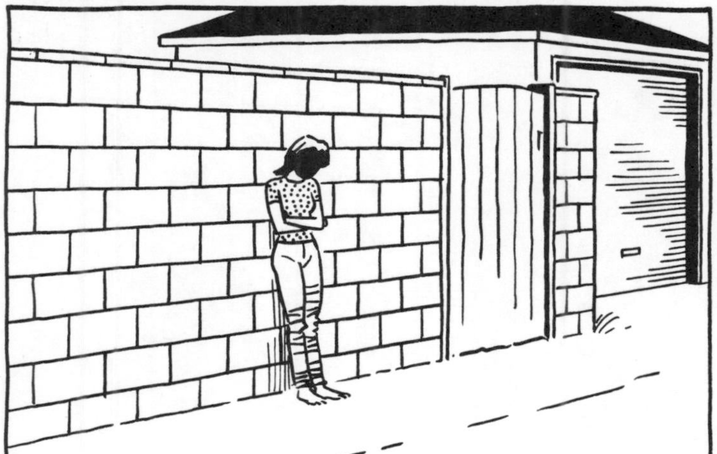

THEN THE STORY GOT WEIRDER. HER MOM WANTED MAGGIE TO STAY IN HOPPERS, AT LEAST UNTIL SCHOOL ENDED AN' GET THIS, 'CAUSE SHE HAD A GOOD JOB! TALK ABOUT CRAZY! I MEAN, I WAS HAPPY SHE GOT TO STAY BUT, TO BE LEFT BEHIND BY YOUR OWN FAMILY, C'MON!

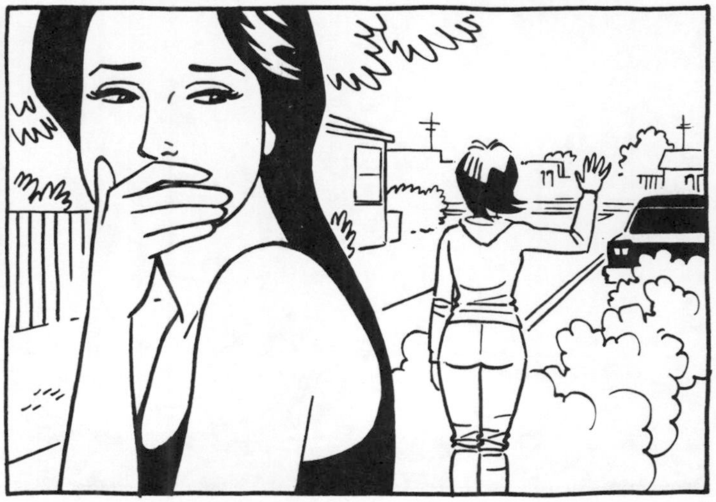

CINTO/BELT

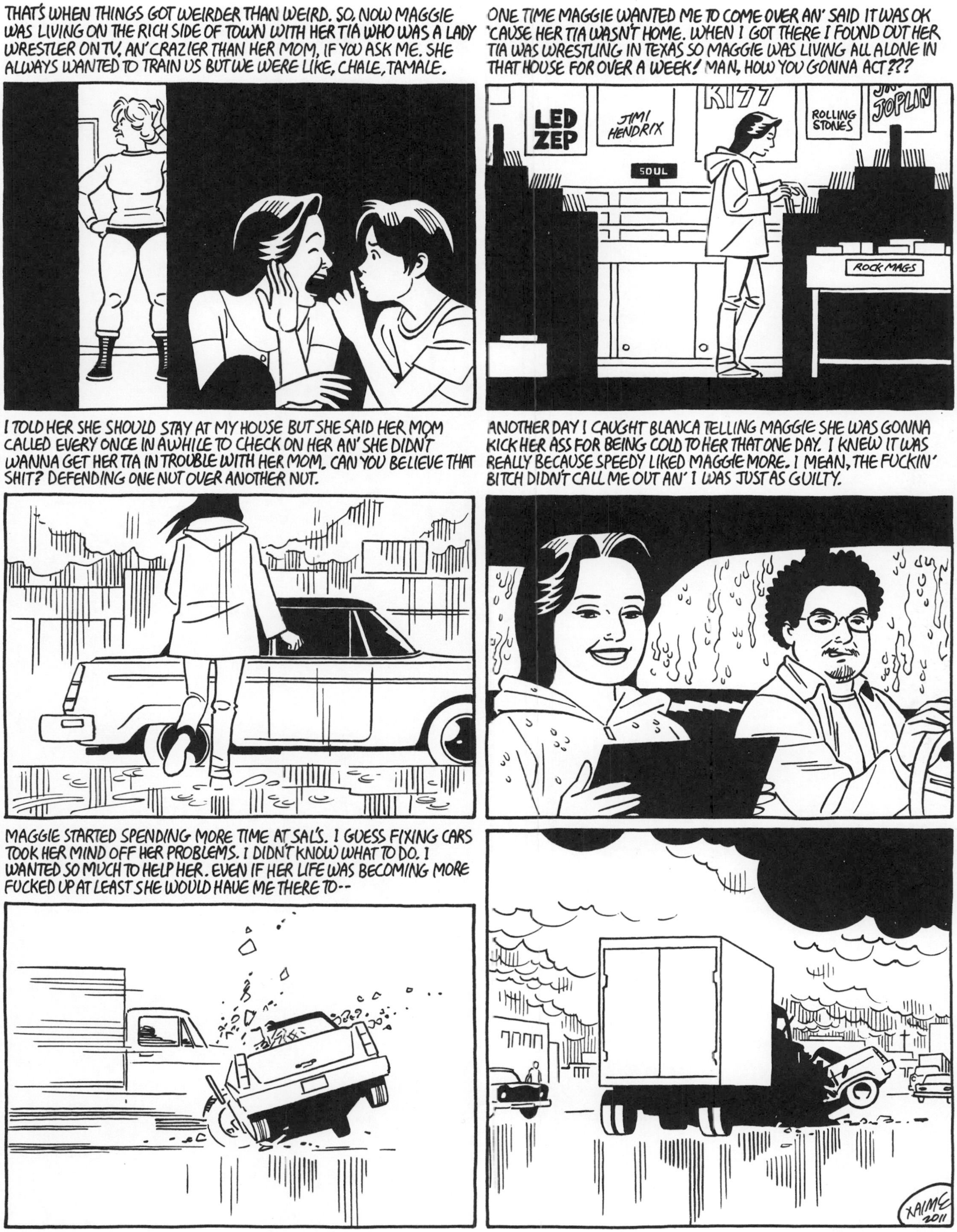
THAT'S WHEN THINGS GOT WEIRDER THAN WEIRD. SO, NOW MAGGIE WAS LIVING ON THE RICH SIDE OF TOWN WITH HER TIA WHO WAS A LADY WRESTLER ON TV, AN' CRAZIER THAN HER MOM, IF YOU ASK ME. SHE ALWAYS WANTED TO TRAIN US BUT WE WERE LIKE, CHALE, TAMALE.
ONE TIME MAGGIE WANTED ME TO COME OVER AN' SAID IT WAS OK 'CAUSE HER TIA WASN'T HOME. WHEN I GOT THERE I FOUND OUT HER TIA WAS WRESTLING IN TEXAS SO MAGGIE WAS LIVING ALL ALONE IN THAT HOUSE FOR OVER A WEEK! MAN, HOW YOU GONNA ACT???
LED ZEP
JIMI HENDRIX
KISS
ROLLING STONES
JOPLIN
SOUL
ROCK MAGS
I TOLD HER SHE SHOULD STAY AT MY HOUSE BUT SHE SAID HER MOM CALLED EVERY ONCE IN A WHILE TO CHECK ON HER AN' SHE DIDN'T WANNA GET HER TIA IN TROUBLE WITH HER MOM. CAN YOU BELIEVE THAT SHIT? DEFENDING ONE NUT OVER ANOTHER NUT.
ANOTHER DAY I CAUGHT BLANCA TELLING MAGGIE SHE WAS GONNA KICK HER ASS FOR BEING COLD TO HER THAT ONE DAY. I KNEW IT WAS REALLY BECAUSE SPEEDY LIKED MAGGIE MORE. I MEAN, THE FUCKIN' BITCH DIDN'T CALL ME OUT AN' I WAS JUST AS GUILTY.
MAGGIE STARTED SPENDING MORE TIME AT SAL'S. I GUESS FIXING CARS TOOK HER MIND OFF HER PROBLEMS. I DIDN'T KNOW WHAT TO DO. I WANTED SO MUCH TO HELP HER. EVEN IF HER LIFE WAS BECOMING MORE FUCKED UP AT LEAST SHE WOULD HAVE ME THERE TO--
XAIME 2011

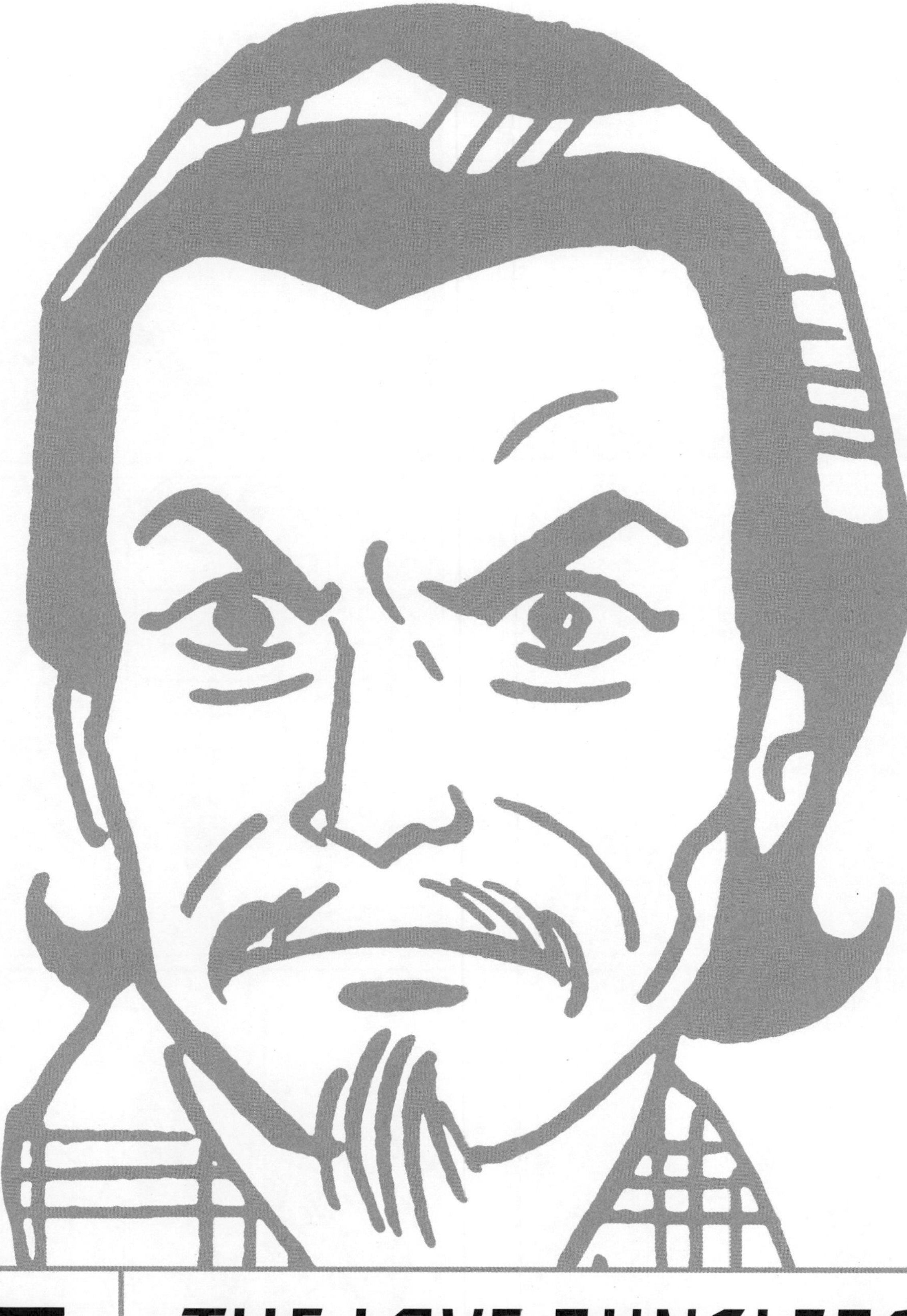

7 THE LOVE BUNGLERS

PART FIVE

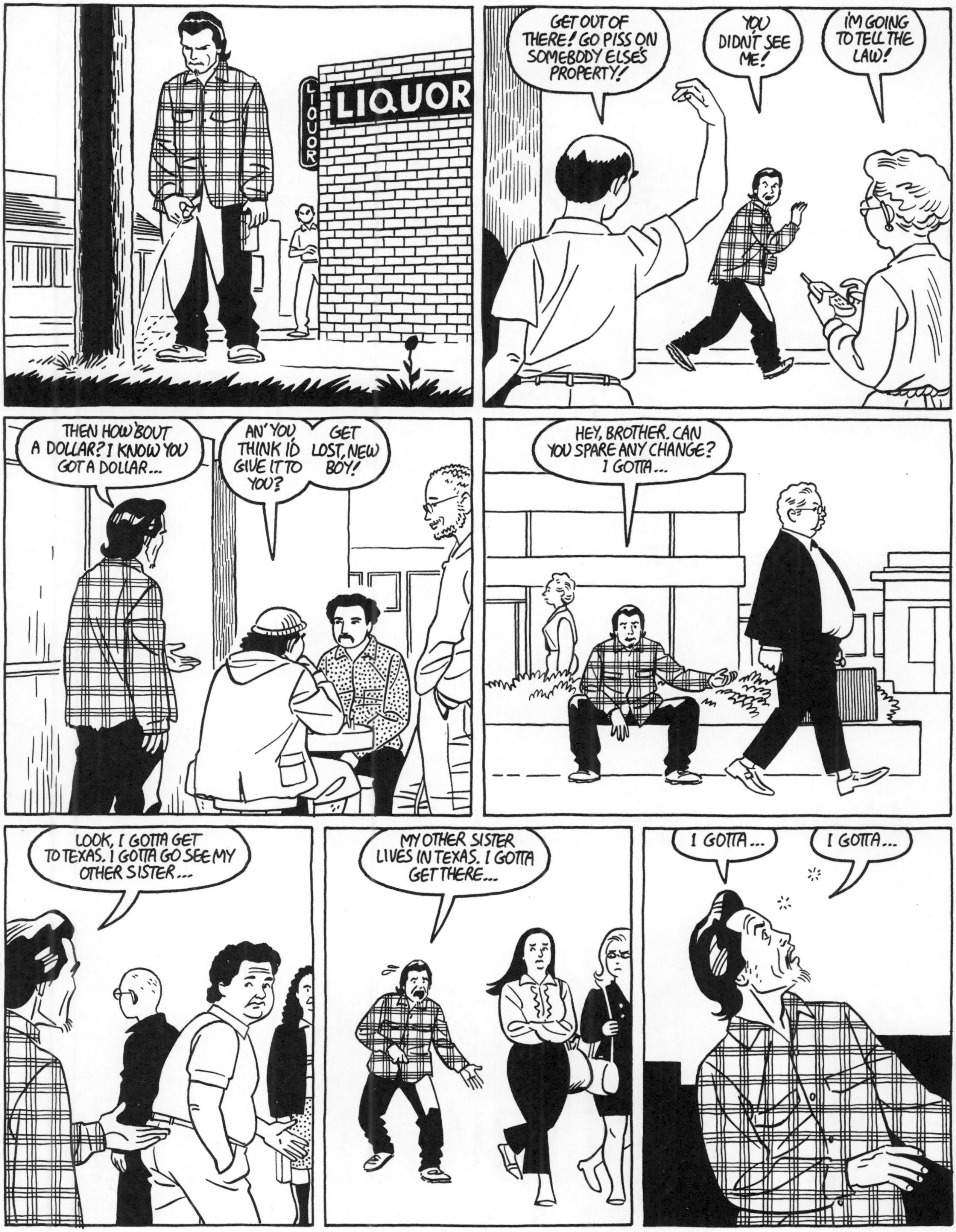
LIQUOR
LIQUOR
GET OUT OF THERE! GO PISS ON SOMEBODY ELSE'S PROPERTY!
YOU DIDN'T SEE ME!
I'M GOING TO TELL THE LAW!
THEN HOW 'BOUT A DOLLAR? I KNOW YOU GOT A DOLLAR...
AN' YOU THINK I'D GIVE IT TO YOU?
GET LOST, NEW BOY!
HEY, BROTHER. CAN YOU SPARE ANY CHANGE? I GOTTA...
LOOK, I GOTTA GET TO TEXAS. I GOTTA GO SEE MY OTHER SISTER...
MY OTHER SISTER LIVES IN TEXAS. I GOTTA GET THERE...
I GOTTA...
I GOTTA...

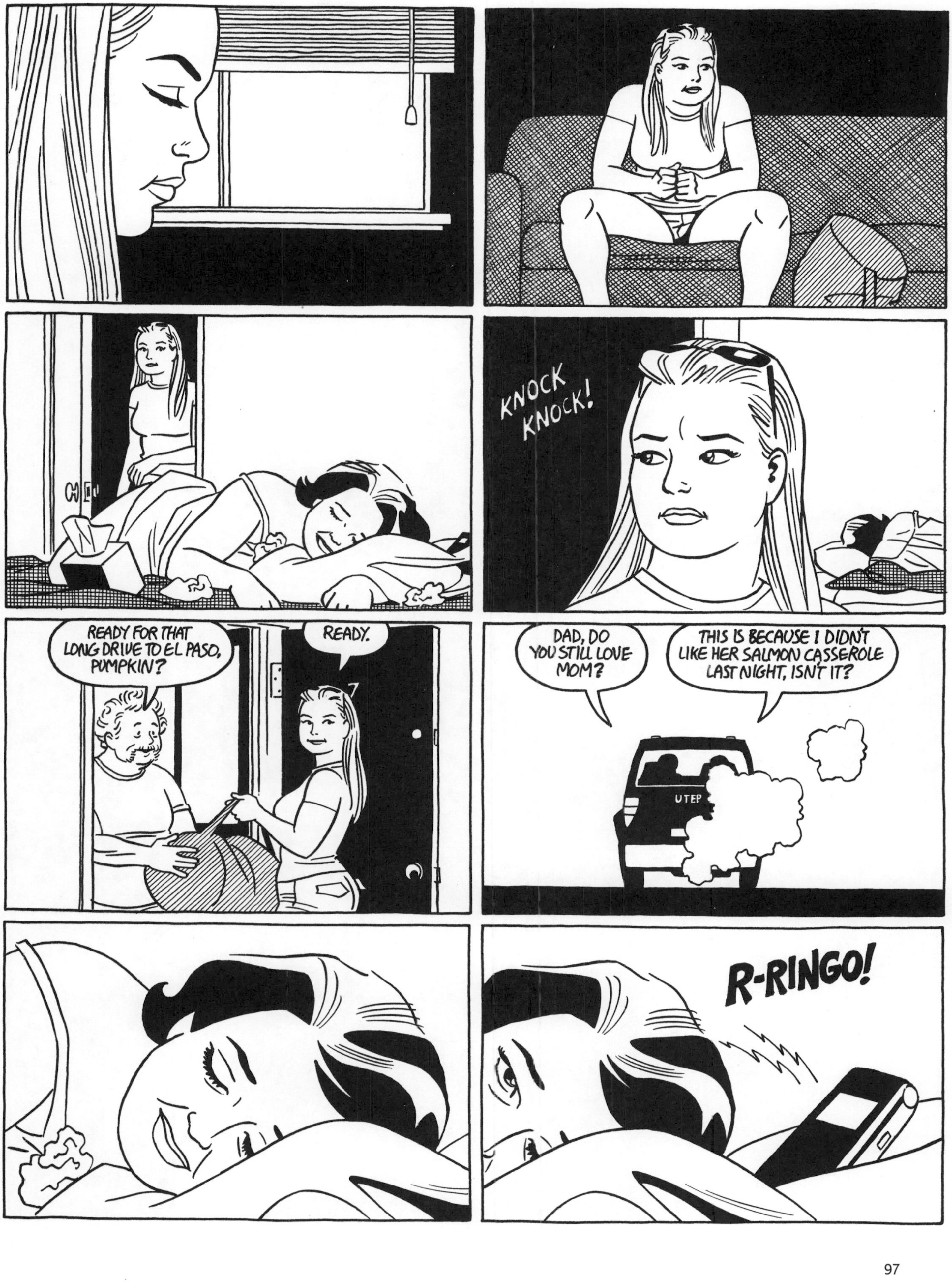
KNOCK
KNOCK!
READY FOR THAT LONG DRIVE TO EL PASO, PUMPKIN?
READY.
DAD, DO YOU STILL LOVE MOM?
THIS IS BECAUSE I DIDN'T LIKE HER SALMON CASSEROLE LAST NIGHT, ISN'T IT?
UTEP
R-RINGO!

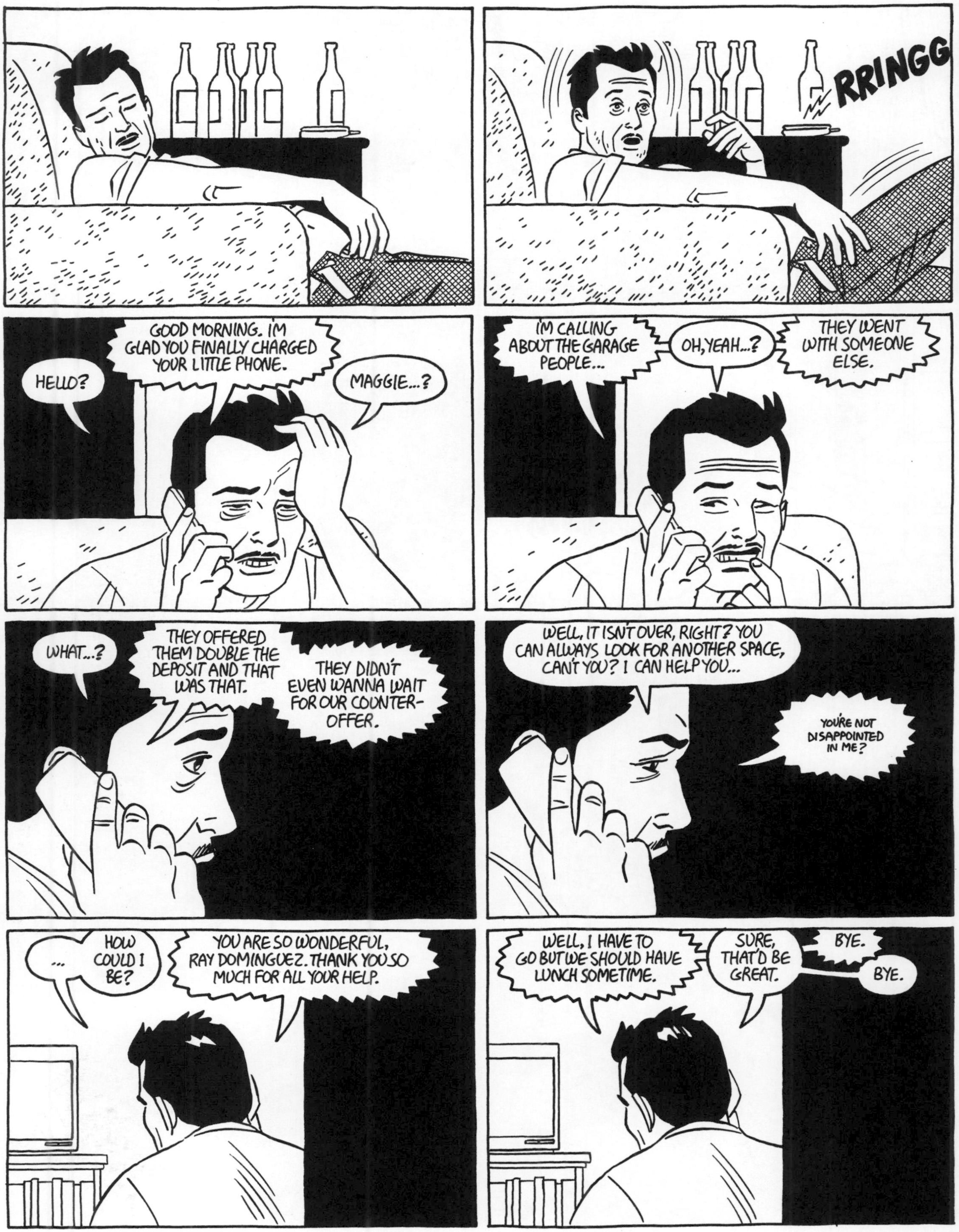
RRINGG
HELLO?
GOOD MORNING. I'M GLAD YOU FINALLY CHARGED YOUR LITTLE PHONE.
MAGGIE...?
I'M CALLING ABOUT THE GARAGE PEOPLE...
OH, YEAH...?
THEY WENT WITH SOMEONE ELSE.
WHAT...?
THEY OFFERED THEM DOUBLE THE DEPOSIT AND THAT WAS THAT.
THEY DIDN'T EVEN WANNA WAIT FOR OUR COUNTER-OFFER.
WELL, IT ISN'T OVER, RIGHT? YOU CAN ALWAYS LOOK FOR ANOTHER SPACE, CAN'T YOU? I CAN HELP YOU...
YOU'RE NOT DISAPPOINTED IN ME?
...
HOW COULD I BE?
YOU ARE SO WONDERFUL, RAY DOMINGUEZ. THANK YOU SO MUCH FOR ALL YOUR HELP.
WELL, I HAVE TO GO BUT WE SHOULD HAVE LUNCH SOMETIME.
SURE, THAT'D BE GREAT.
BYE.
BYE.

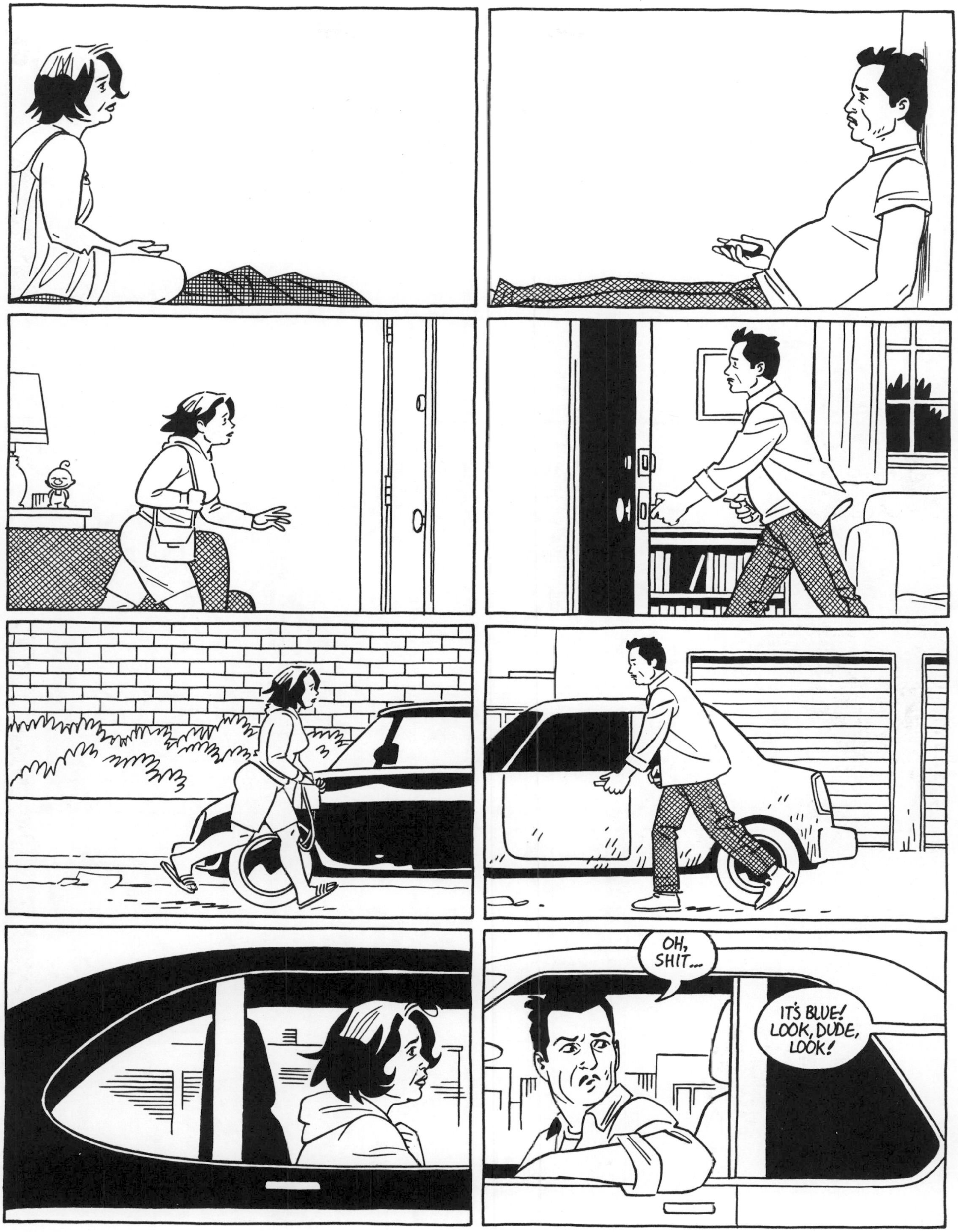
OH, SHIT...
IT'S BLUE! LOOK, DUDE, LOOK!

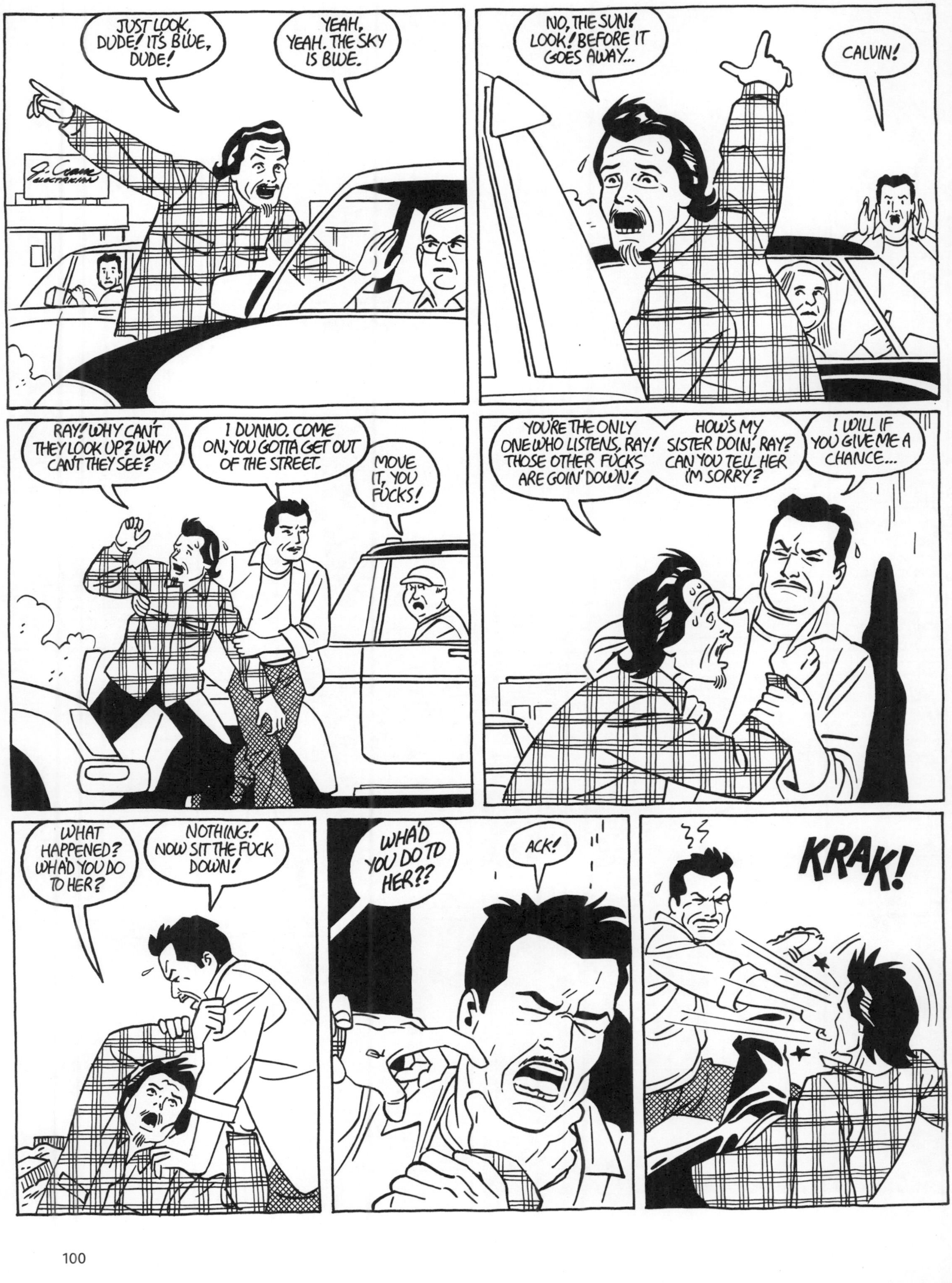
JUST LOOK, DUDE! IT'S BLUE, DUDE!
YEAH, YEAH. THE SKY IS BLUE.
NO, THE SUN! LOOK! BEFORE IT GOES AWAY...
CALVIN!
RAY! WHY CAN'T THEY LOOK UP? WHY CAN'T THEY SEE?
I DUNNO. COME ON, YOU GOTTA GET OUT OF THE STREET.
MOVE IT, YOU FUCKS!
YOU'RE THE ONLY ONE WHO LISTENS, RAY! THOSE OTHER FUCKS ARE GOIN' DOWN!
HOW'S MY SISTER DOIN', RAY? CAN YOU TELL HER I'M SORRY?
I WILL IF YOU GIVE ME A CHANCE...
WHAT HAPPENED? WHA'D YOU DO TO HER?
NOTHING! NOW SIT THE FUCK DOWN!
WHA'D YOU DO TO HER??
ACK!
KRAK!

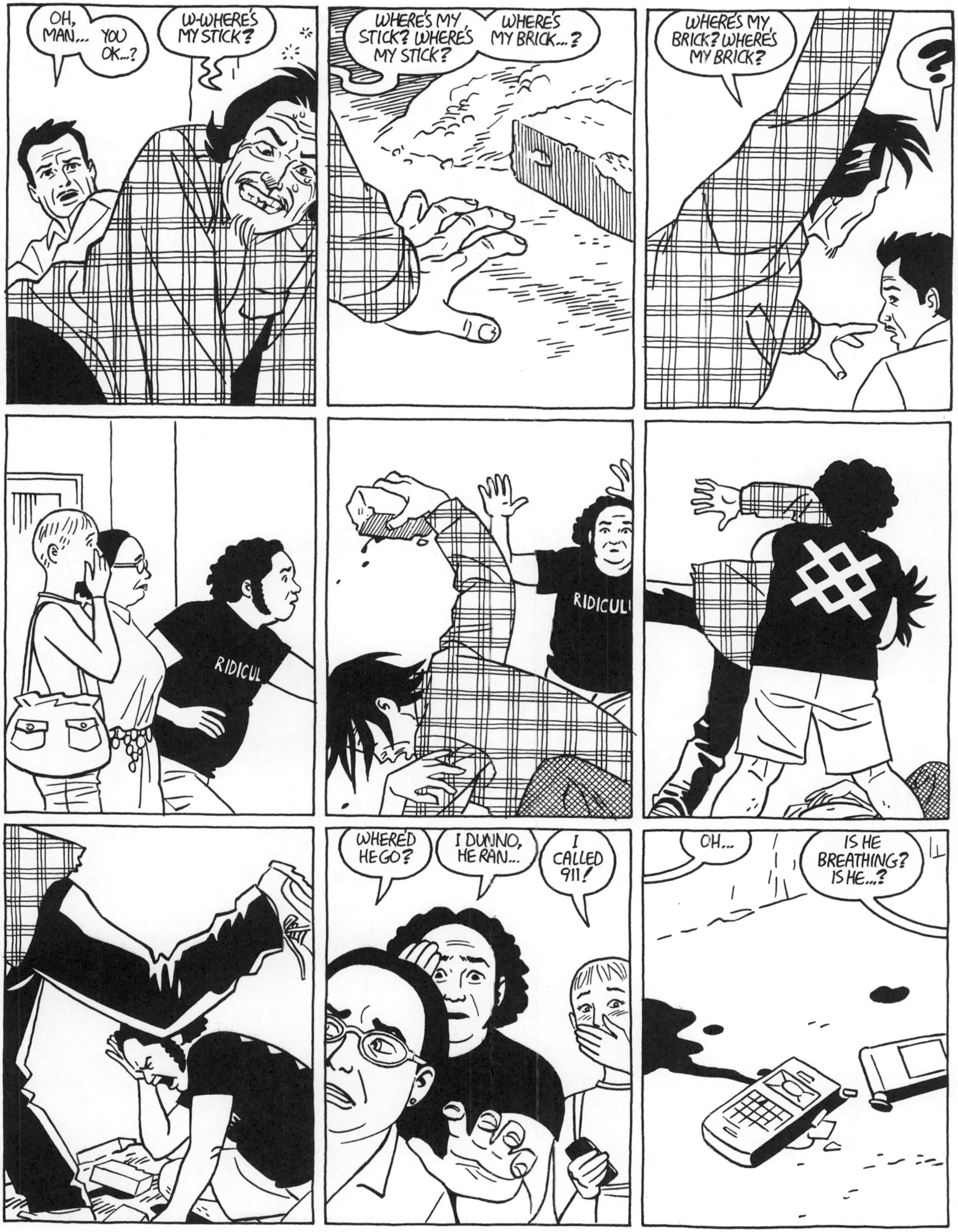
OH, MAN... YOU OK...?
W-WHERE'S MY STICK?
WHERE'S MY STICK? WHERE'S MY STICK?
WHERE'S MY BRICK...?
WHERE'S MY BRICK? WHERE'S MY BRICK?
?
RIDICUL
RIDICUL
WHERE'D HE GO?
I DUNNO, HE RAN...
I CALLED 911!
OH...
IS HE BREATHING? IS HE...?

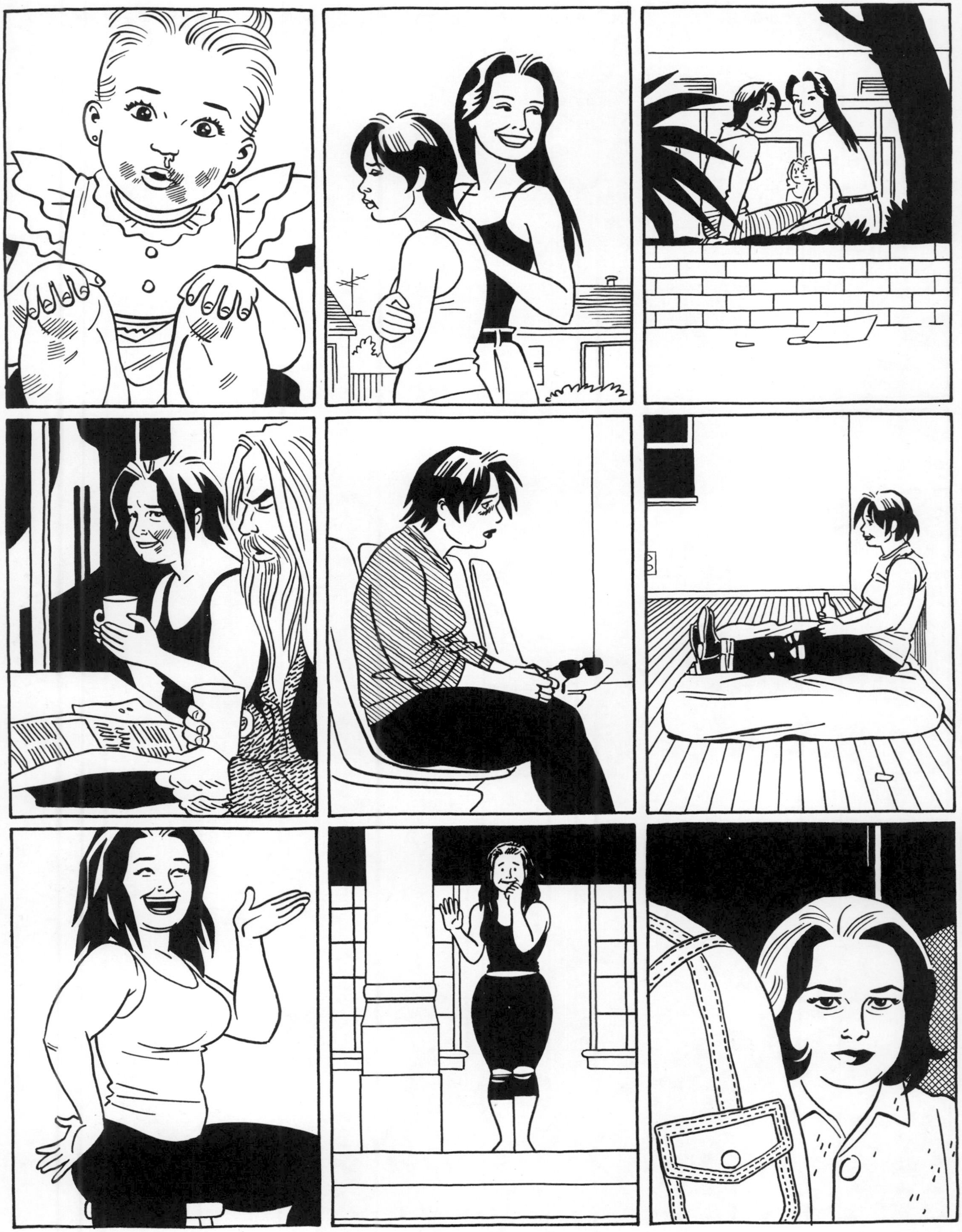

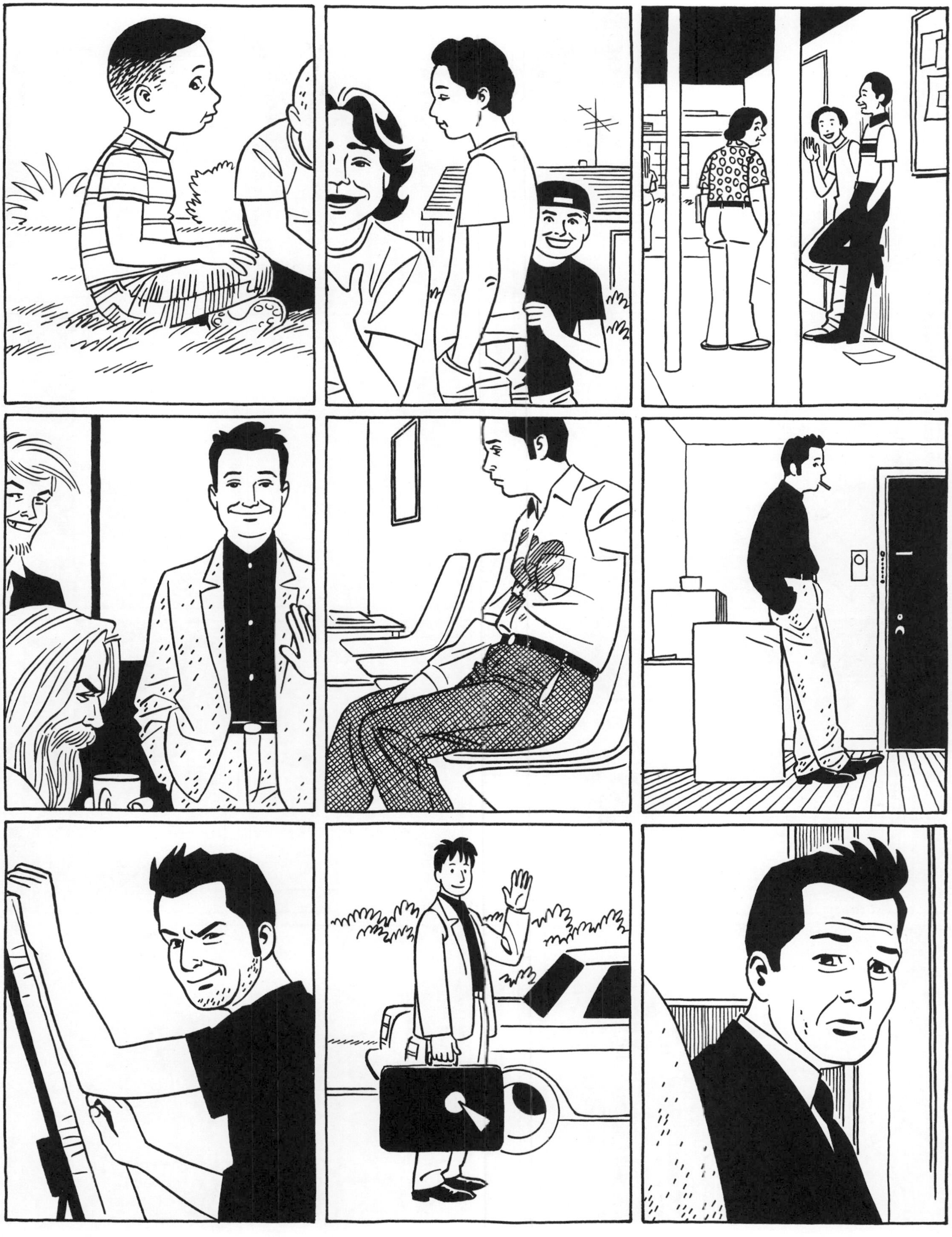

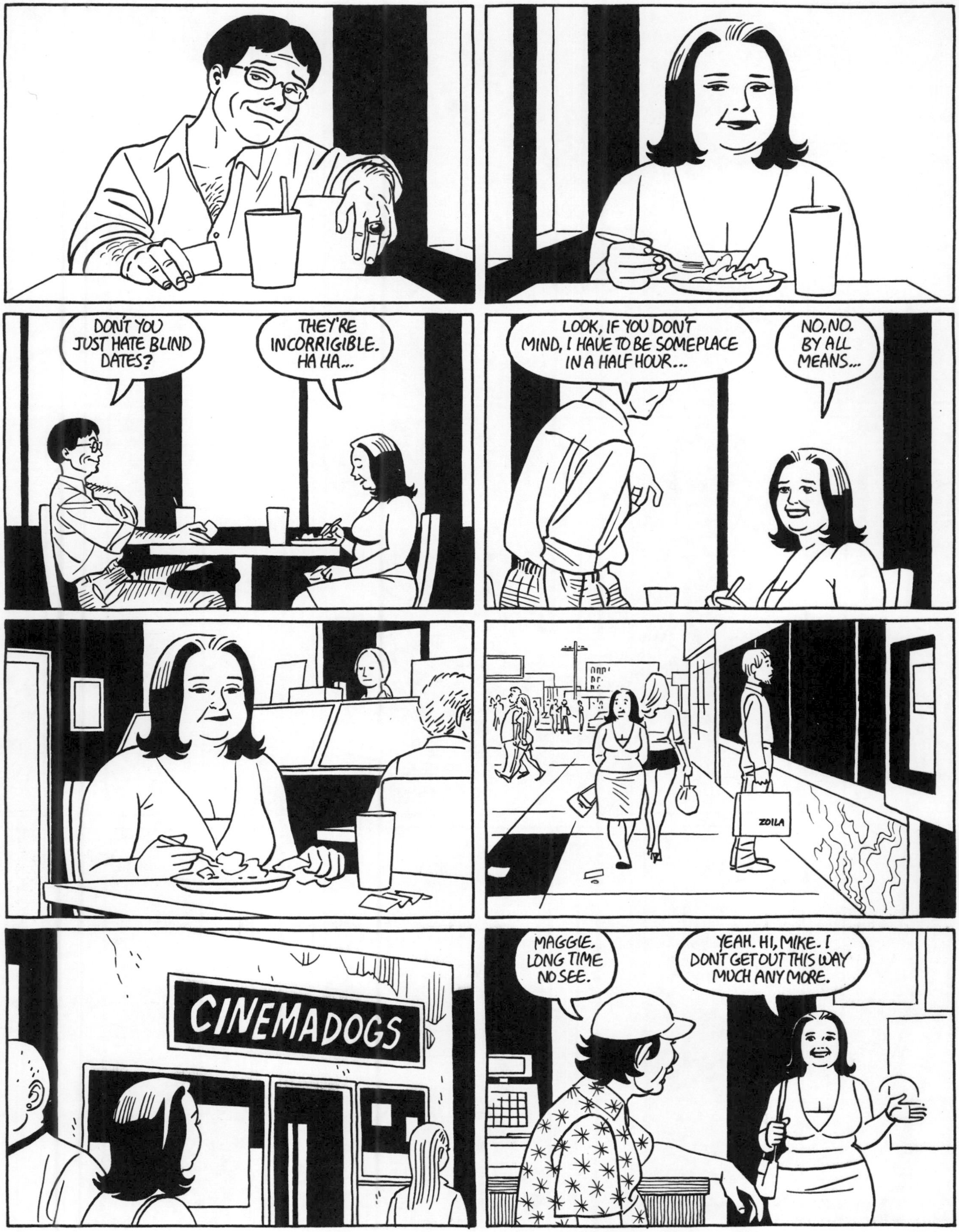
DON'T YOU JUST HATE BLIND DATES?
THEY'RE INCORRIGIBLE. HA HA...
LOOK, IF YOU DON'T MIND, I HAVE TO BE SOMEPLACE IN A HALF HOUR...
NO, NO. BY ALL MEANS...
ZOILA
CINEMADOGS
MAGGIE. LONG TIME NO SEE.
YEAH. HI, MIKE. I DONT GET OUT THIS WAY MUCH ANY MORE.

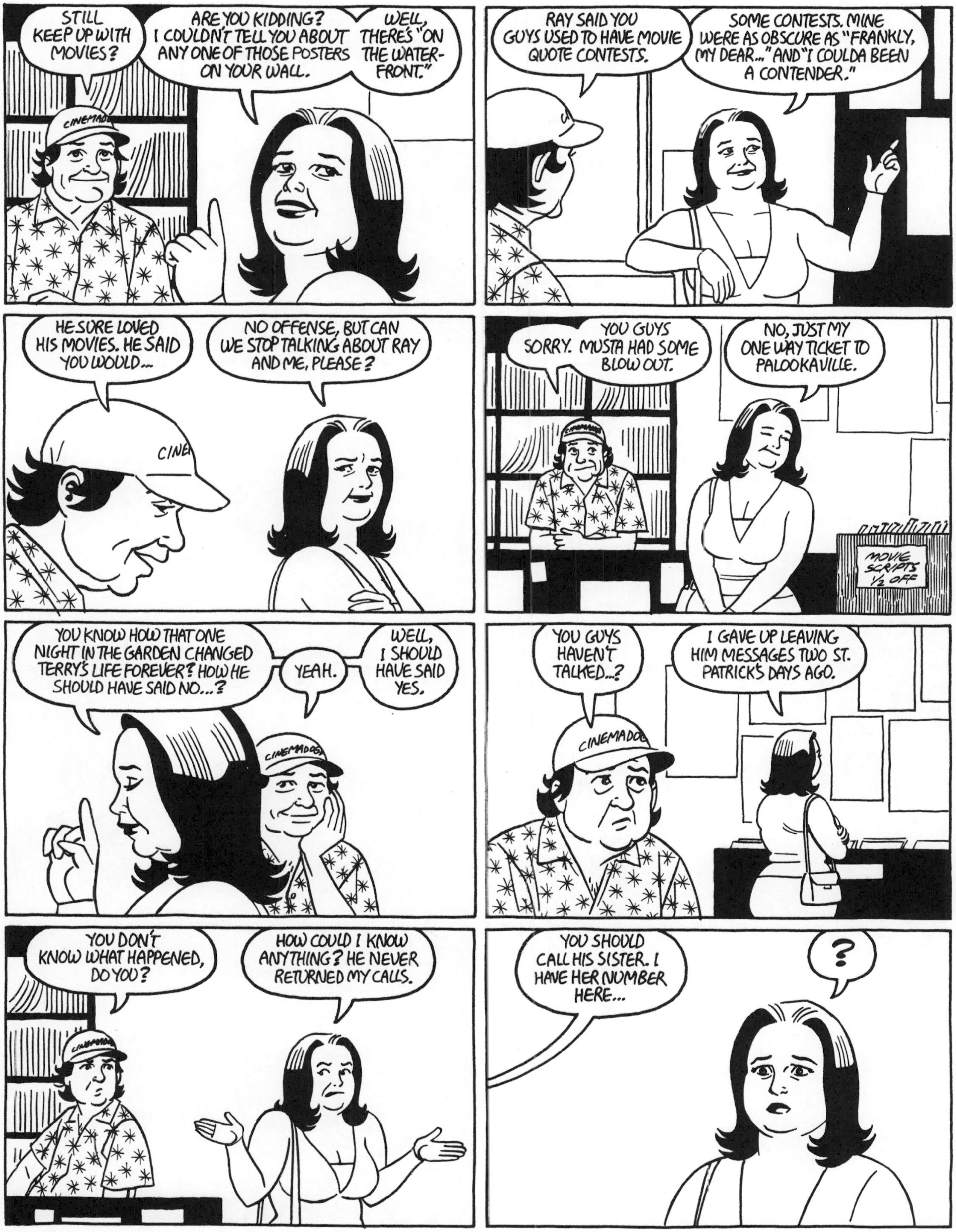
STILL KEEP UP WITH MOVIES?
ARE YOU KIDDING? I COULDN'T TELL YOU ABOUT ANY ONE OF THOSE POSTERS ON YOUR WALL.
WELL, THERE'S "ON THE WATER-FRONT."
CINEMADO
RAY SAID YOU GUYS USED TO HAVE MOVIE QUOTE CONTESTS.
SOME CONTESTS. MINE WERE AS OBSCURE AS "FRANKLY, MY DEAR..." AND "I COULDA BEEN A CONTENDER."
HE SURE LOVED HIS MOVIES. HE SAID YOU WOULD...
NO OFFENSE, BUT CAN WE STOP TALKING ABOUT RAY AND ME, PLEASE?
CINE
SORRY.
YOU GUYS MUSTA HAD SOME BLOW OUT.
NO, JUST MY ONE WAY TICKET TO PALOOKAVILLE.
MOVIE SCRIPTS 1/2 OFF
YOU KNOW HOW THAT ONE NIGHT IN THE GARDEN CHANGED TERRY'S LIFE FOREVER? HOW HE SHOULD HAVE SAID NO...?
YEAH.
WELL, I SHOULD HAVE SAID YES.
CINEMADOGS
YOU GUYS HAVEN'T TALKED...?
I GAVE UP LEAVING HIM MESSAGES TWO ST. PATRICK'S DAYS AGO.
CINEMADOG
YOU DON'T KNOW WHAT HAPPENED, DO YOU?
HOW COULD I KNOW ANYTHING? HE NEVER RETURNED MY CALLS.
YOU SHOULD CALL HIS SISTER. I HAVE HER NUMBER HERE...
?

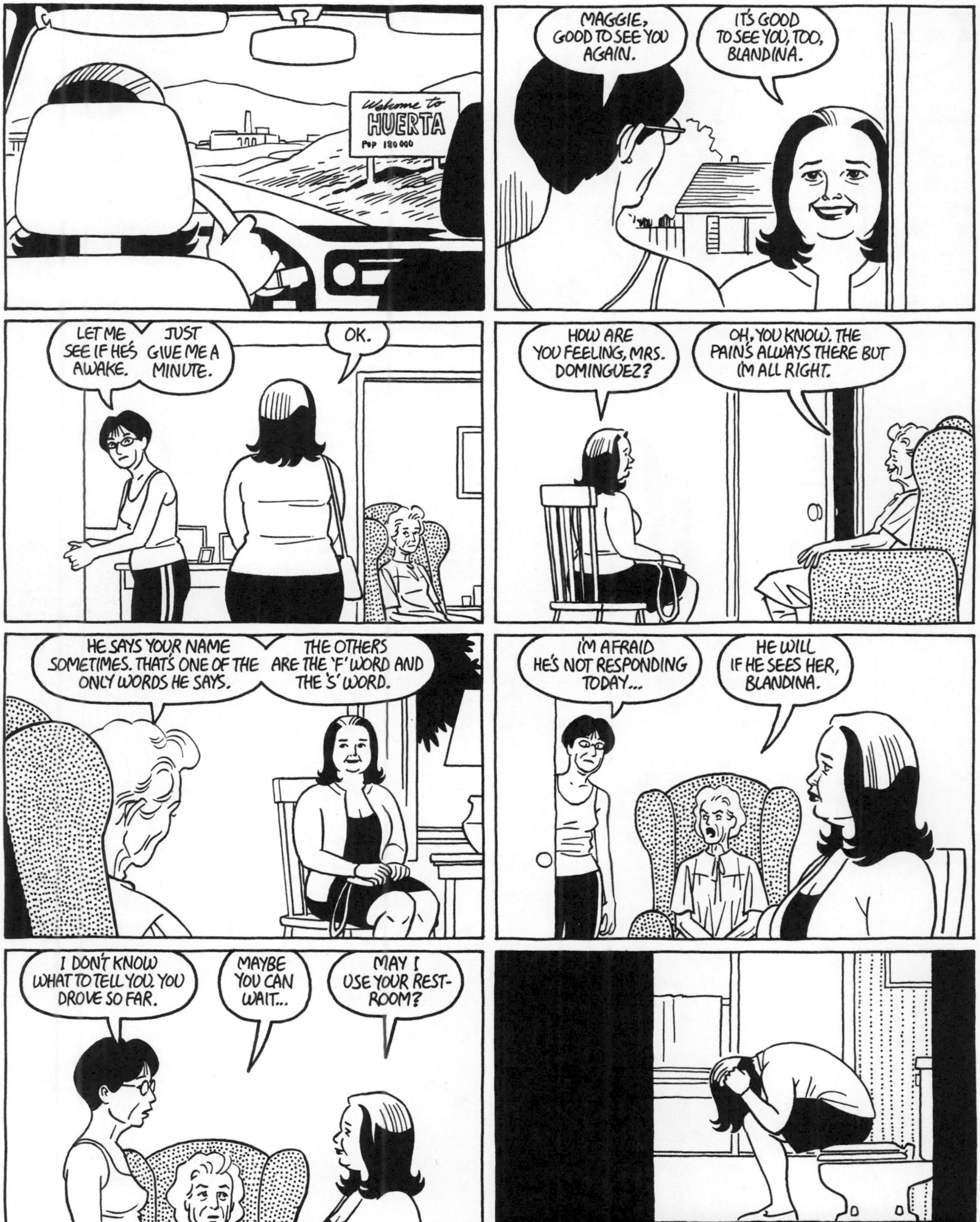
Welcome to
HUERTA
POP 180 000
MAGGIE, GOOD TO SEE YOU AGAIN.
IT'S GOOD TO SEE YOU, TOO, BLANDINA.
LET ME SEE IF HE'S AWAKE.
JUST GIVE ME A MINUTE.
OK.
HOW ARE YOU FEELING, MRS. DOMINGUEZ?
OH, YOU KNOW. THE PAIN'S ALWAYS THERE BUT I'M ALL RIGHT.
HE SAYS YOUR NAME SOMETIMES. THAT'S ONE OF THE ONLY WORDS HE SAYS.
THE OTHERS ARE THE 'F' WORD AND THE 'S' WORD.
I'M AFRAID HE'S NOT RESPONDING TODAY...
HE WILL IF HE SEES HER, BLANDINA.
I DON'T KNOW WHAT TO TELL YOU. YOU DROVE SO FAR.
MAYBE YOU CAN WAIT...
MAY I USE YOUR REST-ROOM?

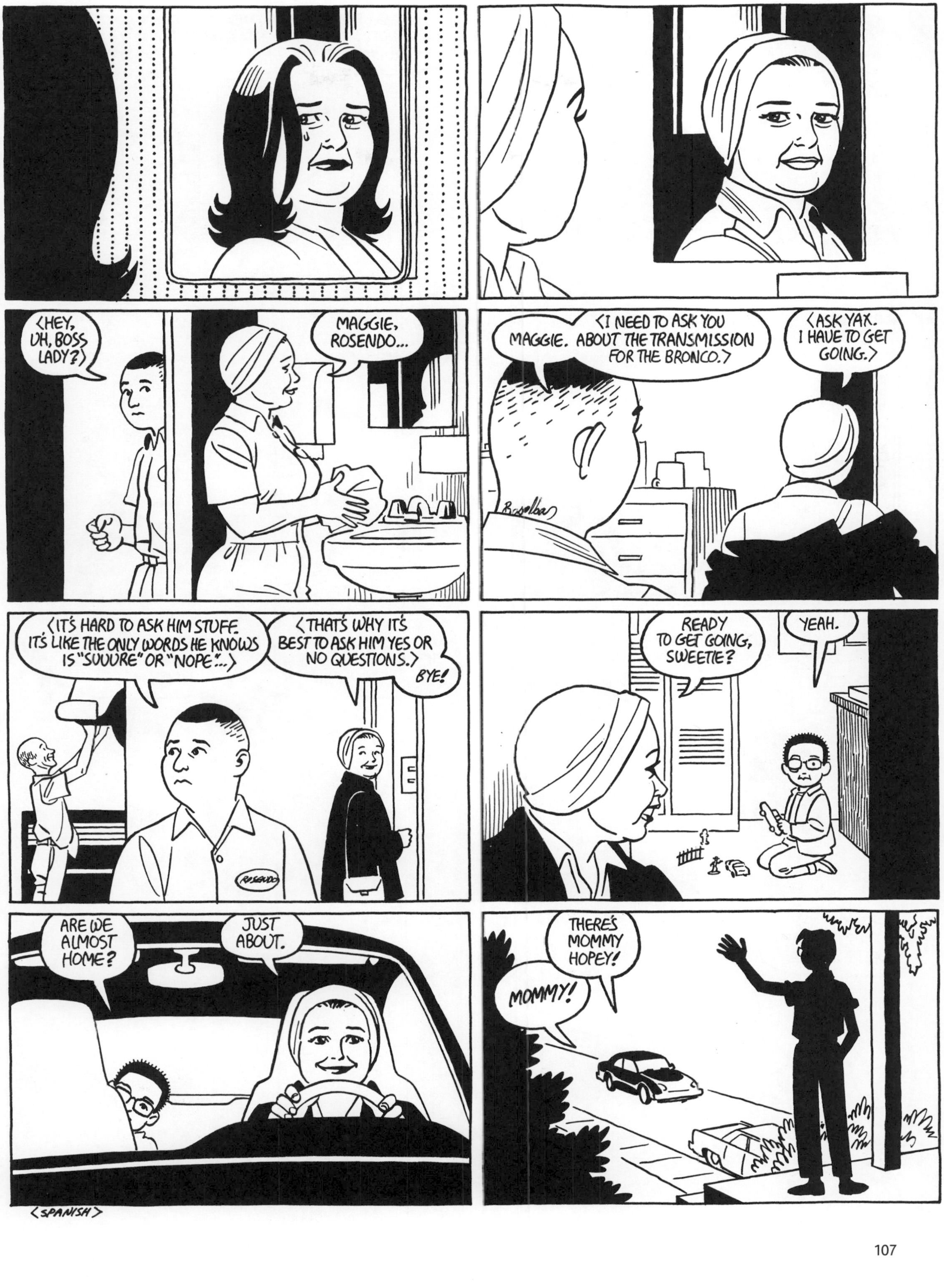
<HEY, UH, BOSS LADY?>
MAGGIE, ROSENDO...
MAGGIE.
<I NEED TO ASK YOU ABOUT THE TRANSMISSION FOR THE BRONCO.>
<ASK YAX. I HAVE TO GET GOING.>
<IT'S HARD TO ASK HIM STUFF. IT'S LIKE THE ONLY WORDS HE KNOWS IS "SUUURE" OR "NOPE."...>
<THAT'S WHY IT'S BEST TO ASK HIM YES OR NO QUESTIONS.>
BYE!
ROSENDO
READY TO GET GOING, SWEETIE?
YEAH.
ARE WE ALMOST HOME?
JUST ABOUT.
THERE'S MOMMY HOPEY!
MOMMY!
<SPANISH>

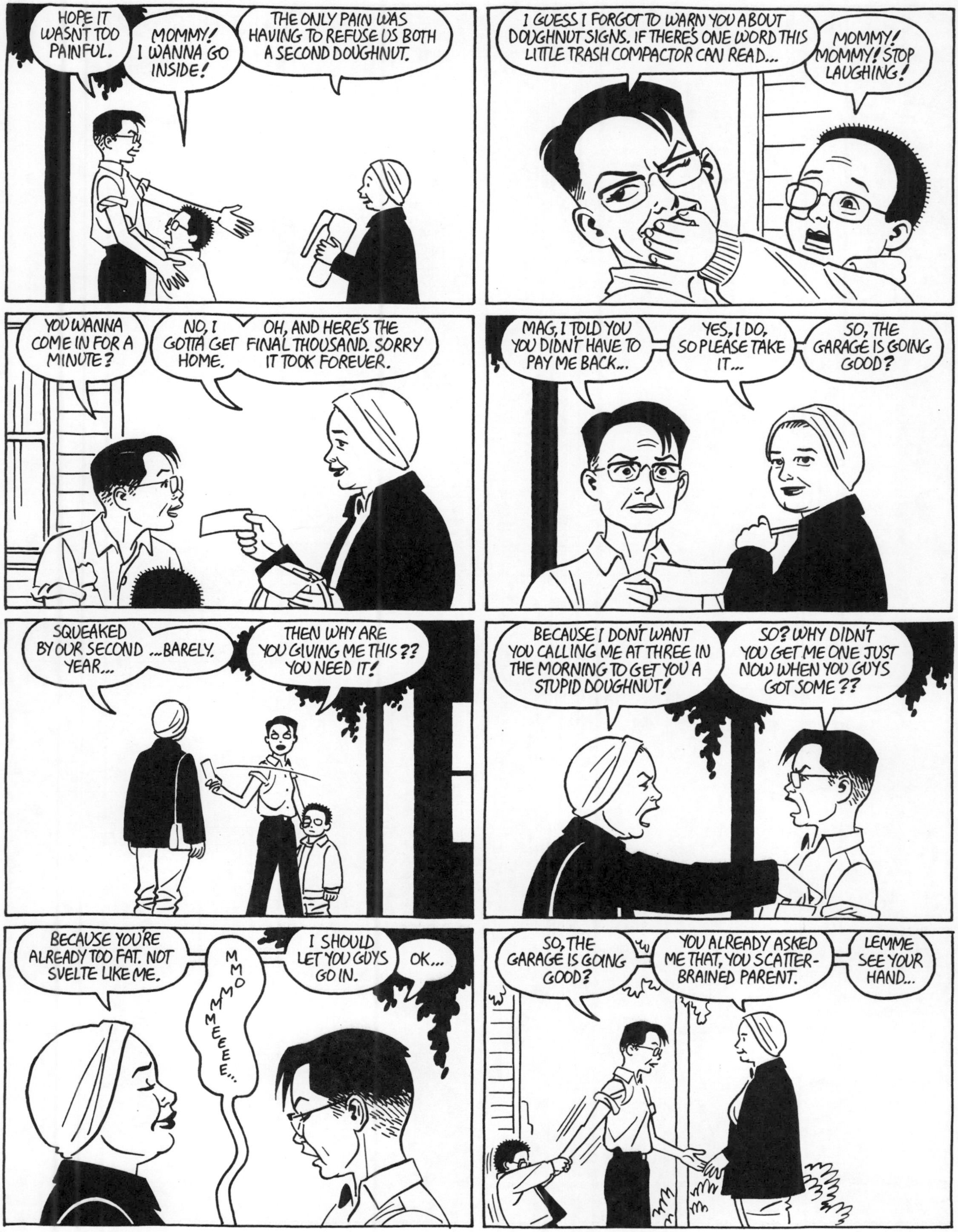
HOPE IT WASN'T TOO PAINFUL.
MOMMY! I WANNA GO INSIDE!
THE ONLY PAIN WAS HAVING TO REFUSE US BOTH A SECOND DOUGHNUT.
I GUESS I FORGOT TO WARN YOU ABOUT DOUGHNUT SIGNS. IF THERE'S ONE WORD THIS LITTLE TRASH COMPACTOR CAN READ...
MOMMY! MOMMY! STOP LAUGHING!
YOU WANNA COME IN FOR A MINUTE?
NO, I GOTTA GET HOME.
OH, AND HERE'S THE FINAL THOUSAND. SORRY IT TOOK FOREVER.
MAG, I TOLD YOU YOU DIDN'T HAVE TO PAY ME BACK...
YES, I DO, SO PLEASE TAKE IT...
SO, THE GARAGE IS GOING GOOD?
SQUEAKED BY OUR SECOND YEAR...
...BARELY.
THEN WHY ARE YOU GIVING ME THIS?? YOU NEED IT!
BECAUSE I DON'T WANT YOU CALLING ME AT THREE IN THE MORNING TO GET YOU A STUPID DOUGHNUT!
SO? WHY DIDN'T YOU GET ME ONE JUST NOW WHEN YOU GUYS GOT SOME??
BECAUSE YOU'RE ALREADY TOO FAT. NOT SVELTE LIKE ME.
MMOMMMEEEE...
I SHOULD LET YOU GUYS GO IN.
OK...
SO, THE GARAGE IS GOING GOOD?
YOU ALREADY ASKED ME THAT, YOU SCATTER-BRAINED PARENT.
LEMME SEE YOUR HAND...

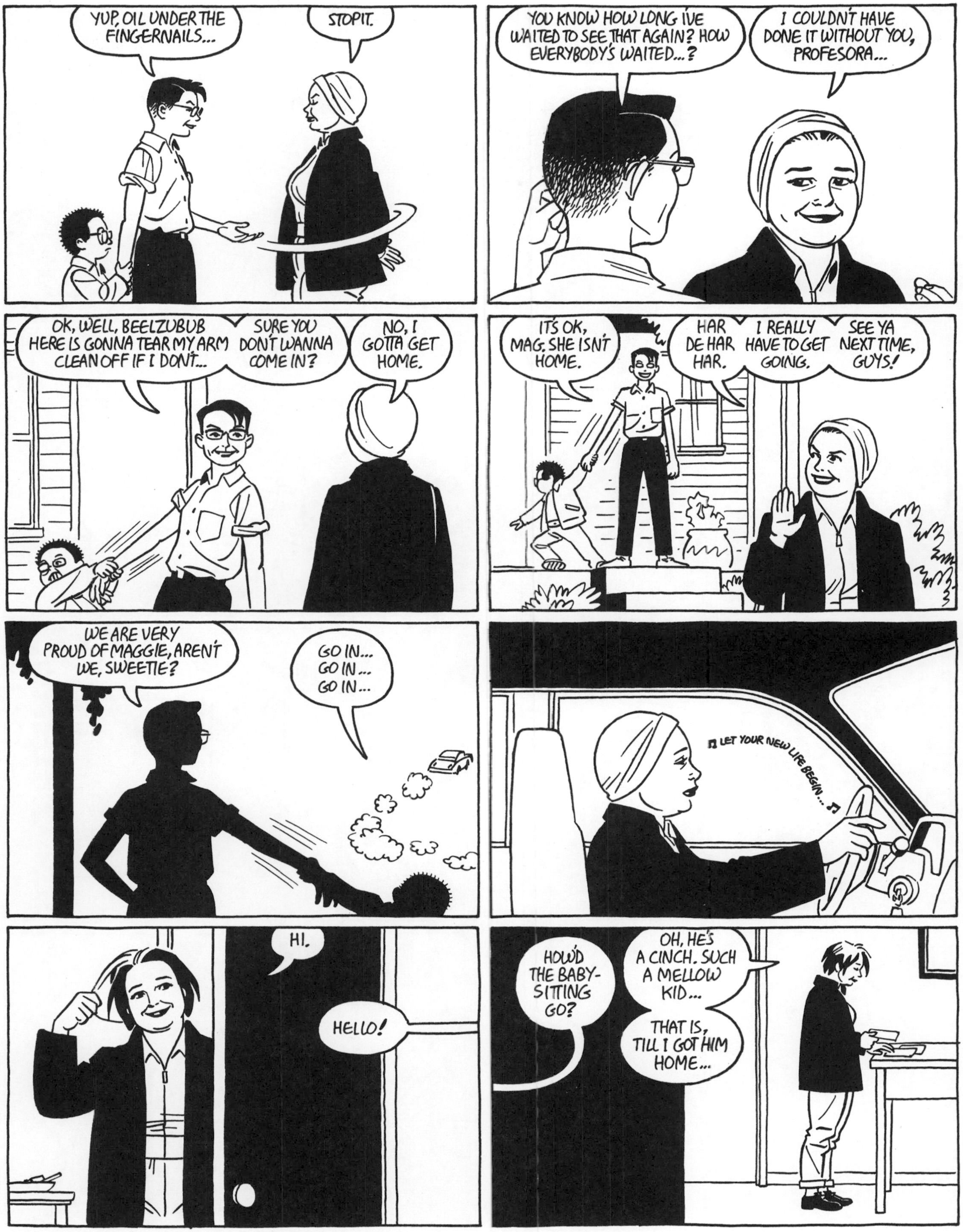
YUP, OIL UNDER THE FINGERNAILS...
STOPIT.
YOU KNOW HOW LONG I'VE WAITED TO SEE THAT AGAIN? HOW EVERYBODY'S WAITED...?
I COULDN'T HAVE DONE IT WITHOUT YOU, PROFESORA...
OK, WELL, BEELZUBUB HERE IS GONNA TEAR MY ARM CLEAN OFF IF I DON'T...
SURE YOU DON'T WANNA COME IN?
NO, I GOTTA GET HOME.
IT'S OK, MAG. SHE ISN'T HOME.
HAR DE HAR HAR.
I REALLY HAVE TO GET GOING.
SEE YA NEXT TIME, GUYS!
WE ARE VERY PROUD OF MAGGIE, AREN'T WE, SWEETIE?
GO IN... GO IN... GO IN...
♫ LET YOUR NEW LIFE BEGIN... ♫
HI.
HELLO!
HOW'D THE BABY-SITTING GO?
OH, HE'S A CINCH. SUCH A MELLOW KID...
THAT IS, TILL I GOT HIM HOME...

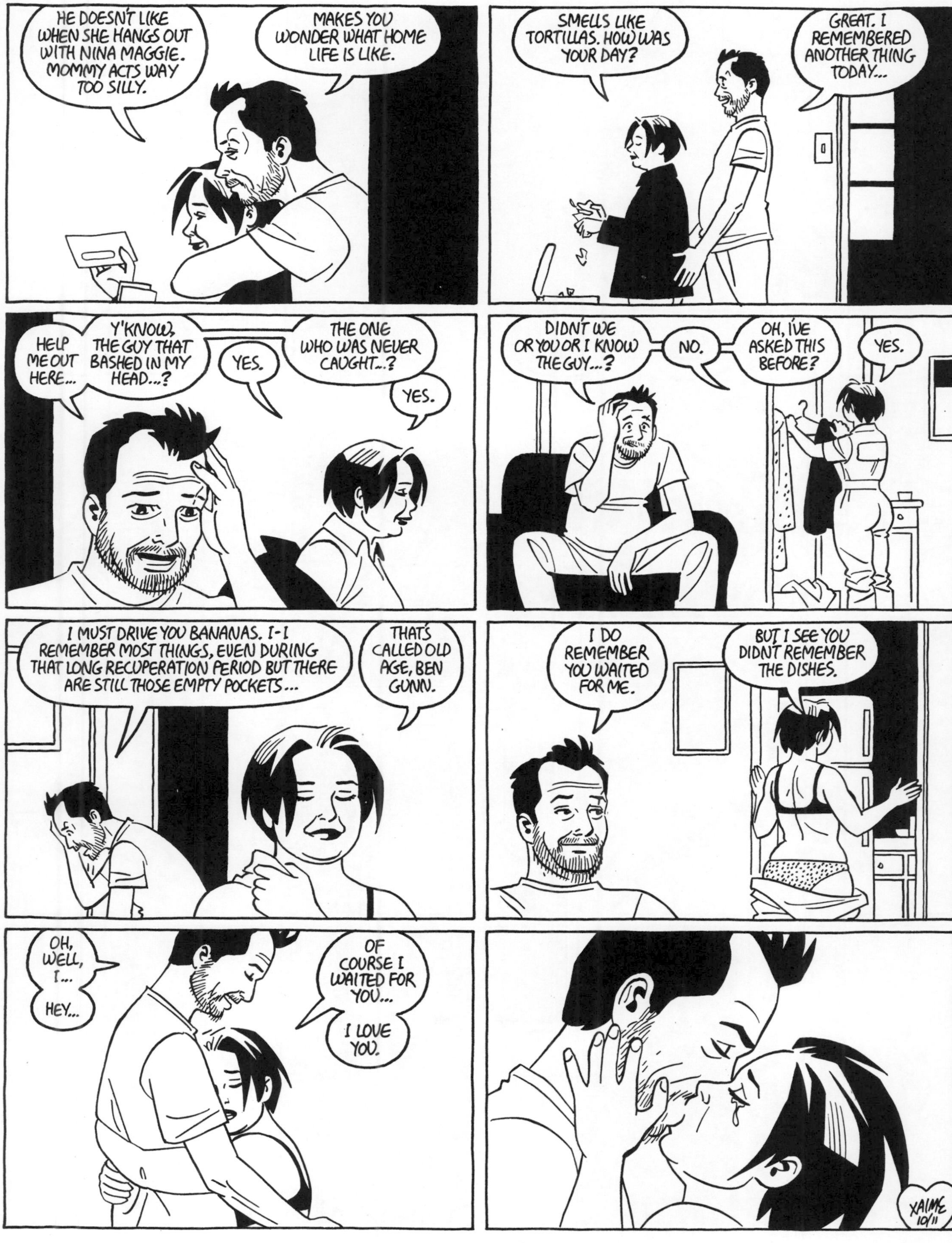
HE DOESN'T LIKE WHEN SHE HANGS OUT WITH NINA MAGGIE. MOMMY ACTS WAY TOO SILLY.
MAKES YOU WONDER WHAT HOME LIFE IS LIKE.
SMELLS LIKE TORTILLAS. HOW WAS YOUR DAY?
GREAT. I REMEMBERED ANOTHER THING TODAY...
HELP ME OUT HERE...
Y'KNOW, THE GUY THAT BASHED IN MY HEAD...?
YES.
THE ONE WHO WAS NEVER CAUGHT...?
YES.
DIDN'T WE OR YOU OR I KNOW THE GUY...?
NO.
OH, I'VE ASKED THIS BEFORE?
YES.
I MUST DRIVE YOU BANANAS. I-I REMEMBER MOST THINGS, EVEN DURING THAT LONG RECUPERATION PERIOD BUT THERE ARE STILL THOSE EMPTY POCKETS...
THAT'S CALLED OLD AGE, BEN GUNN.
I DO REMEMBER YOU WAITED FOR ME.
BUT I SEE YOU DIDN'T REMEMBER THE DISHES.
OH, WELL, I...
HEY...
OF COURSE I WAITED FOR YOU...
I LOVE YOU.
XAIME 10/11

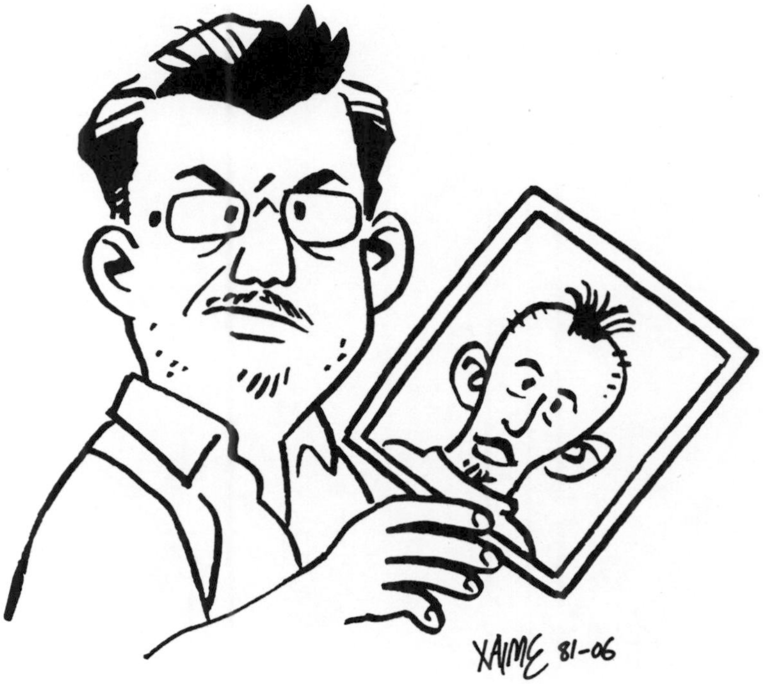
XAIME 81-06

ABOUT THE AUTHOR

Jaime Hernandez was one of six siblings born and raised in Oxnard, California. His mother had been an avid comic book fan as a girl, and she passed onto them a love of Jack Kirby and Steve Ditko's Marvel comics, Hank Ketcham's *Dennis the Menace*, Charles Schulz's *Peanuts* and the Archie comics line. A further strain was added when the family's eldest sibling, Mario, smuggled R. Crumb's *ZAP* into the house.

As adolescence and other interests invaded, Jaime's enthusiasm for mainstream comics waned. The Los Angeles punk rock scene began to thrive, and the anarchistic and gritty aesthetic invaded Jaime's approach to writing and drawing. Mostly self-taught, Jaime assimilated these influences, and in his hands the much-hyped and often misunderstood punk netherworld became a very real, habitable place populated with human beings rather than stereotypes.

Such were the humble beginnings of *Love and Rockets*, the internationally acclaimed series Jaime created with his brother, Gilbert, in 1981. Over 30 years later, *Love and Rockets* still continues (now published annually as *Love and Rockets: New Stories*) and is one of the defining post-underground comic book titles of the last four decades.

Hernandez resides in Altadena, California, with his wife and daughter.